Communications
in Computer and Information Science 2354

Series Editors

Gang Li , *School of Information Technology, Deakin University, Burwood, VIC, Australia*

Joaquim Filipe , *Polytechnic Institute of Setúbal, Setúbal, Portugal*

Zhiwei Xu, *Chinese Academy of Sciences, Beijing, China*

Rationale

The CCIS series is devoted to the publication of proceedings of computer science conferences. Its aim is to efficiently disseminate original research results in informatics in printed and electronic form. While the focus is on publication of peer-reviewed full papers presenting mature work, inclusion of reviewed short papers reporting on work in progress is welcome, too. Besides globally relevant meetings with internationally representative program committees guaranteeing a strict peer-reviewing and paper selection process, conferences run by societies or of high regional or national relevance are also considered for publication.

Topics

The topical scope of CCIS spans the entire spectrum of informatics ranging from foundational topics in the theory of computing to information and communications science and technology and a broad variety of interdisciplinary application fields.

Information for Volume Editors and Authors

Publication in CCIS is free of charge. No royalties are paid, however, we offer registered conference participants temporary free access to the online version of the conference proceedings on SpringerLink (http://link.springer.com) by means of an http referrer from the conference website and/or a number of complimentary printed copies, as specified in the official acceptance email of the event.

CCIS proceedings can be published in time for distribution at conferences or as postproceedings, and delivered in the form of printed books and/or electronically as USBs and/or e-content licenses for accessing proceedings at SpringerLink. Furthermore, CCIS proceedings are included in the CCIS electronic book series hosted in the SpringerLink digital library at http://link.springer.com/bookseries/7899. Conferences publishing in CCIS are allowed to use Online Conference Service (OCS) for managing the whole proceedings lifecycle (from submission and reviewing to preparing for publication) free of charge.

Publication process

The language of publication is exclusively English. Authors publishing in CCIS have to sign the Springer CCIS copyright transfer form, however, they are free to use their material published in CCIS for substantially changed, more elaborate subsequent publications elsewhere. For the preparation of the camera-ready papers/files, authors have to strictly adhere to the Springer CCIS Authors' Instructions and are strongly encouraged to use the CCIS LaTeX style files or templates.

Abstracting/Indexing

CCIS is abstracted/indexed in DBLP, Google Scholar, EI-Compendex, Mathematical Reviews, SCImago, Scopus. CCIS volumes are also submitted for the inclusion in ISI Proceedings.

How to start

To start the evaluation of your proposal for inclusion in the CCIS series, please send an e-mail to ccis@springer.com.

Yitong Yin · Jialin Zhang · Zhiping Cai
Editors

Theoretical Computer Science

42nd National Conference, NCTCS 2024
Qingdao, China, July 19–21, 2024
Revised Selected Papers

Editors
Yitong Yin
Nanjing University
Nanjing, China

Jialin Zhang
Institute of Computing Technology
Beijing, China

Zhiping Cai
National University of Defense Technology
Changsha, China

ISSN 1865-0929　　　　　　　　　ISSN 1865-0937 (electronic)
Communications in Computer and Information Science
ISBN 978-981-96-1489-9　　　　　ISBN 978-981-96-1490-5 (eBook)
https://doi.org/10.1007/978-981-96-1490-5

© The Editor(s) (if applicable) and The Author(s), under exclusive license to Springer Nature Singapore Pte Ltd. 2025

This work is subject to copyright. All rights are solely and exclusively licensed by the Publisher, whether the whole or part of the material is concerned, specifically the rights of translation, reprinting, reuse of illustrations, recitation, broadcasting, reproduction on microfilms or in any other physical way, and transmission or information storage and retrieval, electronic adaptation, computer software, or by similar or dissimilar methodology now known or hereafter developed.
The use of general descriptive names, registered names, trademarks, service marks, etc. in this publication does not imply, even in the absence of a specific statement, that such names are exempt from the relevant protective laws and regulations and therefore free for general use.
The publisher, the authors and the editors are safe to assume that the advice and information in this book are believed to be true and accurate at the date of publication. Neither the publisher nor the authors or the editors give a warranty, expressed or implied, with respect to the material contained herein or for any errors or omissions that may have been made. The publisher remains neutral with regard to jurisdictional claims in published maps and institutional affiliations.

This Springer imprint is published by the registered company Springer Nature Singapore Pte Ltd.
The registered company address is: 152 Beach Road, #21-01/04 Gateway East, Singapore 189721, Singapore

If disposing of this product, please recycle the paper.

Preface

The National Conference of Theoretical Computer Science (NCTCS) has emerged as a pivotal academic platform for the field in China. Over the years, NCTCS has been successfully convened in over 20 regions across the country, fostering an environment conducive to exchange and collaboration among researchers in theoretical computer science and allied disciplines.

NCTCS 2024, held from July 19–21, 2024 in Qingdao, Shandong, was hosted by the China Computer Federation (CCF) and organized jointly by the Theoretical Computer Science Committee of China Computer Society and the School of Computer Science and Technology, Shandong University. This event showcased the latest advancements in the field by inviting esteemed scholars to present their work and engaging in a broad spectrum of academic endeavors.

A total of 242 participants registered for NCTCS 2024, with 204 authors submitting 75 papers, of which 52 were ultimately accepted. The peer-review process, conducted in a single-blind format, involved 85 reviewers from esteemed institutions, with each reviewer assigned an average of 3 papers, and each paper receiving an average of 3 reviews. The submission and review process was facilitated by the Online Submission System (CCF Consys), accessible at https://conf.ccf.org.cn/TCS2024 for further details.

This publication comprises 13 selected papers from NCTCS 2024, categorized under five thematic sections: Algorithm Design, Approximation Algorithms, Logics, Artificial Intelligence Theory and Algorithms, and Algorithm Applications. These contributions reflect the depth and breadth of research in theoretical computer science today.

The proceedings editors extend their heartfelt gratitude to the diligent Program Committee members and external reviewers for their meticulous efforts in evaluating and selecting the papers. We are also indebted to Springer for their unwavering support and trust in publishing the proceedings of NCTCS 2024.

October 2024

Yitong Yin
Jialin Zhang
Zhiping Cai

Organization

Program Committee Chairs

Yitong Yin	Nanjing University, China
Jialin Zhang	Institute of Computing Technology, Chinese Academy of Sciences, China
Zhiping Cai	National University of Defense Technology, China

Area Chairs

Yijia Chen	Fudan University, China
Qilong Feng	Central South University, China
Zhiguo Fu	Northeast Normal University, China
Kun He	Huazhong University of Science and Technology, China
Jian Li	Tsinghua University, China
Lvzhou Li	Sun Yat-sen University, China
Xinwang Liu	National University of Defense Technology, China
Zhihao Tang	Shanghai University of Finance and Economics, China

Program Committee

Kerong Ben	Naval University of Engineering, China
Qingqiong Cai	Nankai University, China
Yongzhi Cao	Peking University, China
Wenbin Chen	Guangzhou University, China
Zhigang Chen	Central South University, China
Baolei Cheng	Soochow University, China
Qilong Feng	Central South University, China
Qi Fu	Hunan University of Science and Technology, China
Zhiguo Fu	Northeast Normal University, China
Kun He	Shenzhen Institute of Computing Sciences, China

Kun He	Huazhong University of Science and Technology, China
Lengxiao Huang	Nanjing University, China
Zhaoming Huang	Guangxi Medical University, China
Hua Jiang	Yunnan University, China
Haitao Jiang	Shandong University, China
Shaofeng Jiang	Peking University, China
Yan Jin	Huazhong University of Science and Technology, China
Xiujuan Lei	Shaanxi Normal University, China
Jian Li	Tsinghua University, China
Longjie Li	Lanzhou University, China
Minming Li	City University of Hong Kong, China
Qian Li	Shenzhen Institutes of Advanced Technology, Chinese Academy of Sciences, China
Xinyu Li	Hunan First Normal University, China
Xuhui Li	Wuhan University, China
Bingkai Lin	Nanjing University, China
Huawen Liu	Zhejiang Normal University, China
Jiyuan Liu	National University of Defense Technology, China
Peiqiang Liu	Shandong University of Finance and Economics, China
Shengxin Liu	Harbin Institute of Technology, Shenzhen, China
Tian Liu	Peking University, China
Yanli Liu	Wuhan University of Science and Technology, China
Yuling Liu	Hunan University, China
Zhendong Liu	Shanghai Polytechnic University, China
Jun Long	National University of Defense Technology, China
Lei Luo	National University of Defense Technology, China
Zhanyou Ma	North Minzu University, China
Dongjing Miao	Harbin Institute of Technology, China
Qiufen Ni	Guangdong University of Technology, China
Haiyu Pan	Guilin University of Electronic Technology, China
Jianmin Pang	Information Engineering University, China
Pan Peng	University of Science and Technology of China, China
Guozhen Rong	Changsha University of Science and Technology, China

Shuai Shao	University of Science and Technology of China, China
Feng Shi	Central South University, China
Haihe Shi	Jiangxi Normal University, China
Yangguang Shi	Shandong University, China
Bosheng Song	Hunan University, China
Feng Tan	Jiangxi Normal University, China
Yun Tan	Central South University of Forestry and Technology, China
Chang Tang	China University of Geosciences, China
Zhihao Tang	Shanghai University of Finance and Economics, China
Biaoshuai Tao	Shanghai Jiao Tong University, China
Changjing Wang	Jiangxi Normal University, China
Gang Wang	Nankai University, China
Liwei Wang	Wuhan University, China
Xiaofeng Wang	North Minzu University, China
Yiyuan Wang	Northeast Normal University, China
Yong Wang	North China Electric Power University, China
Zihe Wang	Renmin University of China, China
Guangwei Wu	Central South University of Forestry and Technology, China
Jigang Wu	Guangdong University of Technology, China
Zhengjun Xi	Shaanxi Normal University, China
Mengji Xia	Institute of Software, Chinese Academy of Sciences, China
Lingyun Xiang	Changsha University of Science and Technology, China
Meihua Xiao	East China Jiaotong University, China
Chao Xu	Changsha University of Science and Technology, China
Yicheng Xu	Shenzhen Institute of Advanced Technology, Chinese Academy of Sciences, China
Jiaoyun Yang	Hefei University of Technology, China
Penghui Yao	Nanjing University, China
Zhen You	Jiangxi Normal University, China
Chihao Zhang	Shanghai Jiao Tong University, China
Guangquan Zhang	Soochow University, China
Jialin Zhang	Institute of Computing Technology, Chinese Academy of Sciences, China
Peng Zhang	Shandong University, China
Yong Zhang	Shenzhen Institute of Advanced Technology, Chinese Academy of Sciences, China

Zhao Zhang	Zhejiang Normal University, China
Zhijie Zhang	Fuzhou University, China
Xiangfu Zhao	Yantai University, China
Hong Zheng	East China University of Science and Technology, China
Shenggen Zheng	Guangdong-Hong Kong-Macao Greater Bay Area Quantum Science Center, China
Cheng Zhong	Guangxi University, China
Shuming Zhou	Fujian Normal University, China
Daming Zhu	Shandong University, China
En Zhu	National University of Defense Technology, China
Zhengkang Zuo	Jiangxi Normal University, China

Contents

Algorithm Design

EFX Graph Division with (Weakly) Lexicographic Preferences 3
   Kuncheng Shao and Hao Guo

Online Bottleneck Matching on a Ring 14
   Man Xiao and Weidong Li

Learning to Design Greedy Algorithm for NP-Complete Problems 30
   Zhenxin Ding, Zihao Huang, Jingyan Sui, Ruizhi Liu, Shizhe Ding,
   Liming Xu, Chao Wang, Haicang Zhang, Chungong Yu, and Dongbo Bu

Approximation Algorithm

Approximation Algorithms on Linear Equalities and Inequalities Mod p 47
   Zhongzheng Tang, Haoyang Zou, and Zhuo Diao

Online Clustering on the Line with θ-th Power Cost Variable Sized
Clustering 58
   Rongchuan Luo

1-Line Minimum λ-Steiner Tree Problem 68
   Yinhua Chen, Jianglin Li, Wencheng Wang, and Tongquan Zhang

Logic

Generalized Possibilistic CTL* Model Checking with Fuzzy Temporal
Logic Operators 81
   Chuanjiang Mu, Wuniu Liu, and Yongming Li

Medical Procedures Based on Bayesian Network and Possibilistic Model
Checking 95
   Ying Wen, Qing He, and Yongming Li

Artificial Intelligence Theory and Algorithm

A Triple-Branch Frequency-Aware Network for Image Manipulation
Detection 111
   Wenyan Pan, Zhihua Xia, and Jiaohua Qin

Advances in Neural Radiance Fields for Large-Scale 3D Scene
Reconstruction: A Comprehensive Review 123
   Yu Du, Fuchun Sun, Xiao Lv, and Xian Zhang

Chinese Medical Spoken Language Understanding Based on Prototypical
Modification Network and Contrastive Learning 140
   Guofeng Zheng, Na Liu, Chen Li, Jie Yang, and Lu Dao

Algorithm Application

Hierarchical Feature Selection Method Based on Sequential Backward
Selection Algorithm for Fasting Blood Glucose Prediction 161
   Wencheng Sun and Xiaoyong Chen

Personalized Recommendation Algorithm Based on Knowledge Graphs
with High-Order Information 169
   Siyao Zhang, Zhihui Wang, Jinru Hu, and Jianrui Chen

Author Index 181

Algorithm Design

EFX Graph Division with (Weakly) Lexicographic Preferences

Kuncheng Shao and Hao Guo[✉]

School of Mathematics and Statistics, Yunnan University, Kunming 650500, Yunnan, People's Republic of China
guoh0221@163.com

Abstract. We study the fair division of indivisible items on undirected graphs under lexicographic preferences, which conside vertices as goods to be allocated to n agents, with the requirement that the bundles have to be connected. We prove that when the graph is a complete bipartite graph and the number of vertices on both sides is greater than n, an envy-free up to any good (EFX) division always exists. By introducing parameter k to relax the classical definition of lexicographic preferences, we prove that when $k \leq n-1$, there does not always exist an EFX division for paths. However, if $k = n$, an envy-free division can always be found for connected graphs. Moreover, under weakly lexicographic preferences, we provide an algorithm based on the maximum weight matching algorithm that can output an EFX division in polynomial time.

Keywords: Fair division · EFX · Undirected graph · Lexicographic preferences

1 Introduction

Fair allocation has been one of the classic and popular topics in the past decade and has attracted many scholars for in-depth research [1]. Such problems can be modeled with simple and clear mathematical models to describe common challenges encountered in many areas of people's lives, including the supply and distribution of scarce materials [2], the multi-resource allocation in cloud computing [3,4] and cloud edge collaborative computing [5], the assignment of course seats at universities [6], crew rostering [7] and so on.

Most research on the allocation of indivisible items primarily focuses on situations in which agents' utility functions are additive. However, in this paper, we primarily investigate lexicographic preferences, which are a subdomain of additive preferences, and agents choose bundles based on the highest-valued item within them. For example, universities prefer to admit all applicants including the top-performing student rather than excluding it. Lexicographic preferences have been extensively studied in various fields [8,9]. Hosseini et al. studied

---

Supported in part by the 14th Postgraduate Innovation Foundation of Yunnan University [No. KC-22221138].

fair allocation under lexicographic preferences, for goods or chores-only [10] and mixed items [11,12].

Combining graph structures with fair division can more specifically and in detail characterize the particular relevance between agents or items. When the valuation functions are additive, the graph is a path, and with the constraint of connected bundles, an EF1 division can always be found if $n \leq 3$ [13]. Bei et al. [14] showed that complete bipartite graphs always admit a division satisfying envy-freeness up to one good (EF1) for three agents. For the division of mixed items under lexicographic preferences, when treating agents as vertices, a G-EFX division can always be found in graphs with diameter ≤ 4 [15]. Aigner-Horev et al. [16] gave a polynomial-time algorithm for finding an envy-free matching of maximum cardinality in a bipartite graph. With ordinal preferences and arbitrary entitlement, Vishwa et al. [17] found there always exist divisions that are weighted necessarily proportional up to one item (WSD-PROP1) by reducing it to a problem of finding perfect matchings in a bipartite graph.

Before us, few have considered the problem that combines lexicographic preferences and graph structure. This problem treats vertices as items and requires that the bundles assigned to each agent be connected. Such scenarios have real-life applications: for instance, in a company's human resource allocation problem, when forming groups, members in the same group are required to have related work directions (corresponding to our connectivity setting), while different groups prioritize having the group leader with the highest corresponding workability.

We find that the structure of the graph significantly limits the existence of EFX divisions. Therefore, by introducing the parameter k, we relaxed the definition of preferences and continued to study the fair division of paths and other connected graphs. We found that when $k \leq n-1$ and n, m are general values, a connected EFX division may not exist in the path. By increasing k to the number of agents (i.e., $k = n$), relatively good results be obtained. In this paper, we mainly consider three typical graph structures: complete bipartite graphs, paths, and connected graphs. For star graphs and tree graphs, we can find counterexamples to demonstrate that EFX divisions do not exist when $k = 1$, specific details can be found in subsequent versions. In our future research, we will also consider the graph partitioning problem for more types of graph structures.

2 Preliminaries

For every k$\in \mathbb{N}$, define [k]$= \{1, 2, \ldots, k\}$. Let $N = [n]$ be a finite set of agents and $G = (V, E)$ be an undirected finite graph, where $V = \{v_1, v_2, \ldots, v_m\}$. The vertices in V correspond to goods. A subset X of V is connected if it induces a connected subgraph of G. We write $\mathcal{C}(V) \subseteq 2^V$ for the set of connected subsets of V, also called bundles. A division $A = (A_1, \ldots, A_n)$ where $A_i \in \mathcal{C}(V)$ is the bundle allocated to agent n and no item is allocated more than once, i.e.,$\cup_{i \in N} A_i = V$ and $A_i \cap A_j = \phi$ when $i \neq j$.

Importance Ordering. For each agent $i \in N$ there is an associated importance ordering $\triangleright_i$ that is a strict linear order over V (we also consider weakly lexicographic preference which is a weak linear order in the following settings). For example,

$$\triangleright_i : v_1 \triangleright v_2 \triangleright v_3 \tag{1}$$

This means that for agent i, v_1 is considered more important than v_2, and v_2 is more important than v_3. Given an importance ordering $\triangleright_i$ and a subset I of V, let $\triangleright_i(l, I)$ denote the item of the l-th position in I according to $\triangleright_i$. In the case where $I = V$, we will write $\triangleright_i(l)$ for brevity. In the example, letting $I = \{v_1, v_3\}$, we have $\triangleright_i(1, I) = v_1$ and $\triangleright_i(2, I) = v_3$. We use a number $pos_i(a)$ to describe the position of good a in $\triangleright_i$ such that $\triangleright_i(pos_i(a)) = a$.

Lexicographic Preference. Lexicographic preference $\succ_i$ is a strict linear order over all possible subsets of items. We consider a relaxation of lexicographic preferences, which are defined by both the number k and the agent's importance ordering: For any pair of $X, Y \subseteq V$: $X \succ_i Y$, if and only if, $pos_i(\triangleright_i(1, Y)) - pos_i(\triangleright_i(1, X)) \geq k$ ($k \in \mathbb{N}$). It should be noted that in our setup only connected bundles are allowed. When $k = 1$, it is the original version of lexicographic preferences.

Weakly Lexicographic Preference. We additionally consider weak lexicographic preferences in this case, which is a weak linear order defined as follows:
For $X, Y \subseteq V$, let $\triangleright_i(1, X) = v_a$, $\triangleright_i(1, Y) = v_b$

(1) $v_a \triangleright_i v_b \Leftrightarrow X \succ_i Y$;
(2) $v_a \trianglerighteq_i v_b \Leftrightarrow X \succeq_i Y$;
(3) v_a and v_b are the same vertex $\Leftrightarrow X \sim_i Y$

For example, giving an importance ordering:

$$\triangleright_i : v_1 \triangleright v_2 \trianglerighteq v_3 \tag{2}$$

This indicates that for agent i, v_2 and v_3 are nearly equally important, but v_1 is more important than both v_2 and v_3. The weakly lexicographic preference on it is: $\{v_1, v_2, v_3\} \sim_i \{v_1, v_3\} \sim_i \{v_1, v_2\} \sim_i \{v_1\} \succ_i \{v_2, v_3\} \sim_i \{v_2\} \succeq_i \{v_3\}$.

Envy-Freeness (EF). Given a pair of $i, j \in N$, we say agent i envies j if $A_j \succ_i A_i$. A division A is EF if $A_i \succeq_i (\sim_i) A_j$ for every pair of $i, j \in N$.

Envy-Free up to Any Good (EFX). This is a widely used relaxation form of EF. A division A satisfies EFX if, for any part of $i, j \in N$ of agents, either $A_j = \phi$ or every good $g \in A_j$, $A_i \succeq_i (\sim_i) A_j \setminus \{g\}$.

3 Lexicographic Preference

In this chapter, we mainly discuss the existence results of connected EFX divisions on connected graphs. However, when we considered paths and other graphs, such existence results did not hold. Therefore, we introduced the parameter k to relax the definition of EFX and discussed the existence results of connected EFX divisions on some graph structures.

3.1 $k = 1$

In this section, we discuss the division for complete bipartite graphs under lexicographic preferences when $k = 1$ and present an existence theorem. To test whether a division under lexicographic preferences is EFX, we quote a propositon which introduced by Hadi Hosseini [10]:

Proposition 1 [10]. *A division A is EFX if and only if each envied agent in A gets exactly one good.*

To check the correctness of the connection, we show a simple observation concerning connected divisions for a complete bipartite graph, which can be proven by contradiction:

Proposition 2. *Given a complete bipartite graph $G = (U, T; E)$, $A = \{A_1, A_2, \ldots, A_n\}$ is a connected division, if and only if, for every A_i in which $|A_i| > 1$, it holds that $\exists v_u \in U, v_u \in A_i$ and $\exists v_t \in T, v_t \in A_i$.*

Here, we here present that an EFX division may not exist in a complete bipartite graph with at least one side of vertices less than n.

Theorem 1. *Let a, b be positive integers with $a \leq b$. The connected EFX division always exists in the complete bipartite graph $K_{a,b}$ if and only if one of the following holds:*

(1) $a = b = 1$;
(2) $a \geq n$.

Proof. If $a = b = 1$, there always exists a connected EFX division since we can assign one vertex to each of two agents, and if there are additional agents, they receive empty bundles. Next we will prove (2) in two steps: (2.1) when $a < n$, there exist instances where no connected EFX division can be found; (2.2) when $a \geq n$, a connected EFX division can always be found. Let us prove (2.1) by giving Examples 1 and 2.

Example 1. Suppose that $N = \{1, 2\}$ have identical ordering. Let G be a complete bipartite graph where $a = 1 < n$ and $b = 2 \geq n$, as shown in Fig. 1:

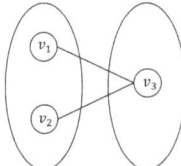

Fig. 1. Complete bipartite graph with $a = 1, b = 2$

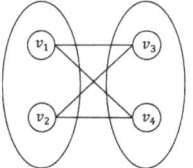

Fig. 2. Complete bipartite graph with $a = 2, b = 2$.

$$\triangleright_i : v_3 \triangleright v_2 \triangleright v_1 \qquad (3)$$

Let v_3 assigned to agent 1. There are four possible results for A_1: $\{v_3\}, \{v_1, v_3\}, \{v_2, v_3\}, \{v_1, v_2, v_3\}$. Thus agent 2 receives the remaining items correspondingly: $\{v_1, v_2\}, \{v_2\}, \{v_1\}, \phi$. The case where $A_1 = \{v_3\}, A_2 = \{v_1, v_2\}$ violates connectivity and any other violates EFX by Propositon 1. Therefore connected EFX divisions are not guaranteed to exist in Example 1.

Example 2. Suppose that $N = \{1, 2, 3\}$ have identical ordering. Let G be a complete bipartite graph $a = 2 < n$ and $b = 2 < n$, as shown in Fig. 2:

$$\triangleright_i : v_4 \triangleright v_3 \triangleright v_2 \triangleright v_1 \qquad (4)$$

Assume that v_4 is assigned to agent 1. If $|A_1| > 1$, then agent 1 will be envied by others and the division is not EFX. If $|A_1| = 1$, it means $A_1 = \{v_4\}$. Next, assume that v_3 is assigned to agent 2. If $|A_2| > 1$, then agent 2 will be envied by agent 3 and the division is not EFX. If $|A_2| = 1$, it means $A_2 = \{v_3\}$, and v_1 and v_2 are both assigned to agent 3, but the undle is not connected in this case. Therefore, there is no connected EFX division in Example 2.

Now we prove (2.2) by giving a simple algorithm process description:

(2.2) If $a \geq n$, let $G = (U, T, E)$ be a complete bipartite graph with $n \leq |U| \leq |T|$. Set the agent sequence $\sigma = (1, \ldots, n)$, starting with agent 1, each agent picks their favorite unallocated vertex, and then all remaining items are assigned to agent n. Let $A = \{A_1, \ldots, A_n\}$. division A is obviously EFX (because agents of $\{1, \ldots, n-1\}$ obtain only one vertex, and they prefer their bundles to agent n's bundle. Therefore, n will not be envied by others. According to Proposition 1, this division is EFX). In what follows, we prove the connectivity of A.

Since everyone only gets one item except agent n, we only need to prove that A_n is connected. For contradiction suppose that A_n is disconnected, therefore A_n is a subset of U or T according to Propositon 2. If $A_n \subset U$, since n receives all unallocated items in step 6, the vertices of T have already been picked by agents preceding n in total in step 4. Hence $T \subseteq \bigcup_{i \in N \setminus \{n\}} A_i$ and $|\bigcup_{i \in N \setminus \{n\}} A_i| = n-1$, but $|T| \geq n$, a contradiction; If $A_n \subset T$, we can get the contradiction in exactly the same way as for $|U| \geq n$. Thus, A_n is connected. It is also a PO division(the proof of PO can be directly derived from the conclusions obtained by Hadi Hosseini [10]).

The complete bipartite graph in Example 1 can be seen as a path with three vertices. If their favorite vertex is v_3, it is impossible to find a connected EFX division. This demonstrates the significant limitations that graph structures impose on lexicographic EFX divisions under the original definition. For this reason, in the next section, we investigate the problem with lexicographic preferences relaxed by parameter k.

3.2 Nonexistence Result of Paths When $k \leq n - 1$

When $k = n - 1$, we consider connected EFX divisions in path, and prove that there exists an instance where no connected EFX division can be found:

Lemma 1. *When the graph is a path in which $|V| = 2n - 1$ and $k = n - 1$, there is an instance where a connected EFX division cannot be found.*

Proof. We will prove Lemma 1 by giving Example 3 as shown in Fig. 3:

Example 3. Suppose that $N = \{1, 2, \ldots, n\}$ have identical ordering. Let $G = (V, E)$ be a path with $|V| = 2n - 1$ and $k = n - 1$:

$$\triangleright_i : v_1 \triangleright v_2 \triangleright \cdots \triangleright v_m - 1 \triangleright v_m$$

Fig. 3. The path $G = (V, E)$ with $|V| = 2n - 1$ and $k = n - 1$.

Assume that v_1 is assigned to agent 1 (the cases where v_1 is assigned to other agents are similar), we discuss this in two cases: $v_m \notin A_1$ and $v_m \in A_1$.

If $v_m \notin A_1$, assume that v_m is assigned to agent 2. According to the definition, agent 2 will envy the agent who gets one or more of $\{v_1, \ldots, v_{m-n+1}\}$. To satisfy EFX, all these envied agents can only be allocated one vertex among the $\{v_1, \ldots, v_{m-n+1}\}$ according to Proposition 1. Since $m = 2n-1$, $m-n+1 > n-1$, which means that if one division is EFX, $\{v_1, \ldots, v_{m-n+1}\}$ cannot be completely allocated. Such a division would only be a partial division. Therefore, no EFX division exists.

If $v_m \in A_1$, this means that $|A_1| > 1$. It only needs to be proven that there is another agent who will envy agent 1. According to the definition, any agent whose bundle does not contain any vertices of $\{v_2, \ldots, v_{n-1}\}$ will envy agent 1. Allocating these $n - 2$ vertices among the other $n - 1$ agents will inevitably leave one agent having none of them. Therefore, the agent will envy agent 1. In conclusion, there is no EFX division in Example 3.

Since there may not be a connected EFX division even in such a specific connected graph as a path, the problem will be even more challenging for general connected graphs. However, we will later prove that if the value of k is increased to n, it is always possible to find a connected envy-free division for general connected graphs.

3.3 $k = n$: Envy-Free Division for Connected Graphs

Next, we prove that when $k = n$ for any connected graph G, there is always a connected envy-free division, and Algorithm 1 can output one of them. The algorithm select an agent with an empty bundle and assign their most preferred unallocated vertex at first. And then, find one spanning tree of the connected graph G. At,last, starting from agent 1 to n, consider all the neighboring vertices of A_i. Check whether the neighboring vertices contain any unallocated vertex: if there is any unallocated vertex, update A_i; otherwise, assign A_i to agent i.

Algorithm 1: Computing a connected EF division

Input: $(G, N, \triangleright)$, where $G = (V, E)$ is a connected graph
Output: a connected EF division

1 $A \leftarrow (\phi, \ldots, \phi), H \leftarrow V, V_i \leftarrow \phi$;
2 **while** $N \neq \phi$ **do**
3 $\quad$ choose any agent $i \in N$;
4 $\quad$ $g_i \leftarrow \triangleright_i(1, H)$;
5 $\quad$ $A_i \leftarrow A_i \cup \{g_i\}$;
6 $\quad$ $N \leftarrow N \setminus \{i\}$;
7 $\quad$ $H \leftarrow H \setminus A_i$;
8 **end**
9 Find the spanning tree $T = (V, F)$ of the connected graph $G = (V, E)$.
10 **for** $i = 1$ *to* n **do**
11 $\quad$ $V_i \leftarrow$ all the neighboring vertices of A_i on $T = (V, F)$.;
12 $\quad$ **if** $V_i \cap H \neq \phi$ **then**
13 $\quad\quad$ $V_i \leftarrow V_i \cup (V_i \cap H)$;
14 $\quad\quad$ $H \leftarrow H \setminus (V_i \cap H)$, return to step 11.
15 $\quad$ **else**
16 $\quad\quad$ $A_i \leftarrow A_i \cup V_i$.
17 $\quad$ **end**
18 $\quad$ $i = i + 1$
19 **end**
20 Return A.

Proposition 3. *In Algorithm 1, all vertices are assigned, and each of them is assigned to only one agent.*

Proof. Based on the algorithm process, it can be clearly inferred that every vertex is assigned to one agent. Next, we will demonstrate that all vertices are assigned in Algorithm 1. For contradiction, suppose that at least one vertex is unallocated. Such a vertex must be unallocated and not connected to any other allocated vertices. This contradicts the fact that the graph G is connected.

The proposition shows that the division returned by Algorithm 1 is certainly complete and disjointed. The following theorem demonstrates that the division returned by Algorithm 1 is also connected and envy-free.

Theorem 2. *Given any connected graph G, Algorithm 1 can return a connected, envy-free division of G.*

Proof. Since in step 12 the search is for the neighbors of all unallocated vertices, it is undoubtedly true that each agent's bundle is connected. Next, we prove that this division is envy-free. For $\forall i, j \in N$, in steps 2–8 each agent gets a favorite unallocated vertex, so that $g_i = \triangleright_i(1, A_i)$ and $\{g_i\} \succ_i (V \setminus \bigcup_{j \in N \setminus \{i\}} g_j)$ where g_j is the vertex allocated to agent j in steps 2–8. We discuss this in two cases: Let $\triangleright_i(1, A_j) = g'_j$, (1) $g_i \triangleright_i g'_j$; (2) $g'_j \triangleright_i g_i$. If (1), then i will not envy j; If (2), since $\{g_i\} \succ_i (A_j \setminus \{g_j\})$, it means $g'_j = g_j$ and $g_j \triangleright_i g_i$. Because there are only n agents, $pos_i(g_i) - pos_i(g_j) \leq n - 1$ holds true. Moreover, agents i and j will not envy each other by $k = n$.

4 Weakly Lexicographic Preferences

In this section, we discuss the division for complete bipartite graphs under lexicographic preferences when $k = 1$. It can always find a connected EFX division if both sides of vertices greater than n (including n).

To describe the algorithm conveniently, we use v_l^i instead of $\triangleright_i(l)(i \in N, l \in [m])$. Let us introduce a weighted complete bipartite graph $G' = ([n-1], M; E; \omega)$ in which ω is based on the agents' preferences. Fixing an ordering of agents $\sigma = (1, \ldots, n)$, in G', one part of the vertices represents the first $n - 1$ agents in the sequence, and the other part represents all the items. The edge set $E = [n-1] \times M$ consists of pairs of agents and items. The weight $\omega : E \to \mathbb{N}$ is defined as follows: from $i = 1$ to $n - 1$, $\omega(i, v_1^i) = m$; for the edge (i, v_l^i) (where $l > 1$), if $v_{l-1}^i \triangleright_i v_l^i$, set $\omega(i, v_l^i) = m - l + 1$; if $v_{l-1}^i \trianglerighteq_i v_l^i$, set $\omega(i, v_l^i) = \omega(i, v_{l-1}^i)$.

The algorithm first finds the maximum weight matching on the complete bipartite graph G', and then assigns agent i the neighboring vertex through its matching edge. At this point, each of the first $n - 1$ agents receives one vertex. Finally, give all unallocated vertices to the last agent n.

Algorithm 2: Computing a connected EFX division

Input: A weakly lexicographic goods-only instance $(N, G, \triangleright)$ where $G = (U, T; E)$ is a complete bipartite graph
Output: a (connected) EFX division A for G

1   $A \leftarrow (\phi, \ldots, \phi)$, $G' = ([n-1], M; E; \omega)$
2   Use the maximum weight matching algorithm on G';
3   **for** $i = 1$ *to* $n - 1$ **do**
4 | $A_i \leftarrow i$'s neighboring vertex through the matching edges
5   **end**
6   $A_n \leftarrow (V \setminus \bigcup_{i=1}^{n-1} A_i)$
7   **return** A.

Theorem 3. *Suppose that $G = (U, T; E)$ is a complete bipartite graph where $n \leq |U| \leq |T|$. A connected EFX division always exists in $G = (U, T; E)$. Moreover, one can compute such a division in polynomial time.*

Proof. Let $(G, N, \triangleright)$ be an instance where $G = (U, T, E)$ is a complete bipartite graph with $n \leq |U| \leq |T|$. We will show that the division A returned by Algorithm 2 is connected EFX division. The process of proving that A is connected is the same as in Theorem 1 (2.2). In what follows, we will prove that A is EFX.

A is EFX. For the first $n-1$ agents, obviously $|A_i| = 1$ holds true. Therefore, they satisfy EFX. For any $j \in [n-1]$, n may envy j, since $|A_j| = 1$, they also satisfy EFX. The following proof we proceed by contradiction: Assume that there is an agent $p \in [n-1]$ such that p envies agent n. Let $A_p = \{v_p\}$. We have $\triangleright_p(1, A_n) \triangleright_p v_p$, which means that $\omega(p, \triangleright_p(1, A_n)) > \omega(p, v_p)$. Since the edge $(p, \triangleright_p(1, A_n))$ was not selected throughout the maximum weight matching algorithm (its corresponding vertex was assigned to agent n), thus replacing (p, v_p) with $(p, \triangleright_p(1, A_n))$ would lead to a matching with greater total weight than before, which is a contradiction. Therefore, for all $j \in [n-1]$, j will not envy n. In conclusion, A is an EFX division.

5 Conclusion

In this paper, We study the fair division of indivisible items on undirected graphs under lexicographic preferences. We demonstrate that for complete bipartite graphs, a connected EFX+PO division is always achievable. Additionally, we introduce a parameter k to relax the preference definition. Our findings reveal that when $k \leq n-1$ and n, m are general values, connected EFX divisions may not exist in paths. However, by increasing k to the number of agents ($k = n$), an envy-free division can always be found in connected graphs.

References

1. Guo, H., Li, W., Deng, B.: A survey on fair allocation of chores. Mathematics **11**(16), 3616 (2023). https://doi.org/10.3390/math11163616
2. Pathak, P.A., Sönmez, T., Ünver, U.M., Yenmez, M.B.: Fair allocation of vaccines, ventilators and antiviral treatments: leaving no ethical value behind in healthcare rationing. Manag. Sci. **70**(6), 3999–4036 (2023). https://doi.org/10.1287/mnsc.2022.00930
3. Deng, B., Li, W.: Maximin share based mechanisms for multi-resource fair allocation with divisible and indivisible tasks. In: Cai, Z., Chen, Y., Zhang, J. (eds.) Theoretical Computer Science. NCTCS 2022. Communications in Computer and Information Science, vol. 1693, pp. 263–272 (2022). https://doi.org/10.1007/978-981-19-8152-4_19
4. Guo, H., Li, W.: Dynamic multi-resource fair allocation with elastic demands. J. Grid Comput. **22**, 35 (2024). https://doi.org/10.1007/s10723-024-09754-6
5. Li, X., Li, W., Zhang, X.: Multi-resource fair allocation with bandwidth requirement compression in the cloud-edge system. Comput. Electr. Eng. **105**, 108510 (2023). https://doi.org/10.1016/j.compeleceng.2022.108510
6. Budish, E., Cachon, G.P., Kessler, J.B., Othman, A.: Course match: a large-scale implementation of approximate competitive equilibrium from equal incomes for combinatorial allocation. Oper. Res. **65**(2), 314–336 (2017). https://doi.org/10.1287/opre.2016.1544
7. Deng, B.: An improved honey badger algorithm by genetic algorithm and levy flight distribution for solving airline crew rostering problem. IEEE Access **10**, 108075–108088 (2022). https://doi.org/10.1109/ACCESS.2022.3213066
8. Saban, D., Sethuraman, J.: A note on object allocation under lexicographic preferences. J. Math. Econ. **50**, 283–289 (2014). https://doi.org/10.1016/j.jmateco.2013.12.002
9. Nguyen, T.T.: How to fairly allocate indivisible resources among agents having lexicographic subadditive utilities. In: Satapathy, S., Bhateja, V., Nguyen, B., Nguyen, N., Le, DN. (eds) Frontiers in Intelligent Computing: Theory and Applications. Advances in Intelligent Systems and Computing, vol. 1013, pp. 156–166 (2020). https://doi.org/10.1007/978-981-32-9186-7_18
10. Hosseini, H., Sikdar, S., Vaish, R., et al.: Fair and efficient allocations under lexicographic preferences. In: Proceedings of the AAAI Conference on Artificial Intelligence, vol. 35, no. 6, pp. 5472–5480 (2021). https://doi.org/10.1609/aaai.v35i6.16689
11. Hosseini, H., Sikdar, S., Vaish, R., Xia, L.: Fairly dividing mixtures of goods and chores under lexicographic preferences. In Proceedings of the 2023 International Conference on Autonomous Agents and Multiagent Systems (AAMAS 2023), pp. 152–160 (2023). https://doi.org/10.5555/3545946.3598632
12. Hosseini, H., Mammadov, A., Was, T.: Fairly allocating goods and (terrible) chores. In Proceedings of the Thirty-Second International Joint Conference on Artificial Intelligence (IJCAI 2023), pp. 2738–2746 (2023). https://doi.org/10.24963/ijcai.2023/305
13. Bilò, V., Caragiannis, I., Flammini, M., et al.: Almost envy-free allocations with connected bundles. Games Econ. Behav. **131**, 197–221 (2016). https://doi.org/10.1016/j.geb.2021.11.006
14. Bei, X., Igarashi, A., Lu, X., et al.: The price of connectivity in fair division. SIAM J. Disc. Math. **36**(2), 1156–1186 (2022). https://doi.org/10.1137/20M1388310

15. Payan, J., Sengupta, R., Viswanathan, V.:Relaxations of envy-freeness over graphs. In Proceedings of the 2023 International Conference on Autonomous Agents and Multiagent Systems (AAMAS 2023), 2652–2654 (2023). https://doi.org/10.5555/3545946.3599032
16. Aigner-Horev, E., Segal-Halevi, E.: Envy-free matchings in bipartite graphs and their applications to fair division. Inf. Sci. **587**, 164–187 (2022). https://doi.org/10.1016/j.ins.2021.11.059
17. HV, Prakash, V., Nimbhorkar, P.: Weighted proportional allocations of indivisible goods and chores: insights via matchings. In: Proceedings of the 23rd International Conference on Autonomous Agents and Multiagent Systems, pp. 780–788 (2024). https://doi.org/10.5555/3635637.3662931

Online Bottleneck Matching on a Ring

Man Xiao and Weidong Li[✉]

School of Mathematics and Statistics, Yunnan University, Kunming 650504, China
weidongmath@126.com

Abstract. On a ring, given m servers and m requests arriving one by one in an online fashion. Upon each request arrival, it needs to be immediately matched to a server, generating a matching distance on the ring. The objective is to find a matching where each server and each request are strictly matched once, minimizing the maximum matching distance. When the m servers are evenly distributed on the ring, we prove that the classical greedy algorithm achieves an optimal competitive ratio of m. When $m = 3$, using polar coordinates to partition the ring into three intervals, we provide optimal online algorithms for four parameter scenarios where the competitive ratio depends on the server spacing ratio.

Keywords: Online bottleneck matching · Ring · Partition · Online algorithm

1 Introduction

The online matching problem in metric spaces has significant applications in scenarios such as matching between ride-hailing services and passengers, or between food delivery orders and couriers [1–3]. In a metric space (X, d), where X is a set of points and $d(\cdot, \cdot)$ is a distance function, the problem involves m servers $s_1, s_2, \cdots, s_m$ and m requests $r_1, r_2, \cdots, r_m$ arriving one by one in an online fashion. Upon the appearance of each request r_j, an online algorithm immediately needs to match it to an unmatched server s_i, generating a matching distance $d(r_j, s_i)$. The objective is to minimize the maximum matching distance in the online bottleneck matching problem.

The performance of online algorithms is typically measured by their competitive ratio. For a given instance I of a minimization online problem and an online algorithm A, let $C^A(I)$ (abbreviated as C^A) denote the output value of algorithm A for instance I, and let $C^{OPT}(I)$ (abbreviated as C^{OPT}) denote the optimal value in the offline setting. If $C^A \leq \rho C^{OPT}$, then algorithm A is said to have a competitive ratio of at most ρ. If the competitive ratio of any algorithm is not less than r, then r is considered a lower bound for the problem. Particularly, when $r = \rho$, algorithm A is called an optimal online algorithm for the problem.

There is relatively limited research on the online bottleneck matching problem. Kalyanasundaram and Pruhs [8] were the first to study this problem, presenting a deterministic online algorithm with a competitive ratio of at most

$2m-1$ and providing a lower bound of $m+1$. Idury and Schaffer [10] improved this lower bound to $1.44m$, which remains the best known lower bound. Anthony and Chung [6] proved that the competitive ratio lower bound for the classic greedy algorithm (which always matches the currently arriving request to the nearest unmatched server) is at least 2^{m-1} and at most $m2^{m-1}$. Subsequently, Anthony and Chung [7] improved the upper bound to $2^m - 1$. They also considered model where requests can be rejected to a certain extent and proposed two threshold greedy algorithms. Xiao and Li [21] designed an optimal online algorithm for the online bottleneck matching problem with two heterogeneous servers.

The online minimum metric matching problem is closely related to the online bottleneck matching problem and aims to minimize the total matching distance. Kalyanasundaram and Pruhs [8] and Khuller [9] independently considered this problem and proposed a deterministic optimal online algorithms with a competitive ratio of $2m-1$. Kalyanasundaram and Pruhs [8] showed that the competitive ratio of the classic greedy algorithm is exactly $2^m - 1$. Raghvendra [11] proposed a deterministic online algorithm with a competitive ratio of $2m - 1 + o(1)$ based on primal-dual method. Meyerson et al. [12] designed a randomized online algorithm with a competitive ratio of at most $O(\log^3 m)$ by appropriately modifying part of the greedy decisions in Meyerson et al.'s work [12]. Bansal et al. [22] proposed a randomized online algorithm with a competitive ratio of at most $O(\log^2 m)$, which is currently the best known randomized online algorithm. They also proved that there is no randomized algorithm with a competitive ratio less than $\ln m$. When requests appear in a uniformly random order, Raghvendra [11] designed a deterministic online algorithm with a competitive ratio of $2H_m - 1 + o(1)$, where $H_m = \sum_{k=1}^{m} \frac{1}{k}$ is the m-th harmonic number. They also proved that there is no randomized online algorithm with a competitive ratio less than $2H_m - 1 - o(1)$. Gairing and Klimm [2] proved that the competitive ratio of the classic greedy algorithm lies in the interval $[m^{0.292}, m]$. Xiao and Li [20] considered the online semi-matching problem with two heterogeneous servers and proposed an optimal online algorithm. When $d(\cdot, \cdot) \in \{0, 1\}$, Duppala et al. [3] proved that the randomized greedy algorithm is optimal, with a competitive ratio of $(1 + \frac{1}{m})(H_{m+1} - 1)$.

Since Kalyanasundaram and Pruhs [25] proposed in 1998 whether it is possible to design an optimal online algorithm for the online minimum metric matching problem on a line, the problem has remained unsolved. For the online minimum metric matching problem on a line, Fuchs et al. [13] provided a deterministic algorithm lower bound of 9.001 through a complex construction. Gupta and Lewi [14] designed a randomized online algorithm with a competitive ratio of at most $O(\log m)$. Antoniadis et al. [15] devised a deterministic online algorithm with a competitive ratio of $O(m^{\log(3+\varepsilon)-1}/\varepsilon)$. Nayyar and Raghvendra [16] proved that the competitive ratio of the deterministic online algorithm in [11] is at most $O(\log^2 m)$, and Raghvendra [17] improved it to $O(\log m)$. Peserico and Scquizzato [18] demonstrated, through clever construction, that there is no randomized online algorithm with a competitive ratio less than $\sqrt{\log_2(m+1)}/15$.

Balkanski et al. [19] analyzed the performance of greedy algorithm for several random models.

Recently, Xiao et al. [23] proposed optimal online algorithms for two specific online bottleneck matching problems on a line based on interval partitioning methods. A ring is a geometric structure closely related to a line. Jawgal [24] considered the online traveling salesman problem on a ring, where rquests always appear online on the ring, and the salesman can only move on the ring. For model requiring a return to the starting point, Jawgal [24] provided a lower bound of $\frac{28}{13}$ and designed an online algorithm with a competitive ratio of 2.5. This paper addresses the online bottleneck matching problem on a ring. Essentially, the online bottleneck matching problem on a ring can also be viewed as on a polygon. The structure of the paper is as follows: In Sect. 2, we introduce preliminaries; In Sect. 3, we consider the case of servers distributed uniformly on the ring; In Sect. 4, we consider the scenario where there are only three non-equidistant servers on the ring; and finally, we summarize the results.

2 Preliminaries

On a ring, $d(\cdot,\cdot)$ is a distance function defined on the ring. Given m servers $s_1, s_2, \cdots, s_m$ and m requests $r_1, r_2, \cdots, r_m$ arriving one by one in an online fashion, when each request r_j arrives, an online algorithm needs to immediately and irrevocably match it to an unmatched server s_i and produce a matching distance $d(r_j, s_i)$. Where $d(r_j, s_i)$ is defined as the shortest arc length between r_j and s_i. As shown in Fig. 1(1), $d(r_j, s_i)$ represents the length of the blue arc. As shown in Fig. 1(2), d_1, d_2, d_3, d_4 respectively represent the lengths of the corresponding four short arcs, and the distances for matching r_1 to s_1 and s_2 are d_4, $d_2 + d_3$ respectively. The distances for matching r_2 to s_1 and s_2 are $d_1 + d_2$ and d_2 respectively. After all requests are matched, each server and each request are matched exactly once, resulting in a matching M. Let $s_{\sigma(j)}$ denote the server matched to request r_j in matching M. The goal is to find a matching M such that the maximum matching distance $\max_j d(r_j, s_{\sigma(j)})$ is minimized.

Without loss of generality, let the radius of the ring be 1, i.e., the circumference of the ring is 2π. For any request r_j and server s_i, it is obvious that

$$d(r_j, s_i) \leq \pi.$$

We use polar coordinates with the center of the ring as the origin. The position of any point on the ring can be represented in polar coordinate as $(1, \theta)$. For simplicity, any polar coordinate $(1, \theta)$ is abbreviated as θ. Let $p(r_j)$ and $p(s_i)$ represent the polar coordinate positions of r_j and s_i on the ring respectively.

3 Adjacent Servers Equidistant

In this section, we consider the scenario where m servers are uniformly distributed on a ring (with equal spacing between any adjacent servers). We prove

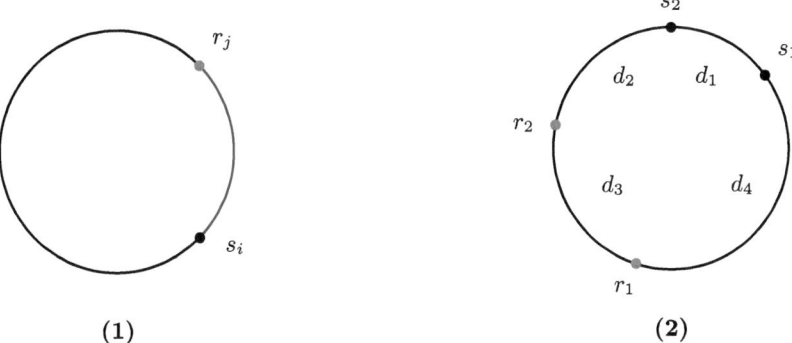

Fig. 1. Matching distance on the ring

that the classical greedy algorithm is an optimal online algorithm with a competitive ratio of m. For convenience, let the polar coordinates of the m servers be

$$p(s_1) = 0, p(s_2) = \frac{2\pi}{m}, p(s_3) = \frac{4\pi}{m}, \cdots, p(s_i) = \frac{2(i-1)\pi}{m}, \cdots, p(s_m) = 2\pi - \frac{2\pi}{m}.$$

Obviously, $d(s_1, s_2) = d(s_2, s_3) = \cdots = d(s_{m-1}, s_m) = d(s_m, s_1) = \frac{2\pi}{m}$.

Theorem 1. *When the distance between each pair of adjacent servers is equal, the competitive ratio of any deterministic online algorithm A for the online bottleneck matching problem on the ring is at least m.*

Proof. As shown in Fig. 2, the first $m-1$ requests appear respectively in $p(r_1) = \frac{\pi}{m}$, $p(r_2) = \frac{3\pi}{m}$, $\cdots$, $p(r_i) = \frac{(2i-1)\pi}{m}$, $\cdots$, $p(r_{m-1}) = 2\pi - \frac{3\pi}{m}$. After $m-1$ requests are matched by an online algorithm A, let s_l be the server that remains unmatched, and $p(s_l) = \frac{2(l-1)\pi}{m}$. The last request r_m arrives at

$$p(r_m) = p(s_l) + \pi = \frac{2(l-1)\pi}{m} + \pi.$$

When m is even, the position $p(r_m)$ of r_m corresponds to the position of a server. Let's assume that $p(r_m)$ is also the position of server s_i. In the optimal solution, the requests $r_1, r_2, \cdots, r_{i-1}, r_m, r_i, r_{i+1}, \cdots, r_m$ are respectively matched to servers $s_1, s_2, \cdots, s_{i-1}, s_i, s_{i+1}, \cdots, s_m$. Thus, $C^{OPT} = \frac{\pi}{m}$, $C^A = d(r_m, s_l) = \pi$. When m is odd, the position $p(r_m)$ of r_m is the midpoint between two adjacent servers. If $p(r_m)$ is the midpoint between servers s_1 and s_m, then in an optimal solution, the requests $r_1, r_2, \cdots, r_m$ are respectively matched to servers $s_1, s_2, \cdots, s_m$. This implies that $C^{OPT} = \frac{\pi}{m}$, $C^A = d(r_m, s_l) = \pi$. Otherwise, let's assume that $p(r_m)$ is the midpoint between servers s_k and s_{k+1}, meaning that $p(r_m)$ is also the position $p(r_k)$ of request r_k. In the optimal solution, requests $r_1, r_2, \cdots, r_k, r_m, r_{k+1}, \cdots, r_{m-1}$ are respectively matched to servers $s_1, s_2, \cdots, s_k, s_{k+1}, s_{k+2}, \cdots, s_m$. It's evident that $C^{OPT} = \frac{\pi}{m}$, $C^A = d(r_m, s_l) = \pi$. Therefore, $\frac{C^A}{C^{OPT}} \geq m$.

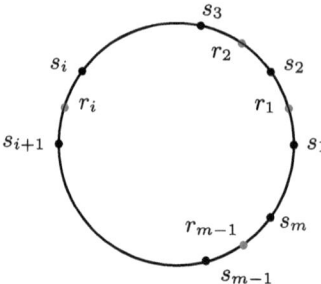

Fig. 2. The position of the first $m-1$ requests on the ring

Theorem 2. *When the distance between each pair of adjacent servers is equal, the competitive ratio of the greedy algorithm for the online bottleneck matching problem on the ring is at most m.*

Proof. Assume that the maximum matching distance of the greedy algorithm occurs when matching request r. According to the distance definition on the ring, the maximum matching distance of the greedy algorithm $C^A \leq \pi$. Let's assume that $p(r) \in [p(s_k) + \frac{\pi}{m}, p(s_{k+1})]$, where $k+1 \leq m$. If r is matched to server s_k (or s_{k+1}) closest to r, then the greedy algorithm achieves optimality.

Next, let's consider that r is matched to server s_k, and that s_k is not the server closest to r. When s_k is not the closest server to r, according to the greedy algorithm, the server s_{k+1} closest to r are matched before r arrives. Let $i_1 = k+1(\mod(m+1)), i_2 = k+2(\mod(m+1)), \cdots, i_t = k+t(\mod(m+1))$, and when r arrives, suppose servers $s_{i_1}, s_{i_2}, \cdots, s_{i_t}$ are all matched, and server s_{i_t+1} is unmatched. That is, when request r arrives, according to the selection of the greedy algorithm, servers $s_{i_1}, s_{i_2}, \cdots, s_{i_t}$ are matched by requests that appeared in the region $[p(s_{i_1}) - \frac{\pi}{m}, p(s_{i_t}) + \frac{\pi}{m}]$. We know $p(r) \in [p(s_k) + \frac{\pi}{m}, p(s_{k+1})]$, in the region $[p(s_{i_1}) - \frac{\pi}{m}, p(s_{i_t}) + \frac{\pi}{m}]$, there are $t+1$ requests and only t servers. Therefore, according to the Pigeonhole Principle, in the optimal solution, there exists a request in the region $[p(s_{i_1}) - \frac{\pi}{m}, p(s_{i_t}) + \frac{\pi}{m}]$ matched to a server in the set $\{s_1, s_2, \cdots, s_m\} \setminus \{s_{i_1}, s_{i_2}, \cdots, s_{i_t}\}$. This implies that $C^{OPT} \geq \frac{\pi}{m}$, thus $\frac{C^A}{C^{OPT}} \leq m$.

If r is matched to a server s by the greedy algorithm other than s_k and s_{k+1}, by the previous proof, a similar argument using the Pigeonhole Principle can be made.

4 Three Non Equidistant Servers

In this section, we consider the online bottleneck matching problem on a ring with only three non equidistant servers. Clearly, the three servers divide the ring into three arcs based on their positions. Without loss of generality, assume that the servers s_1, s_2, s_3 on the ring have polar coordinates $p(s_1) = 0$, $p(s_2) = a$ and $p(s_3) = a + b$, where $0 < a \leq b \leq c = 2\pi - a - b$. Obviously, $a \leq \frac{2\pi}{3}$. Since the radius of the ring is 1, $d(s_1, s_2) = a$, $d(s_2, s_3) = b$, $d(s_1, s_3) = \min\{c, a+b\}$ where the positions of the three servers are shown in Fig. 3. In fact, when $c < a + b$, this is also an online bottleneck matching problem on a triangle, where the three servers are fixed at the vertices of the triangle, and the three requests appear online along the edges of the triangle. When $\frac{b}{a} \leq \sqrt{2}$ and $\frac{a^2+ab}{2a+b} + b + a \leq \pi$, the problem is equivalent to the online bottleneck matching problem on a line for $\alpha \leq \sqrt{2}$ [23]. When $\frac{b}{a} \leq \sqrt{2}$ and $\frac{a^2+ab}{2a+b} + b + a > \pi$, we provide a lower bound $\max\{3, \min\{1 + \frac{\sqrt{\pi^2+4a^2}+\pi}{2a}, \frac{2\pi}{b}\}\}$ and design an optimal online algorithm based on interval partitioning. When $\frac{b}{a} > \sqrt{2}$ and $\frac{3b}{2}+a \leq \pi$, the problem is equivalent to the online bottleneck matching problem on a line for $\alpha > \sqrt{2}$ [23]. When $\alpha > \sqrt{2}$ and $\frac{3b}{2} + a > \pi$, we provide a lower bound $\max\{3, \frac{2\pi}{b}\}$ and design an optimal online algorithm based on interval partitioning.

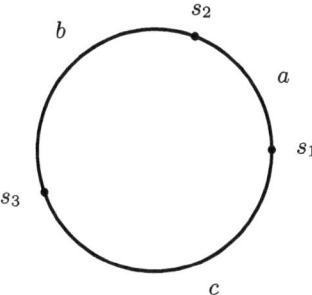

Fig. 3. Three non equidistant servers on the ring

Theorem 3. *The competitive ratio of any online algorithm A for the online bottleneck matching problem on the ring is at least 3.*

Proof. The first request r_1 appears at the position of server s_3, i.e., $p(r_1) = p(s_3)$. If r_1 is matched to server s_2 or s_1 by algorithm A, then the last two requests r_2 and r_3 appear at the positions of servers s_2 and s_1, respectively, i.e., $p(r_2) = p(s_2)$ and $p(r_3) = p(s_1)$. In the optimal solution, requests r_1, r_2, and r_3 are matched to servers s_3, s_2, and s_1, respectively. Therefore, $C^{OPT} = 0$ and $C^A \geq b$. If r_1 is matched to server s_3, then the second request r_2 appears at $p(r_2) = \frac{a}{2}$. There are two possible matches for request r_2.

Case 1. r_2 is matched to server s_1 by algorithm A.

The last request r_3 appears at position $p(r_3) = -\frac{a}{2}$. In the optimal solution, requests r_1, r_2, and r_3 are matched to servers s_3, s_2, s_1, respectively. Therefore, $C^{OPT} = \frac{a}{2}$, $C^A = \frac{3a}{2}$, and $\frac{C^A}{C^{OPT}} = 3$.

Case 2. r_2 is matched to server s_2 by algorithm A.

The last request r_3 appears at position $p(r_3) = \frac{3a}{2}$. In the optimal solution, requests r_1, r_2 and r_3 are matched to servers s_3, s_1 and s_2, respectively. Therefore, $C^{OPT} = \frac{a}{2}$, $C^A = \frac{3a}{2}$, $\frac{C^A}{C^{OPT}} = 3$. According to the above analysis, we have $\frac{C^A}{C^{OPT}} \geq 3$.

4.1 $\frac{b}{a} \leq \sqrt{2}$

Theorem 4. *When $\frac{b}{a} \leq \sqrt{2}$ and $\frac{a^2+ab}{2a+b}+b+a \leq \pi$, this problem is equivalent to the online bottleneck matching problem on a line for $\alpha \leq \sqrt{2}$.*

Proof. When $\frac{b}{a} \leq \sqrt{2}$ and $\frac{a^2+ab}{2a+b}+b+a \leq \pi$, let $\frac{b}{a} = \alpha$. In this case, the online bottleneck matching problem on the ring is equivalent to the online bottleneck matching problem on the line for $\alpha \leq \sqrt{2}$ [23]. □

Theorem 5. *When $\frac{b}{a} \leq \sqrt{2}$ and $\frac{a^2+ab}{2a+b}+b+a > \pi$, the competitive ratio of any online algorithm A for the online bottleneck matching problem on the ring is at least $\max\{3, \min\{1 + \frac{\sqrt{\pi^2+4a^2}+\pi}{2a}, \frac{2\pi}{b}\}\}$.*

Proof. When $\frac{b}{a} \leq \sqrt{2}$, we have

$$\frac{a^2+ab}{2a+b}+b+a \geq \frac{4ab-b^2}{4a-2b}.$$

Let

$$x = \min\{\frac{\sqrt{\pi^2+4a^2}-\pi}{2}, a - \frac{b}{2}\} \leq \frac{a}{2},$$

and

$$y = \min\{\frac{\sqrt{\pi^2+4a^2}+2b-2a-\pi}{2}, \frac{b}{2}\} \leq \frac{b}{2}.$$

When $\pi \leq \frac{4ab-b^2}{4a-2b}$, we have

$$x = a - \frac{b}{2}, y = \frac{b}{2}, \min\{1 + \frac{\sqrt{\pi^2+4a^2}+\pi}{2a}, \frac{2\pi}{b}\} = \frac{2\pi}{b}.$$

When $\pi > \frac{4ab-b^2}{4a-2b}$, we have

$$x = \frac{\sqrt{\pi^2+4a^2}-\pi}{2}, y = \frac{\sqrt{\pi^2+4a^2}+2b-2a-\pi}{2},$$

and

$$\min\{1 + \frac{\sqrt{\pi^2+4a^2}+\pi}{2a}, \frac{2\pi}{b}\} = 1 + \frac{\sqrt{\pi^2+4a^2}+\pi}{2a}.$$

The first request r_1 appears at position $p(r_1) = a-x$, and there are three possible matches for r_1.

Case 1. r_1 is matched to server s_1 by algorithm A.

The second request r_2 appears at position $p(r_2) = -x$. If r_2 is matched to server s_2 by algorithm A, then the last request r_3 appears at position $p(r_3) = p(s_3)$, thus $C^A = d(r_2, s_2) = a + x$. In the optimal solution, requests r_1, r_2, r_3

are matched to servers s_2, s_1, s_3 respectively, $C^{OPT} = d(r_1, s_2) = d(r_2, s_1) = x$. If r_2 is matched to server s_3 by algorithm A, then the last request r_3 appears at position $p(r_3) = a + b + x$, thus $C^A \geq d(r_3, s_2) = b + x$. In the optimal solution, requests r_1, r_2, r_3 are matched to servers s_2, s_1, s_3 respectively, $C^{OPT} = d(r_1, s_2) = d(r_2, s_1) = d(r_3, s_3) = x$. Since $b \geq a$, then,

$$\frac{C^A}{C^{OPT}} \geq \frac{a+x}{x} = 1 + \frac{a}{\min\{\frac{\sqrt{\pi^2+4a^2}-\pi}{2}, a-\frac{b}{2}\}}$$

$$= 1 + \max\{\frac{2a}{\sqrt{\pi^2+4a^2}-\pi}, \frac{2a}{2a-b}\}$$

$$\geq 1 + \frac{\sqrt{\pi^2+4a^2}+\pi}{2a}$$

$$\geq \min\{\frac{2\pi}{b}, 1 + \frac{\sqrt{\pi^2+4a^2}+\pi}{2a}\}.$$

Case 2. r_1 is matched to server s_2 by algorithm A.

The second request r_2 appears at position $p(r_2) = a + y$. If r_2 is matched to server s_1 by algorithm A, then the third request r_3 appears at position $p(r_3) = a + b - \pi$. When $\frac{4ab-b^2}{4a-2b} < \pi < \frac{a^2+ab}{2a+b} + b + a$, there exists

$$|\pi - b - a| < \frac{2a + \pi - \sqrt{\pi^2+4a^2}}{2} = b - y.$$

When $\pi \leq \frac{4ab-b^2}{4a-2b}$, since $\frac{b}{a} \leq \sqrt{2}$, it follows that

$$\pi \leq \frac{4ab-b^2}{4a-2b} \leq a + \frac{3b}{2},$$

which implies that $|\pi - b - a| \leq \frac{b}{2} = b - y$. In the optimal solution, requests r_1, r_2, r_3 are matched to servers s_2, s_3, s_1 respectively. Thus, $C^{OPT} = d(r_2, s_3) = b - y$. Since $C^A \geq d(r_3, s_3) = \pi$, then,

$$\frac{C^A}{C^{OPT}} \geq \frac{\pi}{b-y} = \frac{\pi}{b - \min\{\frac{\sqrt{\pi^2+4a^2}+2b-2a-\pi}{2}, \frac{b}{2}\}}$$

$$= \frac{\pi}{\max\{\frac{2a+\pi-\sqrt{\pi^2+4a^2}}{2}, \frac{b}{2}\}}$$

$$= \min\{\frac{2\pi}{b}, 1 + \frac{\sqrt{\pi^2+4a^2}+\pi}{2a}\}.$$

If r_2 is matched to server s_3 by algorithm A, then the third request r_3 appears at position $p(r_3) = \pi$, thus $C^A \geq d(r_3, s_1) = \pi$. In the optimal solution, requests r_1, r_2, r_3 are matched to servers s_1, s_2, s_3 respectively. This implies $C^{OPT} \leq$

$d(r_1, s_1) = a - x$, therefore,

$$\frac{C^A}{C^{OPT}} \geq \frac{\pi}{a-x} = \frac{\pi}{a - \min\{\frac{\sqrt{\pi^2+4a^2}-\pi}{2}, a-\frac{b}{2}\}}$$

$$= \frac{\pi}{\max\{\frac{2a+\pi-\sqrt{\pi^2+4a^2}}{2}, \frac{b}{2}\}}$$

$$= \min\{\frac{2\pi}{b}, 1 + \frac{\sqrt{\pi^2+4a^2}+\pi}{2a}\}.$$

Case 3. r_1 is matched to server s_3 by algorithm A.

The last two requests r_2 and r_3 appear at positions $p(r_2) = p(s_1)$ and $p(r_3) = p(s_3)$ respectively, $C^A \geq d(r_1, s_3) = b + x$. In the optimal solution, requests r_1, r_2, r_3 are matched to servers s_2, s_1, s_3 respectively, thus $C^{OPT} = d(r_1, s_2) = x$. Since $b \geq a$, similar to Case 1, we have

$$\frac{C^A}{C^{OPT}} \geq \frac{b+x}{x} \geq \frac{a+x}{x} \geq \min\{\frac{2\pi}{b}, 1 + \frac{\sqrt{\pi^2+4a^2}+\pi}{2a}\}.$$

By Theorem 3, it follows that any online algorithm A has a competitive ratio of at least 3 for the online bottleneck matching problem on a ring. Therefore, the competitive ratio of any online algorithm A is at least $\max\{3, \min\{1 + \frac{\sqrt{\pi^2+4a^2}+\pi}{2a}, \frac{2\pi}{b}\}\}$.

To facilitate the description of the algorithm in this section, we first divide the ring into three intervals I_1, I_2, and I_3 using polar coordinates, to further determine the arrival positions of the requests. When $\frac{b}{a} \leq \sqrt{2}$, let

$$x = \min\{\frac{a}{2}, \max\{\frac{ab}{2\pi - b}, \frac{\sqrt{\pi^2+4a^2}-\pi}{2}\}\} \leq \frac{a}{2}$$

and

$$y = \min\{\frac{b}{2}, \frac{\sqrt{\pi^2+4a^2}+2b-2a-\pi}{2}\} \leq \frac{b}{2}.$$

Let the intervals I_1, I_2, and I_3 be

$$I_1 = (-\frac{c}{2}, a-x],$$
$$I_2 = (a-x, a+y],$$
$$I_3 = (a+y, a+b+\frac{c}{2}].$$

After dividing the ring into three intervals as shown in Fig. 4, algorithm $A1$ allocates a server sequence for each request r_j based on its arrival position, to find the first unmatched server and perform the matching. Note that when $\frac{4ab-b^2}{4a-2b} \leq \pi < \frac{a^2+ab}{2a+b} + b + a$, we have

$$\max\{\frac{ab}{2\pi - b}, \frac{\sqrt{\pi^2+4a^2}-\pi}{2}\} = \frac{\sqrt{\pi^2+4a^2}-\pi}{2}, y = \frac{\sqrt{\pi^2+4a^2}+2b-2a-\pi}{2}.$$

When $\pi < \frac{4ab-b^2}{4a-2b}$, we have

$$\max\{\frac{ab}{2\pi-b}, \frac{\sqrt{\pi^2+4a^2}-\pi}{2}\} = \frac{ab}{2\pi-b}, y = \frac{b}{2}.$$

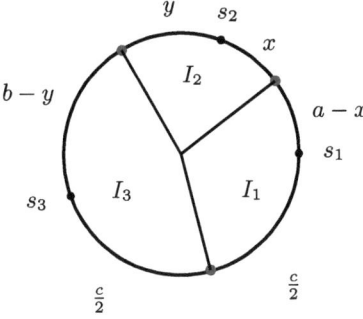

Fig. 4. Three intervals on the ring

Algorithm 1: *A1*
---
1 When a new request r_j arrives, it is matched according to the following three cases:
2 **Case 1.** $p(r_j) \in I_1$. Match r_j to the first unmatched server in the sequence (s_1, s_2, s_3).
3 **Case 2.** $p(r_j) \in I_2$. Match r_j to the first unmatched server in the sequence (s_2, s_1, s_3).
4 **Case 3.** $p(r_j) \in I_3$. Match r_j to the first unmatched server in the sequence (s_3, s_2, s_1).

Theorem 6. *When $\frac{b}{a} \leq \sqrt{2}$ and $\pi < \frac{a^2+ab}{2a+b} + b + a$, the competitive ratio of algorithm A1 for online bottleneck matching problem on the ring is at most $\max\{3, \min\{1 + \frac{\sqrt{\pi^2+4a^2}+\pi}{2a}, \frac{2\pi}{b}\}\}$.*

Proof. Note that when $\pi < \frac{a^2+ab}{2a+b}+b+a$, $x = \min\{\frac{a}{2}, \max\{\frac{ab}{2\pi-b}, \frac{\sqrt{\pi^2+4a^2}-\pi}{2}\}\} \leq \frac{a}{2}$, and $y = \min\{\frac{b}{2}, \frac{\sqrt{\pi^2+4a^2}+2b-2a-\pi}{2}\} \leq \frac{b}{2}$. Suppose algorithm $A1$ produces the maximum matching distance C^{A1} when matching request r. Below, we analyze three cases for the occurrence of r.

Case 1. $p(r) \in I_1 = (-\frac{c}{2}, a-x]$.

Subcase 1.1. r is matched to server s_1 by algorithm $A1$. If $p(r) \in (-\frac{c}{2}, a-\frac{a}{2}]$, then because s_1 is the server closest to r, algorithm $A1$ achieves optimality. If $p(r) \in (a-\frac{a}{2}, a-x]$, then $C^{OPT} \geq d(r, s_2) \geq x$. Since $C^{A1} = d(r, s_1) \leq a-x$, we have

$$\frac{C^{A1}}{C^{OPT}} \le \frac{a-x}{x} = \frac{a}{\min\{\frac{a}{2}, \max\{\frac{ab}{2\pi-b}, \frac{\sqrt{\pi^2+4a^2}-\pi}{2}\}\}} - 1$$

$$\le \max\{3, \min\{\frac{2\pi}{b}, 1 + \frac{\sqrt{\pi^2+4a^2}+\pi}{2a}\}\}.$$

Subcase 1.2. r is matched to server s_2 by algorithm $A1$. If $p(r) \in (-\frac{c}{2}, -x]$, then $C^{OPT} \ge d(r, s_1) \ge x$. Since $C^{A1} = d(r, s_2) = d(r, s_1) + d(s_1, s_2) = d(r, s_1) + a$, we have

$$\frac{C^{A1}}{C^{OPT}} \le \frac{d(r, s_1) + a}{d(r, s_1)} = 1 + \frac{a}{d(r, s_1)} \le 1 + \frac{a}{x}$$

$$= 1 + \frac{a}{\min\{\frac{a}{2}, \max\{\frac{ab}{2\pi-b}, \frac{\sqrt{\pi^2+4a^2}-\pi}{2}\}\}}$$

$$\le \max\{3, \min\{\frac{2\pi}{b}, 1 + \frac{\sqrt{\pi^2+4a^2}+\pi}{2a}\}\}.$$

If $p(r) \in (-x, a-x]$, then according to the selection of algorithm $A1$, before r appears, server s_1 is matched while s_2 is not. Moreover, s_1 can only be matched to a request appearing in the interval I_1, indicating that in the optimal solution, there exists a request appearing in the interval $I_1 = (-\frac{c}{2}, a-x]$ matched to either server s_2 or s_3. Hence, $C^{OPT} \ge \min\{\frac{c}{2}, x\} = x$. Since $C^{A1} = d(r, s_2) \le a + x$, we have

$$\frac{C^{A1}}{C^{OPT}} \le \frac{a+x}{x} = 1 + \frac{a}{x} \le \max\{3, \min\{1 + \frac{\sqrt{\pi^2+4a^2}+\pi}{2a}, \frac{2\pi}{b}\}\}.$$

Subcase 1.3. r is matched to server s_3 by algorithm $A1$.

According to the selection of algorithm $A1$, it is known that before r arrives, servers s_1 and s_2 are matched. Additionally, s_1 and s_2 can only be matched to requests appearing in the $I_1 \cup I_2$. This implies that in the optimal solution, there exists a request appearing in the $I_1 \cup I_2 = (\frac{\pi}{2} - b - a - \frac{c}{2}, \frac{\pi}{2} - b + y]$ matched to server s_3. Hence, $C^{OPT} \ge \min\{\frac{c}{2}, b-y\}$. When $y = \frac{b}{2}$, since $b \le c$, we have $\min\{\frac{c}{2}, b-y\} = b-y$. When $y = \frac{\sqrt{\pi^2+4a^2}+2b-2a-\pi}{2}$, we have $\pi \ge \frac{4ab-b^2}{4a-2b}$. Because $a \le b \le c = 2\pi - b - a$, this can be calculated to obtain

$$3a + b - \pi \le \sqrt{\pi^2 + 4a^2}.$$

We have $2a + \pi - \sqrt{\pi^2 + 4a^2} \le 2\pi - a - b$, which also implies

$$b - y = \frac{2a + \pi - \sqrt{\pi^2+4a^2}}{2} \le \frac{2\pi - a - b}{2} = \frac{c}{2}.$$

This implies that $C^{OPT} \geq \min\{\frac{c}{2}, b-y\} = b-y$. Since $C^{A1} \leq \pi$, we have

$$\frac{C^{A1}}{C^{OPT}} \leq \frac{\pi}{b-y} = \frac{\pi}{\max\{\frac{b}{2}, \frac{2a+\pi-\sqrt{\pi^2+4a^2}}{2}\}}$$

$$= \min\{\frac{2\pi}{b}, 1 + \frac{\sqrt{\pi^2+4a^2}+\pi}{2a}\}.$$

Case 2. $p(r) \in I_2 = (a-x, a+y]$.

Subcase 2.1. r is matched to server s_2 by algorithm $A1$. Since $x \leq \frac{a}{2}$ and $y \leq \frac{b}{2}$, s_2 is the server closest to r, and the algorithm achieves optimality.

Subcase 2.2. r is matched to server s_1 by algorithm $A1$. According to the selection of algorithm $A1$, s_2 is matched before r arrives. If s_3 is matched before r arrives, then in the optimal solution, there exists a request appearing in $I_2 \cup I_3 = (a-x, a+b+\frac{c}{2}]$ matched to server s_1, implying that $C^{OPT} \geq \min\{a-x, \frac{c}{2}\}$. If s_3 is not matched before r arrives, then in the optimal solution, there exists a request appearing in $I_2 = (a-x, a+y]$ matched to either server s_1 or s_3, implying that $C^{OPT} \geq \min\{a-x, b-y\}$.

When $\pi \geq \frac{4ab-b^2}{4a-2b}$, we have $a-x = b-y$ and $y = \frac{\sqrt{\pi^2+4a^2}+2b-2a-\pi}{2}$. Similarly to Subcase 1.3, we obtain $C^{OPT} \geq \min\{a-x, b-y, \frac{c}{2}\} = b-y$. Since $C^{A1} = d(r, s_1) \leq a+y$ and $a+y \leq a+\frac{b}{2} \leq \pi$, we have

$$\frac{C^{A1}}{C^{OPT}} \leq \frac{a+y}{\min\{a-x, b-y, \frac{c}{2}\}} \leq \frac{a+y}{b-y}$$

$$\leq \frac{\pi}{b-y} = 1 + \frac{\sqrt{\pi^2+4a^2}+\pi}{2a}$$

$$= \min\{1 + \frac{\sqrt{\pi^2+4a^2}+\pi}{2a}, \frac{2\pi}{b}\}.$$

When $\pi < \frac{4ab-b^2}{4a-2b}$, we have $y = \frac{b}{2}$. If $p(r) \in (a-x, 2a-x]$, then $C^{A1} = d(r, s_1) \leq 2a - x$. Because

$$C^{OPT} \geq \min\{a-x, b-y, \frac{c}{2}\} = \min\{a-x, \frac{b}{2}, \frac{c}{2}\} = a-x > \frac{a}{2},$$

thus, by $x = \frac{a}{2}$,

$$\frac{C^{A1}}{C^{OPT}} \leq \frac{2a-x}{a-x} = 1 + \frac{a}{a-x} \leq 3.$$

If $p(r) \in (2a-x, a+y]$, then $C^{OPT} \geq d(r, s_2) \geq a - x \geq \frac{a}{2}$. Because $C^{A1} = d(r, s_1) = d(r, s_2) + d(s_1, s_2) \leq d(r, s_2) + a$, we have

$$\frac{C^{A1}}{C^{OPT}} \leq \frac{d(r, s_2) + a}{d(r, s_2)} \leq 1 + \frac{a}{a-x} \leq 3.$$

Subcase 2.3. r is matched to server s_3 by algorithm $A1$. From the choice of algorithm $A1$, it is evident that servers s_2 and s_1 are matched before r arrives.

This implies that in the optimal solution, there exists a request occurring in the $I_1 \cup I_2 = (\frac{\pi}{2} - b - a - \frac{c}{2}, \frac{\pi}{2} - b + y]$ matched to server s_3. By similar analysis to Subcase 1.3, we obtain $C^{OPT} \geq \min\{\frac{c}{2}, b - y\} = b - y$. Since $x \leq \frac{a}{2}$ and $a \leq b \leq c = 2\pi - a - b$, we have $C^{A1} = d(r, s_3) \leq b + x \leq \pi$, thus,

$$\frac{C^{A1}}{C^{OPT}} \leq \frac{b+x}{b-y} \leq \frac{\pi}{b-y} \leq \min\{1 + \frac{\sqrt{\pi^2 + 4a^2} + \pi}{2a}, \frac{2\pi}{b}\}.$$

Case 3. $p(r) \in I_3 = (a + y, a + b + \frac{c}{2}]$

Subcase 3.1. r is matched to server s_3 by algorithm $A1$. If $p(r) \in (a + \frac{b}{2}, a + b + \frac{c}{2}]$, then s_3 is the server closest to r, and algorithm $A1$ achieves optimality. If $p(r) \in (a + y, a + \frac{b}{2}]$, then $C^{OPT} \geq d(r, s_2) \geq y$. Since $C^{A1} = d(r, s_3) \leq b - y$, and $y = \frac{\sqrt{\pi^2 + 4a^2} + 2b - 2a - \pi}{2}$, we have $\frac{b+y}{y} \leq 1 + \frac{\sqrt{\pi^2 + 4a^2} + \pi}{2a} \leq \frac{2\pi}{b}$. Thus,

$$\frac{C^{A1}}{C^{OPT}} \leq \frac{b-y}{y} \leq \frac{b+y}{y} \leq \max\{3, \min\{1 + \frac{\sqrt{\pi^2 + 4a^2} + \pi}{2a}, \frac{2\pi}{b}\}\}.$$

Subcase 3.2. r is matched to server s_2 by algorithm $A1$. From the choice of algorithm $A1$, it follows that server s_3 is matched before r arrives, thus, a request r_j appears in the interval I_3 before r arrives. If both requests r and r_j appear in $(a + b + y, a + b + \frac{c}{2}]$, then $C^{OPT} \geq \min\{\frac{c}{2}, b + y\}$. Since $C^{A1} \leq \pi$, we have

$$\frac{C^{A1}}{C^{OPT}} \leq \frac{\pi}{\min\{\frac{c}{2}, b+y\}} = \max\{\frac{2\pi}{c}, \frac{\pi}{b+y}\}$$

$$\leq \max\{3, \min\{1 + \frac{\sqrt{\pi^2 + 4a^2} + \pi}{2a}, \frac{2\pi}{b}\}\}.$$

If both requests r and r_j appear in $(a + y, a + b + y]$, then $C^{OPT} \geq y$ and $C^{A1} = d(r, s_2) \leq b + y$. When $y = \frac{\sqrt{\pi^2 + 4a^2} + 2b - 2a - \pi}{2}$, we have $\frac{b+y}{y} \leq 1 + \frac{\sqrt{\pi^2 + 4a^2} + \pi}{2a} \leq \frac{2\pi}{b}$. Thus,

$$\frac{C^{A1}}{C^{OPT}} \leq \frac{b+y}{y} \leq \max\{3, \min\{1 + \frac{\sqrt{\pi^2 + 4a^2} + \pi}{2a}, \frac{2\pi}{b}\}\}.$$

If r_j appear in $(a + y, \frac{\pi}{2} + y]$ and r appear in $(a + b + y, a + b + \frac{c}{2}]$, then $C^{OPT} \geq \min\{\frac{c}{2}, d(r, s_3)\} = d(r, s_3) \geq y$. Since $C^{A1} = d(r, s_2) \leq d(r, s_3) + d(s_3, s_2) = d(r, s_3) + b$, we have

$$\frac{C^{A1}}{C^{OPT}} \leq \frac{d(r, s_3) + b}{d(r, s_3)} = 1 + \frac{b}{d(r, s_3)} \leq 1 + \frac{b}{y}$$

$$\leq \max\{3, \min\{1 + \frac{\sqrt{\pi^2 + 4a^2} + \pi}{2a}, \frac{2\pi}{b}\}\}.$$

If r appear in $(a+y, a+b+y]$ and r_j appear in $(a+b+y, a+b+\frac{c}{2}]$, then $C^{OPT} \geq \min\{\frac{c}{2}, d(r_j, s_3)\} = d(r_j, s_3) \geq y$. Since $C^{A1} = d(r, s_2) \leq b+y$, we have

$$\frac{C^{A1}}{C^{OPT}} \leq \frac{b+y}{y} \leq \max\{3, \min\{1+\frac{\sqrt{\pi^2+4a^2}+\pi}{2a}, \frac{2\pi}{b}\}\}.$$

Subcase 3.3. r is matched to server s_1 by algorithm $A1$. According to the choice of algorithm $A1$, servers s_3 and s_2 are matched before the arrival of r. This indicates that in the optimal solution, there exists a request occurring in $I_2 \cup I_3 = (a-x, a+b+\frac{c}{2}]$ that is matched to server s_1. Thus, $C^{OPT} \geq \min\{\frac{c}{2}, a-x\}$. Furthermore, based on the choice of algorithm $A1$, at least two requests appear in the interval $I_3 = (a+y, a+b+\frac{c}{2}]$. Therefore, in the optimal solution, there exists a request occurring in I_3 that is matched to either server s_2 or s_1. This implies that $C^{OPT} \geq \min\{\frac{c}{2}, y\} = y$.

When $\frac{4ab-b^2}{4a-2b} \leq \pi < \frac{a^2+ab}{2a+b}+b+a$, we have $a-x = b-y = \frac{2a+\pi-\sqrt{\pi^2+4a^2}}{2}$ and $\min\{1+\frac{\sqrt{\pi^2+4a^2}+\pi}{2a}, \frac{2\pi}{b}\} = 1+\frac{\sqrt{\pi^2+4a^2}+\pi}{2a}$. Moreover, according to the similar analysis of Subcase 1.3, $a-x = b-y \leq \frac{c}{2}$. Therefore, from $C^{A1} \leq \pi$, we have

$$\frac{C^{A1}}{C^{OPT}} \leq \frac{\pi}{\min\{\frac{c}{2}, a-x\}} = \frac{\pi}{a-x} \leq \max\{3, \min\{1+\frac{\sqrt{\pi^2+4a^2}+\pi}{2a}, \frac{2\pi}{b}\}\}.$$

When $\pi < \frac{4ab-b^2}{4a-2b}$, we have $y = \frac{b}{2}$ and $\min\{1+\frac{\sqrt{\pi^2+4a^2}+\pi}{2a}, \frac{2\pi}{b}\} = \frac{2\pi}{b}$. Thus,

$$\frac{C^{A1}}{C^{OPT}} \leq \frac{\pi}{\min\{\frac{c}{2}, y\}} = \frac{2\pi}{b} \leq \max\{3, \min\{1+\frac{\sqrt{\pi^2+4a^2}+\pi}{2a}, \frac{2\pi}{b}\}\}.$$

4.2 $\frac{b}{a} > \sqrt{2}$

Theorem 7. *When $\frac{b}{a} > \sqrt{2}$ and $a+\frac{3b}{2} \leq \pi$, this problem is equivalent to the online bottleneck matching problem on a line for $\alpha > \sqrt{2}$.*

Proof. When $\frac{b}{a} > \sqrt{2}$ and $a+\frac{3b}{2} \leq \pi$ let $\frac{b}{a} = \alpha$, then the online bottleneck matching problem on the ring is equivalent to the online bottleneck matching problem on the line when $\alpha > \sqrt{2}$ [23].

Theorem 8. *When $a+\frac{3b}{2} > \pi$, the competitive ratio of any online algorithm A for the online bottleneck matching problem on the ring is at least $\max\{3, \frac{2\pi}{b}\}$.*

Proof. We omitted the proof due to space constraints.

When $\frac{b}{a} > \sqrt{2}$ and $\pi < a+\frac{3b}{2}$, similar to the case where $\frac{b}{a} \leq \sqrt{2}$ and $\pi < \frac{a^2+ab}{2a+b}+b+a$, let $x = \frac{a}{2}$ and $y = \frac{b}{2}$. Let intervals I_1, I_2, I_3 be

$$I_1 = (-\frac{c}{2}, a-x],$$
$$I_2 = (a-x, a+y],$$
$$I_3 = (a+y, a+b+\frac{c}{2}],$$

Algorithm $A1$ is also used to solve this problem.

Theorem 9. *When $\pi < a + \frac{3b}{2}$, the competitive ratio of algorithm A1 for the online bottleneck matching problem on the ring is at most $\max\left\{3, \frac{2\pi}{b}\right\}$.*

Proof. We omitted the proof due to space constraints.

5 Conclusion

In this paper, we investigate the online bottleneck matching problem on a ring and provide optimal online algorithms for two special cases. The interval partitioning method used in this paper has some reference value for similar online problems involving important geometric structures. However, solving this problem using interval partitioning becomes challenging when there are many servers and complex inter server distance information. In the future, new methods need to be considered to design optimal online algorithms for the general case of the online bottleneck matching problem on a ring.

Acknowledgement. This work was supported by the National Natural Science Foundation of China (Grant No. 12071417).

References

1. Mehta, A.: Online matching and ad allocation. Found. Trends Theor. Comput. Sci. **8**(4), 265–368 (2013)
2. Gairing, M., Klimm, M.: Greedy metric minimum online matchings with random arrivals. Oper. Res. Lett. **47**, 88–91 (2019)
3. Duppala, S.V.S., Sankararaman, K.A., Xu, P.: Online minimum matching with uniform metric and random arrivals. Oper. Res. Lett. **50**, 45–49 (2022)
4. Karp, R.M., Vazirani, U.V., Vazirani, V.V.: An optimal algorithm for on-line bipartite matching. In: Proceedings of the 22th Annual ACM Symposium on Theory of Computing (STOC), pp. 352–358 (1990)
5. Mahdian, M., Yan, Q.: Online bipartite matching with random arrivals: an approach based on strongly factor-revealing lps. In: Proceedings of the 43th Annual ACM Symposium on Theory of Computing (STOC), pp. 597–606 (2011)
6. Anthony, B.M., Chung, C.: Online bottleneck matching. J. Comb. Optim. **27**(1), 100–114 (2014)
7. Anthony, B.M., Chung, C.: Serve or skip: the power of rejection in online bottleneck matching. J. Comb. Optim. **32**(4), 1232–1253 (2016)
8. Kalyanasundaram, B., Pruhs, K.: Online weighted matching. J. Algor. **14**(3), 478–488 (1993)
9. Khuller, S., Mitchell, S.G., Vazirani, V.V.: On-line algorithms for weighted bipartite matching and stable marriages. Theor. Comput. Sci. **127**(2), 255–267 (1994)
10. Idury, R., Schaffer, A.: A better lower bound for on-line bottleneck matching (1992)
11. Raghvendra, S.: A robust and optimal online algorithm for minimum metric bipartite matching. In: Proceedings of Approximation, Randomization, and Combinatorial Optimization, Algorithms and Techniques (APPROX/RANDOM), p. 18:1 (2016)

12. Meyerson, A., Nanavati, A., Poplawski, L.: Randomized online algorithms for minimum metric bipartite matching. In: Proceedings of the 17th Annual ACM-SIAM Symposium on Discrete Algorithm (SODA), pp. 954–959 (2006)
13. Fuchs, B., Hochstattler, W., Kern, W.: Online matching on a line. Theor. Comput. Sci. **332**(1), 251–264 (2005)
14. Gupta, A., Lewi, K.: The online metric matching problem for doubling metrics. In: Proceedings of International Colloquium on Automata, Languages, and Programming (ICALP), pp. 424–435 (2012)
15. Antoniadis, A., Barcelo, N., Nugent, M., Pruhs, K., Scquizzato, M.: A $o(n)$-competitive deterministic algorithm for online matching on a line. Algorithmica **81**, 2917–2933 (2019)
16. Nayyar, K., Raghvendra, S.: An input sensitive online algorithm for the metric bipartite matching problem. In: Proceedings of IEEE 58th Annual Symposium on Foundations of Computer Science, pp. 505–515 (2017)
17. Raghvendra, S.: Optimal analysis of an online algorithm for the bipartite matching problem on a line. In: Proceedings of the 34th International Symposium on Computational Geometry, pp. 67:1–67:14 (2018)
18. Peserico, E., Scquizzato, M.: Matching on the line admits no $o(\sqrt{\log n})$-competitive algorithm. In: Proceedings of the 48th International Colloquium on Automata, Languages, and Programming(ICALP), pp. 103:1–103:3 (2021)
19. Balkanski, E., Faenza, Y., Perivier, N.: The power of greedy for online minimum cost matching on the line. In: Proceedings of the 24th ACM Conference on Economics and Computation (EC), pp. 185–205 (2023)
20. Xiao, M., Li, W.: Online semi-matching problem with two heterogeneous sensors in a metric space. In: Proceedings of the 28th International Computing and Combinatorics Conference (COCOON), pp. 444–451 (2022)
21. Xiao, M., Yang, Y., Li, W.: Online bottleneck matching problem with two heterogeneous sensors in a metric space. Computation **10**, 217 (2022)
22. Bansal, N., Buchbinder, N., Gupta, A., Naor, J.S.: A randomized $O(\log^2 k)$-competitive algorithm for metric bipartite matching. Algorithmica **68**, 390–403 (2014)
23. Xiao, M., Zhao, S., Li, W., Yang, J.: Online bottleneck matching on aline. J. Comb. Optim. **45**, 108 (2023)
24. Jawgal, V.A., Muralidhara, V.N., Srinivasan, P.S.: Online travelling salesman problem on a circle. In: Proceeding of the 15th Theory and Applications of Models of Computation (TAMC), pp. 325–336 (2019)
25. Kalyanasundaram, B., Pruhs, K.: Online network optimization problems. Lect. Notes Comput. Sci. **1442**, 268–280 (1998)

Learning to Design Greedy Algorithm for NP-Complete Problems

Zhenxin Ding[1,3], Zihao Huang[2,3], Jingyan Sui[1,3], Ruizhi Liu[1,3], Shizhe Ding[1,3], Liming Xu[1,3], Chao Wang[1,3], Haicang Zhang[1,3], Chungong Yu[1,3], and Dongbo Bu[1,3(✉)]

[1] Institute of Computing Technology, Chinese Academy of Sciences, Beijing, China
dbu@ict.ac.cn
[2] Institute of Information Engineering, Chinese Academy of Sciences, Beijing, China
[3] University of Chinese Academy of Sciences, Beijing, China

Abstract. Algorithm design is an art that heavily requires human designers' intuition, expertise, and insights into the combinatorial structure of the problems under consideration. In particular, while greedy algorithms for NP-complete problems are generally straightforward, finding an effective greedy-selection rule is consistently challenging. In the study, we introduce an approach called *artificial intelligence algorithmist for set cover problem* (AIA-SC), which leverages neural networks as greedy-selection rules to solve the minimum weighted set cover problem (WSCP), an NP-complete problem. Initially, we formulate a given WSCP as a 0–1 integer linear program (ILP), in which each variable x_i is binary: $x_i = 0$ indicating the exclusion of set s_i, and $x_i = 1$ indicating the selection of the set. Subsequently, we design a generic search framework to identify the optimal solution to the ILP. At each search step, the value of a variable is determined with the aid of neural networks. The key ingredients of our neural network involve the design of its loss function and training process: the original ILP problem and the sub-problems generated by assigning a variable x_i should satisfy the Bellman-Ford equation, which enables us to set the violation of Bellman-Ford equation as loss function of our neural network. Experimental results on representative instances indicate that the neural network-based greedy selection rule effectively identifies optimal solutions and surpasses the performance of the human-crafted Chvatal's greedy algorithm. Furthermore, the basic idea of our approach can be readily extended to design greedy algorithms for other NP-hard problems without significant modification. The source code of AIA-SC and data sets are available at https://github.com/zxding94/aia-sc.

Keywords: Algorithm Design · Greedy-selection Rules · Neural Networks · Minimum Weighted Set Cover Problem

---

Z. Ding and Z. Huang—Contributed equally to this study.

1 Introduction

NP-complete problems, the hardest ones within the NP class, are characterized by the property that the solutions to these problems can be verified in polynomial time, yet no polynomial-time algorithms have been found to solve them efficiently [1]. These problems encompass a wide range of practical applications, including strategic planning, production planning, facility locating, and various scheduling and routing problems [2]. Consequently, the quest for efficient solving algorithms for NP-complete problems remains a paramount pursuit.

The exact algorithms for NP-complete problems, like branch-and-bound and branch-and-cut, exhibit promising performance in some cases but suffer from the limitation in the size of instances that these algorithms can solve. Significant efforts have been devoted to designing heuristic and meta-heuristic approaches to efficiently find optimal or nearly optimal solutions for large instances within reasonable computing time. Prominent among these heuristic techniques are genetic algorithms, ant colony optimization, simulated annealing, and tabu search [3].

The breakthrough of deep learning techniques has led to a growing interest in utilizing these techniques to solve NP-complete problems. However, it is challenging to tackle NP-complete problems using an end-to-end neural network with supervised learning due to the following reasons: *i*) Traditional algorithms and mathematical methods possess a well-established theoretical foundation, while neural networks lack a comparable insight into the combinatorial structure of problems. *ii*) The practical instances of NP-complete problems often exhibit distinct characteristics, which may not align well with the typical data requirements of deep learning models. *iii*) Deep learning models often demand a substantial amount of labeled data under specific distributions, whereas many combinatorial optimization problems, particularly NP-complete problems, necessitate computationally expensive calculations to derive optimal solutions [4].

In the study, we present an approach (called *artificial intelligence algorithmist for set cover problem*, AIA-SC) to learn algorithm design with the aid of neural networks. The specific goal of this paper is to use machine learning to find greedy rules and then design an efficient and practical greedy algorithm for the weighted set cover problem. Experimental results on multiple datasets demonstrate that the proposed AIA approach outperforms human-designed greedy algorithms, such as the Chvatal's greedy algorithm [5], by achieving superior solutions.

2 Related Works and Background

The algorithms to solve combinatorial optimization problems can be divided into exact and approximate/heuristic algorithms. Exact algorithms are known for their capability to guarantee optimal solutions. However, these exact algorithms become computationally intractable as the size of problem instances increases, rendering them unsuitable for handling large instances. In contrast, approximate/heuristic algorithms trade the quality of solution for increased computational efficiency by applying heuristic rules [6].

The design of effective heuristic rules relies heavily on insights into the problem characteristics and problem-solving process. The efficacy of different heuristic rules and their associated parameters varies across different datasets and solution stages. Thus, data-driven machine learning techniques, including supervised learning and reinforcement learning, have emerged as promising strategies for designing effective heuristic rules and algorithms to solve NP-complete combinatorial optimization problems [7–9]. These efforts are briefly described below.

Supervised learning has shown promising performance in aiding the design of the solver for integer linear programming. For example, Alvarez et al. [10] employed a specialized decision tree to learn the branch variable selection strategy of the strong branch technique [11]. Khalil et al. [12] trained a support vector machine on the choice of strong branching technique collected on some sub-problems and then used this support vector machine to guide variable selection on other sub-problems. Gasse et al. [13] utilized a graph convolutional neural network to learn the choice of strong branching strategies by extracting information on variables and constraints. He et al. [14] devised a machine learning algorithm to identify the sub-problem that contains the optimal solution. To speed up solving the traveling salesman problem, Chaitanya et al. predicted the probabilities for each edge appearing in the optimal tour by using a deep graph network [15].

Unlike supervised learning, reinforcement learning does not require calculating labels in advance, which is time-consuming and practically infeasible for NP-complete problems. This property makes reinforcement learning promising for designing algorithms for NP-complete problems. For example, to solve the traveling salesman problem (TSP), Bello et al. trained a network using the total distance of a tour as reward [16]. To extract the essential information from the given TSP instance, Kool et al. incorporated a graph neural network into the reinforcement learning framework [17], whereas Xavier et al. utilized a transformer together with beam search for decoding [18].

Together, these achievements suggest that the use of machine learning techniques paves a new way to understand the combinatorial structure of the problem under consideration, and subsequently design suitable algorithms to solve the problem.

3 Method

In the study, we focus on the weighted set cover problem (WSCP) as it is a representative NP-complete problem. The basic idea of our approach to WSCP is as follows: we first transform the solving process into a multi-step decision-making process and then design a neural network to learn the optimal decision at each step. The decisions thus acquired constitute a solution to WSCP. The key components of our approach involve the training process and the loss function. The loss function exploits the recursion between consecutive decisions rather than the difference between the neural network's output and the optimal solution as finding the optimal solution itself is our objective and is usually time-consuming.

We describe the multi-step decision-making process, network architecture, loss function, and training procedure below.

3.1 Multi-step Decision-Making Process to Solve WSCP

The weighted set cover problem can be described as follows: given a set of m elements (called the universe U) and a collection of n weighted subsets of U, the goal is to identify a sub-collection of sets such that: i) the universe U should be covered, i.e., the union of the sub-selection equals U, and ii) the weight-sum of the sub-collection is minimized. We formulate the problem as the following 0-1 integer linear program:

$$\begin{aligned} \min z &= \boldsymbol{c}^T \boldsymbol{x} \\ \text{s.t.} \, \boldsymbol{A}\boldsymbol{x} &\geq \boldsymbol{b} \\ x_j &= \text{0-1} \quad (j = 1, 2, \cdots, n). \end{aligned} \tag{1}$$

Here, x_j is a binary variable such that $x_j = 1$ if the j-th set is selected into the sub-collection and $x_j = 0$ otherwise. The constant c_j denotes the weight of the j-th set. Thus, the objective function $\boldsymbol{c}^T \boldsymbol{x}$ represents the sum weight of the sub-collection. In the constraints, $\boldsymbol{A}$ denotes an $m \times n$ matrix in which A_{ij} is 1 if the j-th set covers the i-th element and 0 otherwise. To guarantee that the identified collection of subsets covers all elements, we initialize $\boldsymbol{b}$ as $\boldsymbol{b} = \boldsymbol{1}$ and appropriately update it in subsequent steps.

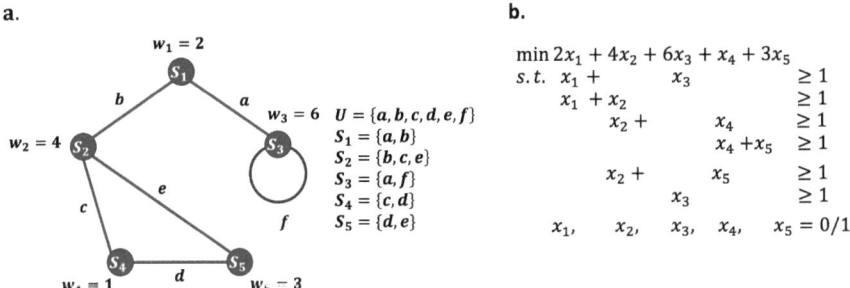

Fig. 1. Weighted set cover problem and its formulation. (a) An example with five subsets over a universe with six elements. (b) Integer linear program for this instance

We further formulate the solving process of the linear program as a multi-step decision-making process: at the k-th step, we attempt to decide whether $x_k = 0$ or 1 with the variables $x_1, \cdots, x_{k-1}$ already determined at previous steps. The problem $\mathcal{P}$ to be solved at the k-th step is:

$$\begin{aligned} \min z &= \boldsymbol{c}_k^T \boldsymbol{x}_k \\ \text{s.t.} \, \boldsymbol{A}_k \boldsymbol{x} &\geq \boldsymbol{b}_k \\ x_j &= \text{0-1}, \quad j = k, k+1 \cdots, n. \end{aligned} \tag{2}$$

Here, $\boldsymbol{x}_k = [x_k\ x_{k+1} \cdots x_n]$ denote the variables, the parameters include $\boldsymbol{c}_k = [c_k\ c_{k+1} \cdots c_n]^T$, $\boldsymbol{b}_k = \boldsymbol{b} - x_1 \alpha_1 - \cdots - x_{k-1}\alpha_{k-1}$, and $\boldsymbol{A}_k = [\alpha_k\ \alpha_{k+1} \cdots \alpha_n]$ in which α_j denotes the j-th column of the matrix $\boldsymbol{A}$. Hereafter, $\mathcal{P}$ and $(\boldsymbol{A}_k, \boldsymbol{b}_k, \boldsymbol{c}_k)$ will be interchangeably used to represent the problem. The optimal objective value of this problem is denoted as $\mathrm{OPT}(\boldsymbol{A}_k, \boldsymbol{b}_k, \boldsymbol{c}_k)$ or $\mathrm{OPT}(\mathcal{P})$ (Fig. 2).

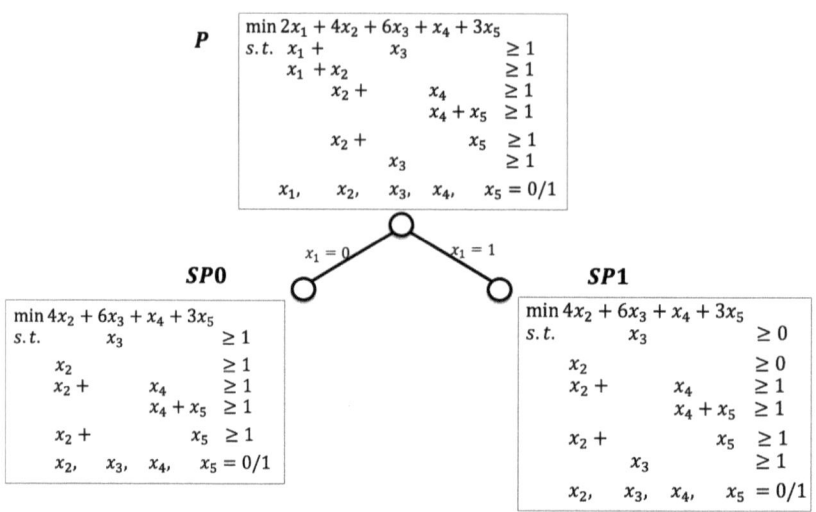

Fig. 2. Multi-step decision-making process to solve the weighted set cover problem. Here, we show the first decision $x_1 = 1$ (selecting subset S_1) and $x_1 = 0$ (abandoning subset S_1). Each option corresponds to a sub-problem of the original problem

The decision $x_k = 1$ will derive a sub-problem of $\mathcal{P} = (\boldsymbol{A}_k, \boldsymbol{b}_k, \boldsymbol{c}_k)$ to be solved at the $k+1$-th step, denoted as $\mathcal{SP}_1 = (\boldsymbol{A}_{k+1}, \boldsymbol{b}_k - \alpha_k, \boldsymbol{c}_{k+1})$. Similarly, the decision $x_k = 0$ will derive another sub-problem denoted as $\mathcal{SP}_0 = (\boldsymbol{A}_{k+1}, \boldsymbol{b}_k, \boldsymbol{c}_{k+1})$. The key observation is that the optimal objective values of a problem $\mathcal{P}$ and its two sub-problems $\mathcal{SP}_0, \mathcal{SP}_1$ satisfy the following recursion:

$$\mathrm{OPT}(\mathcal{P}) = \min\{\mathrm{OPT}(\mathcal{SP}_0), c_k + \mathrm{OPT}(\mathcal{SP}_1)\}. \tag{3}$$

Reversely, we can make correct decision on x_k if we know the optimal solutions $\mathrm{OPT}(\mathcal{SP}_0)$ and $\mathrm{OPT}(\mathcal{SP}_1)$, i.e.,

$$x_k = \begin{cases} 0 & \text{if } \mathrm{OPT}(\mathcal{SP}_0) \leq c_k + \mathrm{OPT}(\mathcal{SP}_1), \\ 1 & \text{otherwise.} \end{cases} \tag{4}$$

3.2 AIA-SC Approach

Equation 4 implies an approach to solving WSCP: we sequentially apply this equation on $x_1, x_2, ..., x_n$, thus acquiring the correct decisions on these variables that constitute the complete solution. This approach is feasible if can exactly calculate, or accurately estimate, the optimal objective values $\text{OPT}(\mathcal{SP}_0)$ and $\text{OPT}(\mathcal{SP}_1)$. For this aim, we design a neural network (denoted as g_θ with θ representing the parameters) to estimate the optimal objective value. The key ingredients of our approach involve the construction of training data, and the design of loss function suitable for learning the objective values for NP-complete problems, which are described in more detail below.

Loss Function: The general loss function, say mean squared error, considers the difference between the neural network prediction $g_\theta(\mathcal{P})$ and the ground-truth value of the objective function $\text{OPT}(\mathcal{P})$. Although widely used, this design strategy of loss function is infeasible as it relies on the ground-truth objective values that are difficult to calculate for NP-complete problems. In addition, it has been reported that a small change of $\boldsymbol{A}, \boldsymbol{b}, \boldsymbol{c}$ might lead to a considerable shift in objective value [19], thus making it challenging to use these values for training.

To overcome this challenge, we resort to the recursive relationship stated in Eq. 3 with the inspiration from Yang et al. [20]. The underlying rationale is that the neural network predictions $g_\theta(\mathcal{P})$ will also satisfy the recursion relationship if they perfectly approximate the ground-truth values $\text{OPT}(\mathcal{P})$, i.e.,

$$g_\theta(\mathcal{P}) = \min\{g_\theta(\mathcal{SP}_0), c_k + g_\theta(\mathcal{SP}_1)\}. \tag{5}$$

This fact enables us to use the violation of the recursion as loss function:

$$\mathcal{L}_\theta = (g_\theta(\mathcal{P}) - \min\{g_\theta(\mathcal{SP}_0), c_k + g_\theta(\mathcal{SP}_1)\})^2. \tag{6}$$

Intuitively, this loss function uses $\min\{g_\theta(\mathcal{SP}_0), c_k + g_\theta(\mathcal{SP}_1)\}\}$ instead of ground-truth value $\text{OPT}(\mathcal{P})$, therefore completely avoiding calculating this value, which is practically infeasible for NP-complete problems.

It should be noted that Eq. 3 does not hold if one of the two sub-problems is infeasible. To amend this deficiency, we pose an extra restriction that $g_\theta(\mathcal{SP}_0)$ is sufficiently large if $\mathcal{SP}_0$ is infeasible (and so is $g_\theta(\mathcal{SP}_0)$). We implement this restriction by augmenting the loss function with a ReLU activation function. The augmented loss function is:

$$\mathcal{L}_\theta^{aug} = \begin{cases} (g_\theta(\mathcal{P}) - c_k - g_\theta(\mathcal{SP}_1))^2 + \text{ReLU}(g_\theta(\mathcal{SP}_1) + c_k - g_\theta(\mathcal{SP}_0)) & \text{if } \mathcal{SP}_0 \text{ is infeasible} \\ (g_\theta(\mathcal{P}) - g_\theta(\mathcal{SP}_0))^2 + \text{ReLU}(g_\theta(\mathcal{SP}_0) - g_\theta(\mathcal{SP}_1) - c_k) & \text{if } \mathcal{SP}_1 \text{ is infeasible} \\ (g_\theta(\mathcal{P}) - \min\{g_\theta(\mathcal{SP}_0), c_k + g_\theta(\mathcal{SP}_1)\})^2 & \text{otherwise.} \end{cases}$$

Here, ReLU nuron is used to force an infeasible sub-problem's predicted objective value to be larger than feasible sub-problems. In this study, a sub-problem is considered infeasible if one or more of its constraints are violated.

Network Architecture: We employ a two-layer fully-connected neural network to predict the optimal function value $g_\theta(\boldsymbol{A}, \boldsymbol{b}, \boldsymbol{c})$ of a WSCP instance $\boldsymbol{A}, \boldsymbol{b}, \boldsymbol{c}$.

The input layer consists of $m \times n + m + n$ input nodes while the hidden layer consists of $m + n$ nodes.

Note that some sub-problems might have negative $\boldsymbol{b}_k$ as $\boldsymbol{b}_k = \boldsymbol{b} - x_1\boldsymbol{\alpha}_1 - x_2\boldsymbol{\alpha}_2 \cdots - x_{k-1}\boldsymbol{\alpha}_{k-1}$ is calculated through subtracting certain $\boldsymbol{\alpha}_i$ from $\boldsymbol{b}$. These negative $\boldsymbol{b}_k$ make the sub-problem differ from the canonical form in which all b_i might be 0 or 1 and thus incur difficulties in predicting the optimal function value for this problem. To circumvent these difficulties, we transform the negative b_i into 0 by applying a ReLU layer onto b_i. It should be noted that this transformation does not change the optimal function value of the problem.

Training Process: To train the neural network used by AIA-SC, we first prepare an instance-specific training dataset constructed specifically from the given instance $(\boldsymbol{A}, \boldsymbol{b}, \boldsymbol{c})$ with network parameters set as θ. The dataset consists of a collection of sub-problem triples with the form $(\mathcal{P}, \mathcal{SP}_0, \mathcal{SP}_1)$, in which $\mathcal{SP}_0$ and $\mathcal{SP}_1$ are sub-problems of $\mathcal{P}$ (Fig. 3).

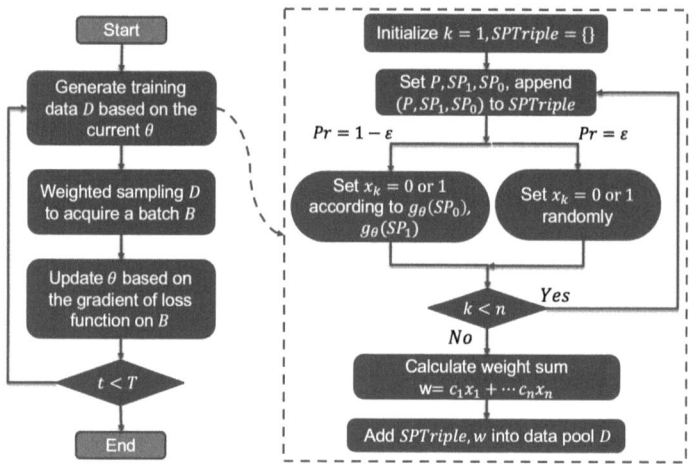

Fig. 3. Training process used by AIA-SC. A collection of sub-problem triples $(\mathcal{P}, \mathcal{SP}_0, \mathcal{SP}_1)$ are first generated as training data, and each triple is assigned with a weight

Specifically, we start from $\mathcal{P} = (\boldsymbol{A}, \boldsymbol{b}, \boldsymbol{c})$, enumerate its two sub-problems $\mathcal{SP}_0$ and $\mathcal{SP}_1$, and insert the triple $(\mathcal{P}, \mathcal{SP}_0, \mathcal{SP}_1)$ into the training dataset. Next, we fix x_1 by distinguishing three cases: i) we fix $x_1 = 1$ if $\mathcal{SP}_0$ is infeasible, ii) we fix $x_1 = 0$ if $\mathcal{SP}_1$ is infeasible, and iii) when both $\mathcal{SP}_0$ and $\mathcal{SP}_1$ are feasible, we fix $x_1 = 0$ if $g_\theta(\mathcal{SP}_0) < c_1 + g_\theta(\mathcal{SP}_1)$ and $x_1 = 1$ otherwise. We further update $\mathcal{P}$ according to the value of x_1. Similarly, we fix $x_2, x_3, \cdots, x_n$ and acquire $n-1$ more triples accordingly. Each triple $(\mathcal{P}, \mathcal{SP}_0, \mathcal{SP}_1)$ is associated with a weight $w = c_1 x_1 + c_2 x_2 + \cdots + c_n x_n$. To increase the diversity of training data and explore more combinations of variables, we introduce randomness into data preparation, i.e., with probability ϵ we fix $x_i = 1$ and 0 uniformly at random.

Then, we sample the training dataset to acquire a batch B of triples. Here, we employ weighted sampling to emphasize the triples with high weight as these triples are more critical to train the neural network. We calculate the gradient of the loss function $\nabla \mathcal{L}_\theta^{aug}$ for all sampled triples and then use it to optimize the network parameters θ. The pseudocode of the training process is presented in Algorithm 1.

Algorithm 1. Training procedure of the neural network for AIA-SC

1: **function** TRAININGNETWORK($\boldsymbol{A}, \boldsymbol{b}, \boldsymbol{c}, n$)
2:     Initialize network parameters θ^0 with random values, data pool $D = \emptyset$, learning rate η;
3:     **for** $t = 1$ to T **do**
4:         $SPTriples, w \leftarrow$ GENERATESUB-PROBLEMTRIPLESANDWEIGHT($\theta^{t-1}, \boldsymbol{A}, \boldsymbol{b}, \boldsymbol{c}, n$);
5:         Append D with all sub-problem triples extracted from $SPTriples$ and associate each triple with a weight w;
6:         Generate a batch B of training data through weighted sampling D;
7:         **for** each $(\mathcal{P}, \mathcal{SP}_0, \mathcal{SP}_1) \in B$ **do**
8:             $\theta^t \leftarrow \theta^{t-1} - \eta \nabla \mathcal{L}_{\theta^{t-1}}^{aug}(\mathcal{P}, \mathcal{SP}_0, \mathcal{SP}_1)$;
9:         **end for**
10:     **end for**
11:     **return** θ^T;
12: **end function**
13: **function** GENERATESUB-PROBLEMTRIPLESWITHWEIGHT($\theta, \boldsymbol{A}, \boldsymbol{b}, \boldsymbol{c}, n$)
14:     Initialize $SPTriples = \emptyset$;
15:     **for** $k = 1$ to n **do**
16:         Set $\mathcal{P} = (\boldsymbol{A}_k, \boldsymbol{b}_k, \boldsymbol{c}_k)$;
17:         Set $\mathcal{SP}_0 = (\boldsymbol{A}_{k+1}, \boldsymbol{b}_k, \boldsymbol{c}_{k+1})$;
18:         Set $\mathcal{SP}_1 = (\boldsymbol{A}_{k+1}, \boldsymbol{b}_k - \alpha_k, \boldsymbol{c}_{k+1})$;
19:         Append $SPTriples$ with the triple $(\mathcal{P}, \mathcal{SP}_0, \mathcal{SP}_1)$;
20:         With probability ϵ set $x_k = 0$ or 1 randomly;
21:         With probability $1 - \epsilon$
22:             set $x_k = 1$ if $\mathcal{SP}_0$ is infeasible;
23:             set $x_k = 0$ if $\mathcal{SP}_1$ is infeasible;
24:             set $x_k = 0$ if $g_\theta(\mathcal{SP}_0) < c_k + g_\theta(\mathcal{SP}_1)$ and 1 otherwise;
25:     **end for**
26:     Calculate the weight sum $w = c_1 x_1 + \cdots + c_n x_n$;
27:     **return** $SPTriples, w$
28: **end function**

Once we have trained the neural network g_θ, we finally decide each variable based on the network predictions for the corresponding sub-problems, i.e., we decide $x_k = 1$ if $g_\theta(\mathcal{SP}_0) < c_1 + g_\theta(\mathcal{SP}_1)$ and $x_k = 0$ otherwise. The pseudo-code is presented in Algorithm 2.

4 Results

4.1 Data Set and Experiment Setting

Following the approach used by Balas and Ho [21], we randomly generated weighted set coverage problems as datasets in two scales, including:

(1) WSCP20: WSCP20 consists of 100 instances and each instance has a total of 20 subsets over a universe U ($|U| = 20$). Here, the elements of each subset were randomly selected from U. Following the convention [21], we set the density as 0.1, i.e., the total number of elements of these subsets is $0.1 \times 20 \times 20 = 40$.
(2) WSCP50: WSCP50 consists of 10 instances and each instance has a total of 50 subsets over a universe U ($|U| = 50$). The density is also set as 0.1.

Algorithm 2. AIA-SC algorithm

1: **function** AIA-SC($\boldsymbol{A}, \boldsymbol{b}, \boldsymbol{c}, n$)
2:     $\theta = $ TRAININGNETWORK($\boldsymbol{A}, \boldsymbol{b}, \boldsymbol{c}, n$)
3:     **for** $k = 1 \to n$ **do**
4:         Set $\boldsymbol{A}_{k+1} = [\alpha_{k+1} \cdots \alpha_n]$;
5:         Set $\boldsymbol{b}_k = \boldsymbol{b} - x_1\alpha_1 \cdots - x_{k-1}\alpha_{k-1}$;
6:         Set $\boldsymbol{c}_{k+1} = [c_{k+1} \cdots c_n]^T$;
7:         Set $\mathcal{SP}_0 = (\boldsymbol{A}_{k+1}, \boldsymbol{b}_k, \boldsymbol{c}_{k+1})$;
8:         Set $\mathcal{SP}_1 = (\boldsymbol{A}_{k+1}, \boldsymbol{b}_k - \alpha_k, \boldsymbol{c}_{k+1})$;
9:         **if** $g_\theta(\mathcal{SP}_0) < c_k + g_\theta(\mathcal{SP}_1)$ **then**
10:           $x_k = 0$;
11:         **else**
12:           $x_k = 1$;
13:         **end if**
14:     **end for**
15:     **return** the solution $x_1, x_2, ..., x_n$ together with the weight sum $\sum_{i=1}^{n} c_i x_i$.
16: **end function**

All experiments were performed on a machine with an Intel CPU i7-8700K and an NVIDIA GeForce GTX 1080Ti GPU card.

4.2 Evaluating the Solution Quality of AIA-SC

We evaluated the solution quality of AIA-SC, and compared it with the established Chvatal's greedy algorithm [5]. Chvatal's greedy algorithm was designed purely based on human experience and heuristics: it repeatedly selects the subset with the highest performance/cost ratio, i.e., the ratio of the number of newly covered elements by the subset over its weight, until the selected subsets cover all elements.

AIA-SC found the optimal solutions on 87 out of the 100 WSCP20 instances; in contrast, Chvatal's greedy algorithm found the optimal solutions for only 11 instances. Furthermore, compared with Chvatal's greedy algorithm, AIA-SC found better solutions for 87 instances and inferior solutions for only 3 instances.

Table 1 shows the performance of the two algorithms for 10 WSCP20 instances. AIA-SC failed to find the optimal solution for only two instances, whereas Chvatal's greedy algorithm failed for seven instances. The gap between the solution by AIA-SC and the optimal solution is much lower than that by the Chvatal's greedy algorithm, e.g., 1.82% vs. 21.05% for WSCP20-3.

Table 1. Performance of AIA-SC and Chvatal's greedy algorithm on WSCP20 and WSCP50 instances

Instance	OPT	Chvatal's Greedy		AIA-SC	
		Objective value	Gap	Objective value	Gap
WSCP20-1	416	416	0	416	0
WSCP20-2	621	676	8.86%	**621**	0
WSCP20-3	494	598	21.05%	**503**	1.82%
WSCP20-4	451	490	10.87%	**451**	0
WSCP20-5	542	542	0	542	0
WSCP20-6	520	553	6.35%	**520**	0
WSCP20-7	570	678	18.95%	**570**	0
WSCP20-8	602	702	16.61%	**602**	0
WSCP20-9	529	549	3.78%	**529**	0
WSCP20-10	427	**427**	0	432	1.17%
WSCP50-1	1559	1742	11.73%	**1725**	**10.65%**
WSCP50-2	2206	2452	11.15%	**2331**	**5.67%**
WSCP50-3	1221	1899	55.53%	**1760**	**44.14%**
WSCP50-4	2548	3203	25.71%	**3067**	**20.37%**
WSCP50-5	2315	2417	4.41%	**2408**	**4.02%**
WSCP50-6	1965	**2294**	**16.74%**	2298	16.95%
WSCP50-7	1933	2128	9.83%	**2030**	**5.02%**
WSCP50-8	1975	2101	6.28%	**2013**	**1.92%**
WSCP50-9	2105	**2439**	**15.87%**	2525	19.95%
WSCP50-10	1630	1888	15.83%	**1630**	0

Both algorithms performed worse for WSCP50 instances than WSCP20; however, AIA-SC still outperforms Chvatal's greedy algorithm. As shown in Table 1, AIA-SC found the optimal solution for one instance WSCP50-10 while Chvatal's greedy algorithm failed for all the ten instances. In addition, AIA-SC generates better solutions for eight instances.

4.3 Evaluating the Decisions Made by AIA-SC

The key for AIA-SC to generate high-quality solutions is its ability to make correct decisions, i.e., $x_k = 1$ or $x_k = 0$, during the solving process. Figure 4 shows how AIA-SC makes decisions for the problem presented in Fig. 1. In the first step, AIA-SC made the correct decision $x_1 = 0$, i.e., abandoning the subset S_1, as $g_\theta(\mathcal{SP}_0) = 16.86$ is less than $c_1 + g_\theta(\mathcal{SP}_1) = 17.43$. Next, AIA-SC selected S_2 and S_3 as they are the only choices to cover the element a. In the fourth step, AIA-SC selected S_4 as $g_\theta(\mathcal{SP}_0) = 1.23$ is greater than $c_4 + g_\theta(\mathcal{SP}_1) = -1.65$. In the fifth step, AIA-SC abandoned S_5 as $g_\theta(\mathcal{SP}_0) = -2.73$ is less than $c_5 + g_\theta(\mathcal{SP}_1) = 0.27$. Finally, AIA-SC selected S_2, S_3, S_4 whose sum of the weights is 11.

Table 2. Confusion matrix of the decisions made by AIA-SC when solving (a) WSCP20 instances and (b) WSCP50 instances. Here, the true values denote whether $OPT(\mathcal{SP}_0) < c_k + OPT(\mathcal{SP}_1)$ or not, and the predictions denote whether $g_\theta(\mathcal{SP}_0) < c_k + g_\theta(\mathcal{SP}_1)$ or not

		True value	
		$x_k = 0$	$x_k = 1$
Predictions	$x_k = 0$	281	33
	$x_k = 1$	28	982

(a)

		True value	
		$x_k = 0$	$x_k = 1$
Predictions	$x_k = 0$	217	139
	$x_k = 1$	128	1494

(b)

In contrast, Chvatal's greedy algorithm selected S_4 as it has the highest performance-cost ratio of $\frac{2}{1}$. Subsequently, it selected S_1, S_3, S_5 and obtained the collection whose sum of the weights is 12. It should be noted that the selection of S_1 is not optimal although S_1 has the highest performance-cost ratio of $\frac{2}{2}$ at the second step. This result demonstrates the drawbacks of human-crafted heuristics.

It is worth pointing out that the relative magnitude between $g_\theta(\mathcal{SP}_0)$ and $c_k + g_\theta(\mathcal{SP}_1)$ rather than their actual values is essential to making correct decisions. As shown in Table 2, AIA-SC made a total of 1324 decisions when solving WSCP20 instances, out of which 1263 decisions are correct, thus achieving an accuracy of 95.39%. Table 2 shows that AIA-SC made 1711 correct decisions when solving WSCP50 instances, also achieving a high accuracy of 86.50% (1978 decisions in total). The high accuracy of correct decisions empowers AIA-SC to generate nearly optimal solutions.

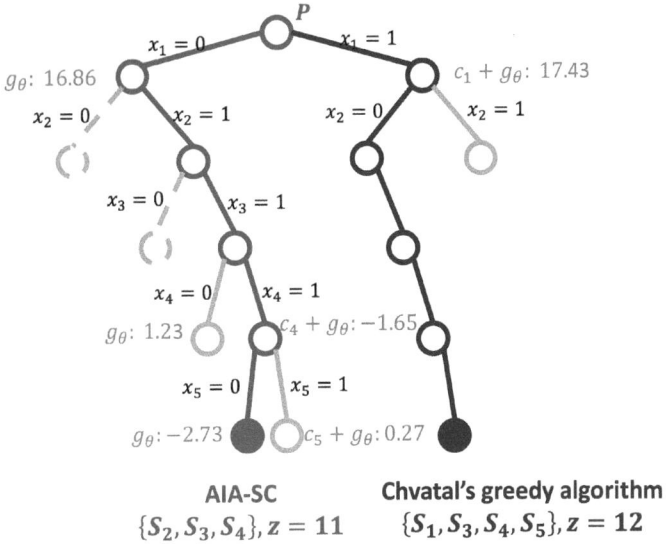

Fig. 4. The solving process of AIA-SC (in red) and Chvatal's greedy algorithm (in blue) for the instance shown in Fig. 1. AIA-SC finds the optimal solution while Chvatal's greedy algorithm fails. (Color figure online)

5 Conclusion and Discussion

The results presented here have highlighted the special features of AIA-SC in designing algorithms aided by deep learning. The abilities of AIA-SC have been clearly demonstrated by the high quality of the generated solutions and the high accuracy of decisions for set cover problems. Experimental results suggested that our AIA-SC approach consistently yields superior solutions than Chvatal's greedy algorithm which was designed using the human experience.

Notably, the fundamental concept of our approach is highly versatile and can be easily extended, requiring minimal modifications, to design efficient greedy algorithms for addressing other NP-hard problems.

AIA-SC approach uses an instance-specific training strategy, thus leading to longer running time than commercial solvers. In addition, the time required for training varies substantially even for WSCP instances of the same scale. Training a general neural network suitable for all WSCP instances remains one of the future studies. The use of transformer instead of the current full connection layers might greatly improve AIA-SC.

This paper represents a pioneering effort in leveraging deep learning technology to aid in algorithm design. Unlike traditional approaches relying on human-crafted heuristics, our approach learns heuristic rules autonomously. This intelligent search algorithm has the potential to surpass the limitations imposed by human experience. We firmly believe that data-driven algorithm design will emerge as a compelling and burgeoning area of research, presenting new opportunities for exploration and advancements in the field.

Acknowledgements. This study was funded by the National Key Research and Development Program of China (2020YFA0907000), the National Natural Science Foundation of China (32370657, 32270657, 32271297) and Youth Innovation Promotion Association, Chinese Academy of Sciences. We appreciate the ComputeX center, ICT, CAS for providing computation service.

References

1. Sipser, M.: Introduction to the theory of computation. ACM SIGACT News **27**(1), 27–29 (1996)
2. Karp, R.M.: Reducibility among combinatorial problems. In: Complexity of Computer Computations, pp. 85–103. Springer, Heidelberg (1972). https://doi.org/10.1007/978-1-4684-2001-2_9
3. Glover, F.: Tabu search-part I. ORSA J. Comput. **1**(3), 190–206 (1989)
4. Russakovsky, O., et al.: Imagenet large scale visual recognition challenge. Int. J. Comput. Vision **115**(3), 211–252 (2015)
5. Chvatal, V.: A greedy heuristic for the set-covering problem. Math. Oper. Res. **4**(3), 233–235 (1979)
6. Papadimitriou, C.H., Steiglitz, K.: Combinatorial Optimization: Algorithms and Complexity. Courier Corporation, Chelmsford (2013)
7. Garmendia, A.I., Ceberio, J., Mendiburu, A.: Neural combinatorial optimization: a new player in the field. arXiv preprint arXiv:2205.01356 (2022)
8. Vinyals, O., Fortunato, M., Jaitly, N.: Pointer networks. Adv. Neural Inf. Process. Syst. **28** (2015)
9. Khalil, E., Dai, H., Zhang, Y., Dilkina, B., Song, L.: Learning combinatorial optimization algorithms over graphs. Adv. Neural Inf. Process. Syst. **30** (2017)
10. Alvarez, A.M., Louveaux, Q., Wehenkel, L.: A supervised machine learning approach to variable branching in branch-and-bound. In: IN ECML (2014)
11. Achterberg, T., Koch, T., Martin, A.: Branching rules revisited. Oper. Res. Lett. **33**(1), 42–54 (2005)
12. Khalil, E.B., Le Bodic, P., Song, L., Nemhauser, G., Dilkina, B.: Learning to branch in mixed integer programming. In: Thirtieth AAAI Conference on Artificial Intelligence (2016)
13. Gasse, M., Chételat, D., Ferroni, N., Charlin, L., Lodi, A.: Exact combinatorial optimization with graph convolutional neural networks. Adv. Neural Inf. Process. Syst., 15580–15592 (2019)
14. He, H., Daume III, H., Eisner, J.M.: Learning to search in branch and bound algorithms. Adv. Neural Inf. Process. Syst., 3293–3301 (2014)
15. Joshi, C.K., Laurent, T., Bresson, X.: An efficient graph convolutional network technique for the travelling salesman problem. arXiv preprint arXiv:1906.01227 (2019)

16. Bello, I., Pham, H., Le, Q.V., Norouzi, M., Bengio, S.: Neural combinatorial optimization with reinforcement learning. arXiv preprint arXiv:1611.09940 (2016)
17. Kool, W., Van Hoof, H., Welling, M.: Attention, learn to solve routing problems. arXiv preprint arXiv:1803.08475 (2018)
18. Bresson, X., Laurent, T.: The transformer network for the traveling salesman problem. arXiv preprint arXiv:2103.03012 (2021)
19. Jensen, R.E.: Sensitivity analysis and integer linear programming. Account. Rev. **43**(3), 425–446 (1968)
20. Yang, F., Jin, T., Liu, T.Y., Sun, X., Zhang, J.: Boosting dynamic programming with neural networks for solving NP-hard problems. In: Asian Conference on Machine Learning, pp. 726–739. PMLR (2018)
21. Balas, E., Ho, A.: Set covering algorithms using cutting planes, heuristics, and subgradient optimization: a computational study. In: Combinatorial Optimization, pp. 37–60 (1980)

Approximation Algorithm

Approximation Algorithms on Linear Equalities and Inequalities Mod p

Zhongzheng Tang[1], Haoyang Zou[2], and Zhuo Diao[2](✉)

[1] School of Science, Beijing University of Posts and Telecommunications, Beijing 100876, China
tangzhongzheng@amss.ac.cn
[2] School of Statistics and Mathematics, Central University of Finance and Economics, Beijing 100081, China
diaozhuo@amss.ac.cn

Abstract. In this paper, we have a set of weighted linear equalities and inequalities of the form $A_1\mathbf{x} \equiv 0 \pmod{p}, A_2\mathbf{x} \not\equiv 0 \pmod{p}$ where all entries of A_1 and A_2 are in $\{-1, 0, 1\}$. The objective is to assign each x_i to $\mathbb{Z}_p = \{0, \ldots, p-1\}$ to maximize the total weight of the satisfied equalities and inequalities. This problem is a generalization of k-Correlation Clustering problem. We design an approximation algorithm with the approximation ratio $\max\{a, \frac{(2-p)a+p-1}{p}\}$, where a is the weighted proportion of equalities in all equalities and inequalities. As a varies from 0 to 1, the approximation ratio varies from $\frac{p-1}{p}$ to 1 and the minimum value is $\frac{1}{2}$ when a is $\frac{1}{2}$.

Keywords: Linear Equalities and Inequalities mod p · Approximation Algorithms · Choosing the Better of Two Solutions

1 Introduction

Systems of linear equations mod p is a basic and very general combinatorial problem, there is a set of weighted linear equations of the form $A\mathbf{x} \equiv b \pmod{p}$. We want to set $x_i \in \mathbb{Z}_p = \{0, \ldots, p-1\}$ to maximize the total weight of the satisfied equalities. This problem is denoted as Max Lin mod p.

Max Lin mod p problem is a generalization of Max-p-Cut problem [13], thus it is NP-hard. For Max Lin mod p problem, the naive randomized algorithm which chooses a solution at random approximates the problem within p. Hastad [15] studied systems of linear equations mod p with exactly k variables in each equation, and showed that it is actually NP-hard to approximate the problem within $1/p + \epsilon$ for all $\epsilon > 0$, $p \geq 2$, and $k \geq 3$.

Supported by National Natural Science Foundation of China under Grant No.11901605, No.12101069, Program for Innovation Research in Central University of Finance and Economics, the disciplinary funding of Central University of Finance and Economics.

© The Author(s), under exclusive license to Springer Nature Singapore Pte Ltd. 2025
Y. Yin et al. (Eds.): NCTCS 2024, CCIS 2354, pp. 47–57, 2025.
https://doi.org/10.1007/978-981-96-1490-5_4

Bansal, Blum and Chawla [2] introduced the correlation clustering problem and motivated it by a document clustering application. There is a trivial 0.5-approximation algorithm for maximizing agreements; putting all vertices in one big cluster, or placing every vertex in a separate cluster, agrees with at least half the edge labels. Bansal et al. also gave an algorithm to approximate agreements with an additive error of $\epsilon|V|^2$, obtaining a PTAS when $|E| = \Omega(|V|^2)$. An equivalent optimization problem is to minimize disagreements - the number of "−" edges within clusters and "+" edges between clusters. In [2], a constant-factor approximation algorithm is given for minimizing disagreements on a complete unweighted graph. In [4,5,8], the authors independently gave $O(\log|V|)$-approximation algorithms for minimizing disagreements on weighted graphs. In [20], Swamy gave a 0.7666-approximation algorithm for maximizing agreements and shown that the problem is APX-Hard.

For every fixed k, there is a polynomial-time approximation scheme for the correlation clustering problem on complete graphs [14]. In contrast, for the general graphs, the best approximation ratio 0.7666 is known due to Swamy [20]. In [6], for arbitrary k, exact [3,12] and heuristic methods [7,16,17] are developed based on a mixed integer programming model. Denoting the order of a graph by n, exact algorithms fail for $n > 21$ [3] and $n > 40$ [12]. While greedy algorithms [7] and local search heuristics [16] are used for larger instances with $n \approx 10^3$ and $n \approx 10^4$ respectively.

After extending the nonlinear energy minimization model suggested by Facchetti et al. [11] to generalised balance, Ma et al. [18,19] has experimented on the correlation clustering problem in networks with $n \approx 10^5$ using various heuristics. Esmailian et al. [9,10] have also extended the work of Facchetti et al. [11] focusing on the role of negative ties in signed graph clustering.

The k-correlation clustering problem is a special case of the Max 2-Lin mod k problem where each equality or inequality contains exactly 2 variables. Swamy [20] got a 0.7666-approximation for the special case of the Max 2-Lin mod k problem where the right-side value of each equality or inequality equals zero. In contrast, for the general case only a $(1/k+\varepsilon(k))$-approximation is known due to Andersson, Engebretsen and Hastad [1].

Our Contributions

- We consider a special case of Max Lin mod p problem, which is called Max Lin-0 mod p problem. We prove Max Lin-0 mod p problem is a generalization of k-correlation clustering problem.
- For Max Lin-0 mod p problem, we design a randomized algorithm and a greedy algorithm. These two algorithms have the same approximation ratio $\frac{(2-p)a+p-1}{p}$, where a is the weighted proportion of equalities in all equalities and inequalities. As a varies from 0 to 1, the approximation ratio varies from $\frac{p-1}{p}$ to $\frac{1}{p}$ and the minimum value is $\frac{1}{p}$.
- By choosing a better one from the greedy algorithm and a trivial algorithm, we get a $\max\{a, \frac{(2-p)a+p-1}{p}\}$. As a varies from 0 to 1, the approximation ratio varies from $\frac{p-1}{p}$ to 1 and the minimum value is $\frac{1}{2}$.

Organization. In Sect. 2, we introduce the formal definitions of the problems. In Sect. 3, we prove the Max k-Lin-0 mod p problem is a generalization of k-correlation clustering problem. In Sect. 4, for the Max Lin-0 mod p problem, we design a randomized algorithm, a greedy algorithm and a choosing better one algorithm.

2 Preliminaries

Denote $\mathbb{Z}_p = \{0, \ldots, p-1\}$. We first give the definition of our problems.

Definition 1. *The* Max Lin mod p *problem is defined as follows. Given n variables $x_1, \ldots, x_n$, a system of m_1 linear equalities mod p and a system of m_2 linear inequalities mod p. Let $A_1 \in \{-1, 0, 1\}^{m_1 \times n}$, $A_2 \in \{-1, 0, 1\}^{m_2 \times n}$ be the coefficient matrices for equality and inequality systems. Let $b_1 \in \mathbb{Z}_p^{m_1}$, $b_2 \in \mathbb{Z}_p^{m_2}$ be the right-side vectors for equality and inequality systems. Denote $[x_1, \ldots, x_n]^T$ as column vector $\mathbf{x}$.*

$$A_1 \mathbf{x} \equiv b_1 (\mod p)$$
$$A_2 \mathbf{x} \not\equiv b_2 (\mod p)$$

for each equality or inequality has a positive weight w_i, $i = 1, \ldots, m_1 + m_2$. The objective is deciding values from $\mathbb{Z}_p$ for all variables to maximize the total weight of satisfied equations.

Definition 2. *The* Max k-Lin mod p *problem is a special case of the* Max Lin mod p *problem with the following constraints: for each equality or inequality, the number of nonzero coefficient equals k. In other word, each equality or inequality contains exactly k variables.*

Definition 3. *The* Max Lin-0 mod p *problem is the* Max Lin mod p *problem satisfies that all entries of b_1 and b_2 are zeros.*

Definition 4. *The* Max k-Lin-0 mod p *problem is the* Max k-Lin mod p *problem satisfies that all entries of b_1 and b_2 are zeros.*

3 Computational Complexity

In this section, we derive the reduction from the k-Correlation Clustering problem to the Max 2-Lin-0 mod p problem to show that the k-Correlation Clustering problem is a special case of the Max 2-Lin-0 mod p problem, which implies the NP-hardness of the Max Lin-0 mod p problem.

k-Correlation Clustering problem: given an edge-weighted graph $G(V, E)$ where the edges are labeled either "+"(similar) or "−"(different) with non-negative weights, we want to partition the vertices at most k-clusters to maximize agreements - the total weights of "+" edges within clusters and "−" edges between clusters.

The k-Correlation Clustering problem is a generalization of Max k-Cut problem. If all edges are labelled "−" with trivial weight 1, the k-Correlation Clustering problem is equivalent to Max k-Cut problem. Thus the k-Correlation Clustering problem is NP-hard.

Theorem 1. *The Max 2-Lin-0 mod p problem is a generalization of k-Correlation Clustering problem.*

Proof. We will give a reduction from k-Correlation Clustering problem to Max 2-Lin-0 mod p problem. Given an instance of k-Correlation Clustering problem, there is an edge-weighted graph $G(V, E)$ where the edges are labeled either "+"(similar) or "−"(different) with non-negative weights and we want to partition the vertices at most k-clusters to maximize agreements - the total weights of "+" edges within clusters and "−" edges between clusters. The reduction from k-Correlation Clustering problem to Max 2-Lin-0 mod $p(=k)$ problem is constructed as following:

- The variables $x_1, \ldots, x_n$ correspond to the vertices $v_1, \ldots, v_n$;
- For each weighted-edge $e = \{v_i, v_j\}$ labelled "+", there is an equation $x_i - x_j \equiv 0 \pmod{k}$ with the same weight w_e;
- For each weighted-edge $e = \{v_i, v_j\}$ labelled "−", there is an equation $x_i - x_j \not\equiv 0 \pmod{k}$ with the same weight w_e;

- The vertices $v_1, \ldots, v_n$ are divided into k clusters, then there is an assignment $x_1, \ldots, x_n$ to $\{0, \ldots, k-1\}$.
- For each weighted-edge $e = \{v_i, v_j\}$ labelled "+", $\{v_i, v_j\}$ are in the same cluster if and only if $x_i - x_j \equiv 0 \pmod{k}$ holds.
- For each weighted-edge $e = \{v_i, v_j\}$ labelled "−", $\{v_i, v_j\}$ are in different clusters if and only if $x_i - x_j \not\equiv 0 \pmod{k}$ holds.

The agreements - the total weights of "+" edges within clusters and "−" edges between clusters are exactly the total weight of the satisfied equalities and inequalities. Thus the k-Correlation Clustering problem is reduced to the Max 2-Lin-0 mod p problem.

The k-Correlation Clustering problem is NP-hard, thus the Max 2-Lin-0 mod p problem is also NP-hard.

Remark 1. The Max Lin-0 mod p problem is NP-hard.

4 Approximation Algorithms

In this section, we design three approximation algorithms to compute the Max Lin-0 problem, which are based on randomized technique, greedy technique and choosing the better of two solutions.

The following definition will be used frequently in our discussions. Denote the set of equalities as E and the set of inequalities as IE. $W(E)$ is the total weight of all equalities and $W(IE)$ is the total weight of all inequalities. Let a denote the weighted proportion of equalities in all equalities and inequalities, i.e. $a = \frac{W(E)}{W(E)+W(IE)}$. Let $\mathbf{x}$ be the output of the variable assignment and $W(\mathbf{x})$ denote the total weight of satisfied equalities and inequalities.

Algorithm 1. Randomized Algorithm for $W(\mathbf{x})$

Input: The coefficient matrices $A_1 \in \{-1, 0, 1\}^{m_1 \times n}$ and $A_2 \in \{-1, 0, 1\}^{m_2 \times n}$, the non-negative weight of all equalities and inequalities.

Output: The assignment value of variables $\{x_1, \ldots, x_n\}$ and the total weight of satisfied equalities and inequalities.

1: Take a variable order $x_1, \ldots, x_n$ arbitrarily.
2: **for** $i = 1$ to n **do**
3:   Assign one of $\mathbb{Z}_p$ to x_i with equal probability $\frac{1}{p}$.
4: Output the assignment value of all variables and the total weight of satisfied equalities and inequalities.

4.1 The Randomized Algorithm

The Randomized Algorithm: Assign values to all variables $\{x_1, x_2, \ldots, x_n\}$ in this order and every variable x_i is assigned a value in $\mathbb{Z}_p$ with equal probability $\frac{1}{p}$ independently. Finally, output the assignment value of variables $\{x_1, \ldots, x_n\}$ and the total weight of satisfied equalities and inequalities $W(\mathbf{x})$. The randomized algorithm is as shown in Algorithm 1.

The next lemma is useful in proving Theorem 2.

Lemma 1. *For any equation $x_1 \pm \cdots \pm x_k \equiv b \pmod{p}$ where $b \in \mathbb{Z}_p$, assign $\{x_1, \ldots, x_k\}$ values from $\mathbb{Z}_p$. There is exactly p^{k-1} solutions satisfying the equation.*

Proof. We will prove this lemma by conduction on k. For the case $k = 1$, the equation is $x_1 \equiv b \pmod{p}$ and the only one solution is $x_1 = b$. Assume for the case $k = t$, the lemma holds. For the case $k = t + 1$, we have

$$x_1 \pm \cdots \pm x_t \pm x_{t+1} \equiv b \pmod{p} \Leftrightarrow x_1 \pm x_2 \cdots \pm x_t \equiv b \mp x_{t+1} \pmod{p}$$

Assign x_{t+1} value in $\mathbb{Z}_p$. For each value x_{t+1}, according to the assumption, the equation $x_1 \pm x_2 \cdots \pm x_t \equiv b \mp x_{t+1} \pmod{p}$ have exactly p^{t-1} solutions. The value x_{t+1} traverses $\mathbb{Z}_p$, thus there are exactly $p^{t-1} \times p = p^t$ solutions satisfying the equation $x_1 \pm \cdots \pm x_t \pm x_{t+1} \equiv b \pmod{p}$.

Theorem 2. *Given a non-negative weighted linear equalities and inequalities of the form $A_1 \mathbf{x} \equiv 0 \pmod{p}, A_2 \mathbf{x} \not\equiv 0 \pmod{p}$. The randomized algorithm is a $\frac{(2-p)a+p-1}{p}$-approximation algorithm in the expectation sense: $E[W(\mathbf{x})] \geq \frac{(2-p)a+p-1}{p} \cdot OPT$.*

Proof. We just need to explain

$$E[W(\mathbf{x})] = \frac{(2-p)a+p-1}{p} \cdot \{W(E) + W(IE)\} \geq \frac{(2-p)a+p-1}{p} \cdot OPT$$

According to the assignment rule: Assign a value in $\mathbb{Z}_p$ to x_i with equal probability $\frac{1}{p}$ for each i independently.

For any equation $a_1^T \mathbf{x} \equiv 0 \pmod{p}$ where $a_1 \in \{-1, 0, 1\}^n$, define a random variable X_e:
$$X_e = \begin{cases} 1, & \text{if the equation is satisfied} \\ 0, & \text{if the equation is not satisfied} \end{cases}$$

For any inequality $a_2^T \mathbf{x} \not\equiv 0 \pmod{p}$ where $a_2 \in \{-1, 0, 1\}^n$, define a random variable X_{ie}:
$$X_{ie} = \begin{cases} 1, & \text{if the inequality is satisfied} \\ 0, & \text{if the inequality is not satisfied} \end{cases}$$

Thus we have
$$W(\mathbf{x}) = \sum_{e \in E} w(e) X_e + \sum_{ie \in IE} w(i.e.) X_{ie}$$

Here E is the set of equalities and IE is the set of inequalities.

- For each equation $a_1^T \mathbf{x} \equiv 0 \pmod{p}$ with exactly k_1 variables, assign a value in $\mathbb{Z}_p$ to x_i with equal probability $\frac{1}{p}$ for each i independently. Thus there are p^{k_1} possibilities. According to Lemma 1, there is exactly p^{k_1-1} solutions satisfying the equation. Thus we have

$$E(X_e) = Pr(X_e = 1) \cdot 1 + Pr(X_e = 0) \cdot 0 = Pr(X_e = 1) = \frac{p^{k_1-1}}{p^{k_1}} = \frac{1}{p}$$

- For each inequality $a_2^T \mathbf{x} \not\equiv 0 \pmod{p}$ with exactly k_2 variables, assign a value in $\mathbb{Z}_p$ to x_i with equal probability $\frac{1}{p}$ for each i independently. Thus there are p^{k_2} possibilities. According to Lemma 1, there is exactly $p^{k_2} - p^{k_2-1}$ solutions satisfying the inequality. Thus we have

$$E(X_{ie}) = Pr(X_{ie} = 1) \cdot 1 + Pr(X_{ie} = 0) \cdot 0 = Pr(X_{ie} = 1) = \frac{p^{k_2} - p^{k_2-1}}{p^{k_2}} = 1 - \frac{1}{p}$$

Thus we have
$$E[W(\mathbf{x})] = \sum_{e \in E} w(e) E[X_e] + \sum_{ie \in IE} w(i.e.) E[X_{ie}]$$
$$= \sum_{e \in E} w(e) \frac{1}{p} + \sum_{ie \in IE} w(i.e.) (1 - \frac{1}{p}) = W(E) \frac{1}{p} + W(IE)(1 - \frac{1}{p})$$

Combined with $W(E) = a[W(E) + W(IE)], W(IE) = (1 - a)[W(E) + W(IE)]$, we have

$$E[W(\mathbf{x})] = \frac{(2-p)a + p - 1}{p} \cdot \{W(E) + W(IE)\} \geq \frac{(2-p)a + p - 1}{p} \cdot OPT$$

Algorithm 2. Greedy Algorithm for $W(\mathbf{x})$

Input: The coefficient matrices $A_1 \in \{-1, 0, 1\}^{m_1 \times n}$ and $A_2 \in \{-1, 0, 1\}^{m_2 \times n}$, the non-negative weight of all equalities and inequalities.

Output: The assignment value of variables $\{x_1, \ldots, x_n\}$ and the total weight of satisfied equalities and inequalities.

1: Take a variable order $x_1, \ldots, x_n$ arbitrarily.
2: **for** $i = 1$ to n **do**
3:     Assign one of $\mathbb{Z}_p$ to x_i to maximize the total weight.
4: Output the assignment value of all variables and the total weight of satisfied equalities and inequalities.

As a varies from 0 to 1, $\frac{(2-p)a+p-1}{p}$ varies from $\frac{p-1}{p}$ to $\frac{1}{p}$ and the minimum value is $\frac{1}{p}$, thus we have the next corollary instantly:

Corollary 1. *The randomized algorithm is a $\frac{1}{p}$-approximation algorithm in the expectation sense for the Max Lin-0 mod p problem.*

Remark 2. The randomized algorithm is easily derandomized by conditional expectation method, which is exactly the greedy algorithm.

Remark 3. This randomized algorithm is also a $\frac{1}{p}$-approximation algorithm in the expectation sense for the Max Lin mod p problem.

4.2 The Greedy Algorithm

The Greedy Algorithm: Consider the assignment value of variables $\{x_1, \ldots, x_n\}$ to $\mathbb{Z}_p$ in this order and the rules for assignment value are as follows: When a variable x_i is assigned a value in $\mathbb{Z}_p$, choose the number to maximize the weights of satisfied equalities and inequalities. Finally, output the assignment value of variables $\{x_1, \ldots, x_n\}$ and the total weight of satisfied equalities and inequalities. The greedy algorithm is as shown in Algorithm 2.

Theorem 3. *Given a non-negative weighted linear equalities and inequalities of the form $A_1\mathbf{x} \equiv 0 \pmod{p}, A_2\mathbf{x} \not\equiv 0 \pmod{p}$. The greedy algorithm is a $\frac{(2-p)a+p-1}{p}$-approximation algorithm: $W(\mathbf{x}) \geq \frac{(2-p)a+p-1}{p} \cdot OPT$.*

Proof. We just need to explain

$$W(\mathbf{x}) \geq \frac{(2-p)a+p-1}{p} \cdot \{W(E) + W(IE)\} \geq \frac{(2-p)a+p-1}{p} \cdot OPT$$

When a variable x_i is assigned a value in $\mathbb{Z}_p$, choose the number to maximize the weights of satisfied equalities and inequalities. Denote $W_0(i), W_1(i), \ldots, W_{p-1}(i)$

as the weights of satisfied equalities and inequalities incident to x_i if x_i is assigned a value in $\mathbb{Z}_p$. $W_E(i)$ is the total weight of equalities incident to x_i and $W_{IE}(i)$ is the total weight of inequalities incident to x_i. Notice the equalities and inequalities incident to x_i means x_i is the last appeared variable in the order. Thus there is a partition of all the equalities and inequalities according to the incident variable $x_i, 1 \leq i \leq n$.

- For each equality incident to x_i, there is exactly 1 assignment number satisfying the equality.
- For each inequality incident to x_i, there is exactly $p-1$ assignment number satisfying the inequality.

Thus we have

$$W_0(i) + W_1(i) + \cdots + W_{p-1}(i) = W_E(i) + (p-1)W_{IE}(i)$$

$$\frac{1}{p}[W_0(i) + W_1(i) + \cdots + W_{p-1}(i)] = \frac{1}{p}[W_E(i) + (p-1)W_{IE}(i)]$$

According to the assignment rule, we choose the number to maximize the weights of satisfied equalities and inequalities, thus the weights of satisfied equalities and inequalities incident to x_i is $\max\{W_0(i), W_1(i), \ldots, W_{p-1}(i)\}$. Thus we have

$$\max\{W_0(i), W_1(i), \ldots, W_{p-1}(i)\} \geq \frac{1}{p}[W_0(i) + W_1(i) + \cdots + W_{p-1}(i)]$$

$$= \frac{1}{p}[W_E(i) + (p-1)W_{IE}(i)]$$

Consider the assignment process from x_1 to x_n and sum these results, we have

$$\sum_{i=1}^{n} \max\{W_0(i), W_1(i), \ldots, W_{p-1}(i)\} \geq \sum_{i=1}^{n} \frac{1}{p}[W_E(i) + (p-1)W_{IE}(i)]$$

$$= \frac{1}{p}[W(E) + (p-1)W(IE)]$$

Combined with $W(E) = a[W(E) + W(IE)], W(IE) = (1-a)[W(E) + W(IE)]$, we have

$$W(\mathbf{x}) = \sum_{i=1}^{n} \max\{W_0(i), W_1(i), \ldots, W_{p-1}(i)\}$$

$$\geq \frac{(2-p)a + p - 1}{p} \cdot \{W(E) + W(IE)\}$$

$$\geq \frac{(2-p)a + p - 1}{p} \cdot OPT$$

As a varies from 0 to 1, $\frac{(2-p)a+p-1}{p}$ varies from $\frac{p-1}{p}$ to $\frac{1}{p}$ and the minimum value is $\frac{1}{p}$, thus we have the next corollary instantly:

Algorithm 3. One Better of Two Algorithms for $W(\mathbf{x})$

Input: The coefficient matrices $A_1 \in \{-1, 0, 1\}^{m_1 \times n}$ and $A_2 \in \{-1, 0, 1\}^{m_2 \times n}$, the non-negative weight of all equalities and inequalities.

Output: The assignment value of variables $\{x_1, \ldots, x_n\}$ and the total weight of satisfied equalities and inequalities.

1: Run Algorithm 2 to get the assignment value of all variables and the total weight $W(\mathbf{x})$.
2: **if** $W(\mathbf{x}) > W(E)$ **then**
3:     Output the assignment value of all variables and the total weight $W(\mathbf{x})$.
4: **else**
5:     Output the all-0 assignment of all variables and the total weight $W(E)$.

Corollary 2. *The greedy algorithm is a $\frac{1}{p}$-approximation algorithm for the Max Lin-0 mod p problem.*

Remark 4. This greedy algorithm is also a $\frac{1}{p}$-approximation algorithm for the Max Lin mod p problem.

4.3 The One Better of Two Algorithms

The greedy algorithm has the approximation ratio - $\frac{(2-p)a+p-1}{p}$. As a varies from 0 to 1, $\frac{(2-p)a+p-1}{p}$ varies from $\frac{p-1}{p}$ to $\frac{1}{p}$ and the minimum value is $\frac{1}{p}$. Obviously, the approximate ratio is an inverse proportional linear function of a. This means that the smaller weighted proportion of equalities, the better approximation ratio. How do we deal with the case of high weighted proportion of equalities ? A trivial algorithm is setting all variables to 0, $x_1 = \cdots = x_n = 0$. In the trivial algorithm, all equalities are satisfied and all inequalities are not satisfied. Thus the trivial algorithm has the better approximation ratio as the higher weighted proportion of equalities. Finally, we consider the greedy algorithm and the trivial algorithm together and choose the one better of two algorithms. This algorithm is as shown in Algorithm 3.

Theorem 4. *Given a non-negative weighted linear equalities and inequalities of the form $A_1\mathbf{x} \equiv 0 (\bmod\ p)$, $A_2\mathbf{x} \not\equiv 0 (\bmod\ p)$. The one better of two algorithms is a $\max\{a, \frac{(2-p)a+p-1}{p}\}$-approximation algorithm: $W(\mathbf{x}) \geq \max\{a, \frac{(2-p)a+p-1}{p}\} \cdot OPT$.*

Proof. Let us denote the variables' assignment result of the greedy algorithm as X_1 and denote the variables' assignment result of the trivial algorithm as X_2. According to Theorem 3, there is

$$W(\mathbf{x}_1) \geq \frac{(2-p)a+p-1}{p} \cdot [W(E) + W(IE)]$$

For the trivial algorithm, set all variables to 0, $x_1 = \cdots = x_n = 0$. All equalities are satisfied and all inequalities are not satisfied. Thus there is

$$W(\mathbf{x}_2) = W(E) = a \cdot [W(E) + W(IE)] \geq a \cdot OPT$$

The final output is choosing the one better of two algorithms. Thus there is

$$\max\{W(\mathbf{x}_1), W(\mathbf{x}_2)\} \geq \max\{\frac{(2-p)a+p-1}{p}, a\} \cdot [W(E) + W(IE)]$$

$$\geq \max\{a, \frac{(2-p)a+p-1}{p}\} \cdot OPT$$

As a varies from 0 to 1, the approximation ratio $max\{a, \frac{(2-p)a+p-1}{p}\}$ varies from $\frac{p-1}{p}$ to 1 and the minimum value is $\frac{1}{2}$ when a is $\frac{1}{2}$. Thus we have the next corollary instantly:

Corollary 3. *The one better of two algorithms is a $\frac{1}{2}$-approximation algorithm for the Max Lin-0 mod p problem.*

Remark 5. If p is a prime, our results can be generalized for more general problems, where the entries of the coefficient matrices A_1 and A_2 belong to $\mathbb{Z}_p$ instead of $\{-1, 0, 1\}$.

Acknowledges. The authors are very indebted to two anonymous referees for their invaluable suggestions and comments.

References

1. Andersson, G., Engebretsen, L., Hastad, J.: A new way of using semidefinite programming with applications to linear equations mod p. J. Algor. **39**(2), 162–204 (2001)
2. Bansal, N., Blum, A., Chawla, S.: Correlation clustering. Mach. Learn. **56**(1/3), 89–113 (2004)
3. Brusco, M., Steinley, D.: K-balance partitioning: an exact method with applications to generalized structural balance and other psychological contexts. Psychol. Methods **15**(2), 145–57 (2010)
4. Charikar, M., Guruswami, V., Wirth, A.: Clustering with qualitative information. J. Comput. Syst. Sci. **71**(3), 360–383 (2003)
5. Demaine, E., Immorlica, N.: Correlation clustering with partial information. In: Proceeding of the 6th International Workshop on Approximation, Randomization and Combinatorial Optimization: Algorithms and Techniques, pp. 1–13 (2003)
6. Demaine, E.D., Emanuel, D., Fiat, A., Immorlica, N.: Correlation clustering in general weighted graphs. Theor. Comput. Sci. **361**(2), 172–187 (2006)
7. Drummond, L., Figueiredo, R., Frota, Y., Levorato, M.: Efficient solution of the correlation clustering problem: an application to structural balance. In: Proceeding of OTM Confederated International Conferences "On the Move to Meaningful Internet Systems", pp. 674–683 (2013)

8. Emanuel, D., Fiat, A.: Correlation clustering - minimizing disagreements on arbitrary weighted graphs. In: Proceeding of the 11th Annual European Symposium on Algorithms, pp. 208–220 (2003)
9. Esmailian, P., Abtahi, S.E., Jalili, M.: Mesoscopic analysis of online social networks: the role of negative ties. Phys. Rev. E **90**(4), 042817 (2014)
10. Esmailian, P., Jalili, M.: Community detection in signed networks: the role of negative ties in different scales. Sci. Rep. **5**, 14339 (2015)
11. Facchetti, G., Iacono, G., Altafini, C.: Computing global structural balance in large-scale signed social networks. Proc. Natl. Acad. Sci. **108**(52), 20953–20958 (2011)
12. Figueiredo, R., Moura, G.: Mixed integer programming formulations for clustering problems related to structural balance. Social Netw. **35**(4), 639–651 (2013)
13. Frieze, A., Jerrum, M.: Improved approximation algorithms for max k-cut and max bisection. Algorithmica **18**(1), 67–81 (1997)
14. Giotis, I., Guruswami, V.: Correlation clustering with a fixed number of clusters. Theory Comput. **2**, 249–266 (2006)
15. Hastad, J.: Some optimal inapproximability results. In: Proceedings Twenty-ninth Annual ACM Symposium on Theory of Computing, pp. 1–10. ACM (1997)
16. Levorato, M., Drummond, L., Frota, Y., Figueiredo, R.: An ils algorithm to evaluate structural balance in signed social networks. In: Proceeding of the 30th Annual ACM Symposium, pp. 1117–1122 (2015)
17. Levorato, M., Figueiredo, R., Frota, Y., Drummond, L.: Evaluating balancing on social networks through the efficient solution of correlation clustering problems. EURO J. Comput. Optim. **5**(4), 467–498 (2017)
18. Ma, L., Gong, M., Du, H., Shen, B., Jiao, L.: A memetic algorithm for computing and transforming structural balance in signed networks. Knowl.-Based Syst. **85**(9), 196–209 (2015)
19. Ma, L., Gong, M., Yan, J., Yuan, F., Du, H.: A decomposition-based multi-objective optimization for simultaneous balance computation and transformation in signed networks. Inf. Sci. Int. J. **378**, 144–160 (2017)
20. Swamy, C.: Correlation clustering: maximizing agreements via semidefinite programming. In: Proceedings of the Fifteenth Annual ACM-SIAM Symposium on Discrete Algorithms, SODA, pp. 526–527 (2004)

Online Clustering on the Line with θ-th Power Cost Variable Sized Clustering

Rongchuan Luo(✉)

School of Mathematics and Statistics, Yunnan University, Kunming 650000,
Yunnan, People's Republic of China
luorongchuana@163.com

Abstract. Online clustering is the process of dynamically partitioning a set of points into clusters in a sequential manner, where points arrive one after another and are assigned to clusters upon arrival. We focus on the one-dimensional clustering scenario, where the cost of a cluster is the unit cost of opening cluster 1 plus the θ-th power cost of the cluster diameter. The objective is to minimize the total cost incurred by the algorithm in opening clusters. We investigate both the strict model and the flexible model, both of which maintain two essential properties: points allocated to a given cluster must remain assigned to that cluster, and clusters cannot be merged or split. In the strict model, cluster diameters and precise positions are predetermined during the initialization of clusters. In the flexible model, the algorithm has the flexibility to move or expand clusters, as long as points allocated to a cluster remain assigned to that cluster. This paper introduces the $GRID_a$ algorithm for the strict model's online problem and the $SOSM_a$ algorithm for the semi-online problem, providing proofs of their approximation ratios. For the flexible model's online problem, we present the $FGRID_a$ algorithm and establish its approximation ratio.

Keywords: Online algorithms · Competitive analysis · Clustering problem

1 Introduction

In clustering problems, the objective is to partition a set of points into subsets, optimizing a given objective function. The offline one-dimensional clustering problem involves partitioning already collected one-dimensional data into clusters, seeking intervals on the real line with a length not exceeding 1 to cover all points, minimizing the number of clusters. This problem can be optimally solved in $O(nlogn)$ time using a greedy algorithm [1].

Similarly, the energy cover problem is a variant of the clustering problem, that aims to cover all points while minimizing the required number of clusters.

Supported by the 15th Postgraduate Innovation Foundation of Yunnan University [No. KC-23233888].

It is commonly encountered in cover optimization problems in fields such as wireless sensor networks. Lev-Tov et al. [2] studied the one-dimensional minimum power coverage problem and obtained a fast algorithm in polynomial time. The minimum power cover problem is also a special case of the minimum power partial cover problem. The minimum power partial cover problem in wireless networks is discussed in detail in [3], with sensors or wireless access points having their coverage scaled by changing the transmit power.

The Minimum Power Cover Problem (MPCP) is known to be NP-hard [4], and the best available approximation algorithm for this problem is the Polynomial-Time Approximation Scheme (PTAS) developed by Biló et al. [5]. Liu et al. [6] introduced the k-Prize-Collecting Minimum Power Cover Problem (k-PCPC). They presented a novel two-phase primal-dual algorithm for the k-PCPC with an approximation ratio of at most 3^α. Building upon this foundation, Zhang et al. [7] proposed a primal-dual-based power control approach aimed at reducing the energy consumption of edge servers while ensuring quality of service (QoS) for a finite number of users.

In a related vein, there is a growing interest in combinatorial optimization problems that involve submodular penalties [8]. Meanwhile, Xu et al. [9] studied submodular vertex cover problems with linear penalties and submodular penalties, which are two variants of the submodular vertex cover problem. When the penalty function is a submodular function, Liu et al. [10] designed polynomial time $5 \cdot 2^\alpha + 1$-approximation algorithm for minimum power cover problem with penalty on a plane based on primitive dual frames. Subsequently, in their recent study [11], Liu et al. considered the MPC problem with submodular and linear penalty terms.

Online unit clustering and energy cover are both variants of the coverage problem. The coverage in online unit clustering problem is that the index points are covered by clusters. Charikar et al. [12] proposed a method for the online partitioning of points into clusters of unit size. This problem is referred to as online unit cover. Given a set of n points that need to be covered by balls of unit radius, the objective is to minimize the number of balls used, and they devised an algorithm with a competitive ratio of $O(2^d d \log d)$.

Chan [13] and Zarrabi-Zadeh [14] introduced the online unit clustering problem, where the goal is to ensure that a set of points assigned to a ball (cluster) can always be covered by that ball, but the ball can be moved if necessary. The objective remains to minimize the number of balls as much as possible. Thus, a cluster in an algorithm may have multiple position choices at any time, including the time when the algorithm terminates. They presented two significant randomized algorithms with competitive ratios of $\frac{15}{8}, \frac{11}{6}$. Subsequently, Epstein et al. [15] and Ehmsen et al. [16] improved the competitive ratio of these two algorithms to $\frac{7}{4}, \frac{8}{5}$. In 2022 Dai et al. [17] assumed that the distance between any two adjacent clusters in the offline optimal solution is greater than 0.5. They proposed two online algorithms and then, with a probability of 0.5, ran the two online algorithms independently, resulting in a combined randomized algorithm with a competitive ratio of 1.5.

In 2013, Csirik and Epstein et al. [18] studied a variant of the online clustering problem where the length of clusters is variable, and the cost of each cluster is the cost of opening the cluster plus its length. They initially considered three online models-strict, flexible, and intermediate-and provided algorithms with approximation ratios of $1+\sqrt{2}, \frac{1+\sqrt{5}}{2}, 1+\sqrt{2}$ for each model, along with tight bounds on the performance of online algorithms. In 2014, Divéki G and Imreh C investigated the unit cover problem with rejection on a grid in one-dimensional space [19], where each cluster has a diameter of a, proving that for the strict model, the competitive ratio of any online algorithm is at least 2.3243. In 2017, Araki T [20] proposed an online unit clustering problem with capacity constraints. For this problem, the authors developed an online algorithm with a competitive ratio not exceeding 3.178 and demonstrated that the lower bound of the competitive ratio for any online algorithm is 2. Building upon this, Divéki G [21] studied online algorithms for variable-sized clusters with square costs and provided the online algorithms $GRID_a$ and $FGRID_a$ for strict and flexible models, respectively. In 2020, Monika et al. [22] studied the problem of dynamic clustering minimizing the sum of radii.

2 Preliminaries

In one-dimensional space, we have n request points located on the real line. Our objective is to partition these points into several sets, also known as clusters. A cluster is identified by the assigned request points and the associated interval with that cluster. The cost of cluster C, denoted as $1+max_{i,j\in C}|i-j|^\theta$, is defined as the fixed cost of opening cluster 1 plus the θ-th power cost of the diameter of the opened cluster (i and j are the endpoints of the interval corresponding to the cluster, and they may or may not be request points). The objective is to find an allocation for this input that minimizes the cost of opened clusters.

We measure the performance of an online algorithm A using standard criteria to compare its competitiveness with that of the optimal offline algorithm. The competitiveness ratio of A is defined as $sup_\sigma \frac{A(\sigma)}{OPT(\sigma)}$, where σ is the input sequence of request points, $OPT(\sigma)$ is the cost incurred by the optimal offline algorithm for the input sequence σ, and $A(\sigma)$ is the cost incurred by algorithm A for this input sequence.

3 The Strict Model of the Online Problem

In this section, we consider online clustering problems. Points arrive one by one at arbitrary locations, to be assigned to clusters at the time of arrival without any information about future points. In [21], the author presented an online algorithm $GRID_a$, whose cluster cost is a fixed cost of 1 plus the square of the diameter. We generalize the algorithm, that is, the costs of the cluster are fixed cost at 1 plus the θ-th power of the diameter, and we give the approximate ratio of the algorithm.

Algorithm $GRID_a$ works as follows. When the first point of the interval $I_k = (ka, (k+1)a]$ is reached, for every integer $-\infty < k < +\infty$, a new cluster is opened in the interval $I_k = (ka, (k+1)a]$ and the future points belonging to this interval are assigned to this cluster. The competitive ratio of $GRID_a$ is determined by the following theorem.

Theorem 1. *The competitive ratio of algorithm $GRID_a$ is $max\{F(k), 2+2a^\theta\}$ where k is solved by $k^{\theta-1}[2\theta + (\theta-1)k] - \frac{1}{a^\theta} = 0$ and $F(k) = \frac{(k+2)(1+a^\theta)}{1+k^\theta a^\theta}$, $\theta \geq 2, k \geq 1, a > \frac{1}{\sqrt{5}}$.*

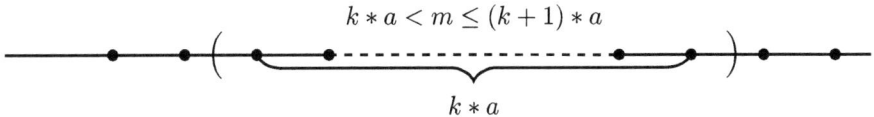

Fig. 1. The optimal cluster intersects at most $k + 2$ clusters from the grid

Proof. We consider an arbitrary sequence of request points. We use OPT to denote the optimal solution. Given that the number of clusters for OPT is unknown, we consider an arbitrary cluster in OPT, denoted by m, representing the length of this cluster.

First, assume that for any integer $k \geq 1$, the inequality $k*a < m \leq (k+1)*a$ holds. This optimal cluster intersects with at most $k + 2$ clusters within the grid (see Fig. 1). Therefore, considering only the request points within this optimal cluster, the cost of the $GRID_a$ algorithm is at most $(1+a^\theta)(k+2)$. Therefore, the competitive ratio of this subsequence is at most $\frac{(1+a^\theta)(k+2)}{m^\theta+1} < \frac{(k+2)(1+a^\theta)}{1+k^\theta a^\theta} = F(k)$
The derivative of this function is

$$F'(k) = \frac{(1+a^\theta) \cdot [1 - 2\theta k^{\theta-1} a^\theta - (\theta-1)k^\theta a^\theta]}{(k^\theta a^\theta + 1)^2} \qquad (1)$$

Considering that both $1 + a^\theta$ and $(k^\theta a^\theta + 1)^2$ are greater than 0, we let $f(k) = 1 - 2\theta k^{\theta-1} a^\theta - (\theta-1)k^\theta a^\theta$. The derivative of $f(k)$ is

$$f'(k) = -\theta(\theta-1)k^{\theta-2} \cdot a^\theta (2+k) < 0 \qquad (2)$$

Therefore, $f(k) \leq f(1) = 1 - (3\theta - 1)a^\theta < 0$ for every $a > \frac{1}{\sqrt{5}}$, and $F'(k)$ is monotonically decreasing. We set $F'(k) = 0$.

$$k^{\theta-1}[2\theta + (\theta-1)k] = \frac{1}{a^\theta} \qquad (3)$$

When $\theta = 2$, the equation is $k(4+k) = \frac{1}{a^2}$, and the solution for k^* is $\inf\{-2 + \sqrt{4 + \frac{1}{a^2}}\}$ or $\sup\{-2 + \sqrt{4 + \frac{1}{a^2}}\}$. This value coincides with the result obtained in reference [21]. Subsequently, when $\theta > 2$, we can infer that $F(k)$ reaches its maximum value at k^*, where k^* is determined by solving $0 = k^{\theta-1}[2\theta + (\theta - 1)k] - \frac{1}{a^\theta}$.

Assuming that $m \leq a$, the sequence intersects with at most two clusters in the grid. Consequently, for this sequence, the cost of the $GRID_a$ algorithm is at most $2(1 + a^\theta)$. Therefore, the competitive ratio of this sequence is at most $\frac{2 + 2a^\theta}{1 + m^\theta} \leq 2 + 2a^\theta$

Now let us prove that the analysis is tight. Take any real number a and a sufficiently small positive number ϵ. If the request sequence consists of points at distances $-\epsilon$ and ϵ, the optimal solution uses only one cluster with a cost of $1+(2\epsilon)^\theta$. Meanwhile, the algorithm employs two clusters with a cost of $2(1+a^\theta)$. Therefore, the competitive ratio is $\frac{2(1 + a^\theta)}{1 + (2\epsilon)^\theta}$. Considering ϵ to be arbitrarily small, we obtain a competitive ratio not smaller than $2 + 2a^\theta$.

Consider a sequence where all points are request points, and the endpoints of the sequence are $-\epsilon$ and $ka+\epsilon$(see Fig. 2). In this context, the $GRID_a$ algorithm utilizes $k+2$ grid cells, corresponding to $k+2$ clusters, with a cost of $(k+2)(1+a^\theta)$. However, if we use only one cluster, the cost is $1+(ka+2\epsilon)^\theta$. Since ϵ is arbitrarily small, the ratio of the cost of the $GRID_a$ algorithm to the cost of the optimal solution is given by $\frac{(k + 2)(1 + a^\theta)}{1 + (ka + 2\epsilon)^\theta} \leq \frac{(k + 2)(1 + a^\theta)}{1 + (ka)^\theta} = F(k)$. Thus, we derive a lower bound for the competitive ratio of the $GRID_a$ algorithm, which is not smaller than F(k) for any integer k, thereby establishing the tightness of our analysis.

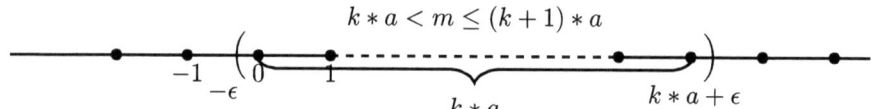

Fig. 2. The sequence with endpoints $-\epsilon$ and $ka + \epsilon$

4 The Semi-online Stict Problem

In the semi-online model, the request points are arranged in ascending order. In Divéki (2013), the semi-online algorithm $SOSM_a$ is proposed to address this problem, where the cost of the considered clusters is a fixed cost of 1 plus the square of the diameter. We have extended this approach, exploring the cost of open clusters as a fixed cost of 1 plus the square of the diameter raised to the power of θ.

The algorithm $SOSM_a$ works as follows. When p is a new request point, if the algorithm already has a cluster that includes p, then p is assigned to the cluster. If none of the algorithm's clusters include p, then a new cluster is opened for p with an interval of $[p, p + a]$, and p is assigned to this new cluster. The competitive ratio of $SOSM_a$ is determined by the following theorem.

Theorem 2. *The competitive ratio of algorithm $SOSM_a$ is $\max\{F(k), 1 + a^\theta\}$ where k is solved by $a^\theta k^\theta(1 - \theta - \frac{\theta}{k}) + 1 = 0$ and $F(k) = \frac{(k+1)(1+a^\theta)}{1+k^\theta a^\theta}$, $\theta \geq 2$, $k \geq 1$, $a > \frac{1}{\sqrt{3}}$.*

Proof. We consider an arbitrary sequence of request points. We use OPT to denote the optimal solution. Given that the number of clusters for OPT is unknown, we consider an arbitrary cluster in OPT, denoted by m, representing the length of this cluster.

First, assume that for any integer $k \geq 1$, the inequality $k*a < m \leq (k+1)*a$ holds. This optimal cluster intersects with at most $k + 2$ clusters within the grid (see Fig. 1). We have to consider clusters with left endpoints greater than or equal to the left endpoint of the optimal cluster. If there is a cluster to the right of the optimal cluster that overlaps with it, this cluster is treated as merged with the clusters to the left of the optimal cluster. Therefore, it is not considered an individual cluster but rather merged with the clusters on the left. Therefore, if we only consider these clusters, the cost of $SOSM_a$ is at most $(1 + a^\theta)(k + 1)$. Consequently, the competitive ratio of this sequence is at most $\frac{(1+a^\theta)(k+1)}{m^\theta+1} < \frac{(k+1)(1+a^\theta)}{1+k^\theta a^\theta} = F(k)$. The derivative of this function is

$$F'(k) = \frac{(1+a^\theta) \cdot [1 - \theta k^{\theta-1} a^\theta - (\theta-1)k^\theta a^\theta]}{(k^\theta a^\theta + 1)^2} \quad (4)$$

Considering that both $1 + a^\theta$ and $(k^\theta a^\theta + 1)^2$ are greater than 0, we let $f(k) = 1 - \theta k^{\theta-1}a^\theta - (\theta-1)k^\theta a^\theta$. Now, let's examine the monotonicity of $f(k)$. The derivative of $f(k)$ is

$$f'(k) = \theta a^\theta k^{\theta-1}(1 - \theta - \frac{\theta-1}{k}) < 0 \quad (5)$$

Therefore, $f(k) \leq f(1) = 1 - (2\theta - 1)u^\theta < 0$ for every $a > \frac{1}{\sqrt{3}}$, and $F'(k)$ is monotonically decreasing. We set $F'(k) = 0$.

$$0 = a^\theta k^\theta(1 - \theta - \frac{\theta}{k}) + 1 \quad (6)$$

When $\theta = 2$, the equation is $a^2 k^2 + 2a^2 k - 1 = 0$, and the solution for k^* is $\inf\{-1 + \sqrt{1 + \frac{1}{a^2}}\}$ or $\sup\{-1 + \sqrt{1 + \frac{1}{a^2}}\}$. This value coincides with the result obtained in reference [20]. Subsequently, when $\theta > 2$, we can infer that $F(k)$ attains its maximum value at k^*, where k^* is determined by solving $0 = a^\theta k^\theta(1 - \theta - \frac{\theta}{k}) + 1$.

Assuming that $m \leq a$, the sequence intersects with at most two clusters in the grid. Consequently, for this sequence, the cost of the $GRID_a$ algorithm is at most $(1+a^\theta)$. Therefore, the competitive ratio of this sequence is at most $\frac{1+a^\theta}{1+m^\theta} \leq 1+a^\theta$.

Now let us prove that the analysis is tight. Take any real number a and a sufficiently small positive number ϵ. If the request sequence consists of one point at distances ϵ, the optimal solution uses only one cluster with a cost of $1+\epsilon^\theta$. Meanwhile, the algorithm employs one cluster with a cost of $(1+a^\theta)$. Therefore, the competitive ratio is $\frac{(1+a^\theta)}{1+\epsilon^\theta}$. Considering ϵ to be arbitrarily small, we obtain a competitive ratio not smaller than $1+a^\theta$.

Consider a sequence where all points are request points, and the endpoints of the sequence are $-\epsilon$ and $ka+\epsilon$. In this context, the $SOSM_a$ algorithm utilizes $k+1$ grid cells, corresponding to $k+1$ clusters, with a cost of $(k+1)(1+a^\theta)$. However, if we use only one cluster, the cost is $1+(ka+2\epsilon)^\theta$. Since ϵ is arbitrarily small, the ratio of the cost of the $SOSM_a$ algorithm to the cost of the optimal solution is given by $\frac{(k+1)(1+a^\theta)}{1+(ka+2\epsilon)^\theta} \leq \frac{(k+1)(1+a^\theta)}{1+(ka)^\theta} = F(k)$. Thus, we derive a lower bound for the competitive ratio of the $SOSM_a$ algorithm, which is not smaller than $F(k)$ for any integer k, thereby establishing the tightness of our analysis.

5 The Flexible Model of the Online Problem

In the context of online problems in flexible models, the competitiveness of the one-dimensional ECC algorithm with linear cost is denoted as $\frac{1+\sqrt{5}}{2}$. Moreover, for the one-dimensional $FGRID_a$ algorithm with a square cost, its competitiveness is established as 2 within a given range of parameter a. Building upon this foundation, we extend the algorithm to consider the one-dimensional FGRIDa algorithm with the θ-th power cost. The proof and methodology closely resemble in [21].

Algorithm $FGRID_a$ works as follows. Let p be a new point. If the algorithm identifies an existing cluster whose interval encompasses point p, then p is allocated to that cluster without altering the associated interval. On the other hand, if the algorithm does not find any existing cluster with an interval covering point p, it examines the grid to locate the cell containing p. If this cell does not contain a cluster, a new cluster is created, and p is assigned to this newly formed cluster. In this scenario, the cluster consists solely of the single point p. Alternatively, if the cell already contains a cluster, the interval of the cluster is expanded to include the point p.

Theorem 3. *The competitive ratio of algorithm $FGRID_a$ is $max\{F(k), 1+a^\theta\}$, where k is solved by $a^\theta k^\theta(1-\theta-\frac{\theta}{k})+1 = 0$ and $F(k) = \frac{(k+1)(1+a^\theta)}{1+k^\theta a^\theta}, \theta \geq 2, k \geq 1, a > 0$.*

Proof. We consider an arbitrary sequence of request points. We use OPT to denote the optimal solution. Given that the number of clusters for OPT is unknown, we consider an arbitrary cluster in OPT, denoted by m, representing the length of this cluster.

Suppose that for any integer $k \geq 1$, the inequality $k*a < m \leq (k+1)*a$ holds. This optimal cluster intersects with at most $k+2$ clusters within the grid. The cells that are not endpoints of optimal clusters may be completely covered by $FGRID_a$. If the endpoint cells of this optimal cluster do not intersect with those of other optimal clusters, then OPT and $FGRID_a$ cover the same portion of this cell. Next, we consider two cases in which the optimal cluster intersects with the grid.

Case 1. If the optimal cluster intersects with k+2 cells.

If the endpoint cell intersects with at least one other optimal cluster, it may be completely covered by $FGRID_a$. However, its online cost is divided between at least two optimal clusters. We only consider half of this cost, denoted as $\frac{1}{2}(1+a^\theta)$. Hence, we assign the entire online cost $2*\frac{1}{2}(1+a^\theta)$, to these endpoint cells. By assigning the cost to the optimal clusters, we cover the entire online cost. Therefore, for the $FGRID_a$ algorithm, we allocate at most $(1+a^\theta)k + (1+a^\theta) = (1+a^\theta)(k+1)$ online cost to this optimal cluster, while the cost of the optimal cluster is at least $1 + m^\theta$. Consequently, the competitive ratio of this sequence is at most $\frac{(1+a^\theta)(k+1)}{m^\theta+1} < \frac{(k+1)(1+a^\theta)}{1+k^\theta a^\theta} = F(k)$.

If $k=1$ then $F(k) = 2$

Case 2. If the optimal cluster intersects with k+1 cells.

Case 2.1

If the optimal cluster has two endpoint cells and a length less than a, and if these two endpoint cells do not intersect with other optimal clusters, then OPT and $FGRID_a$ cover the same portion of this cell. If the endpoint cell intersects with at least one other optimal cluster, then its online cost is divided between at least two optimal clusters, and we consider half of the cost. Therefore, for the GRIDa algorithm, the cost of this optimal cluster is at most $(k-1)(1+a^\theta) + 1 + a^\theta = k(1+a^\theta)$. The cost of the optimal cluster is at least $1 + m^\theta$. Consequently, the competitive ratio of this sequence is at most $\frac{k(1+a^\theta)}{m^\theta+1} < \frac{k(1+a^\theta)}{1+k^\theta a^\theta} = F_1(k)$.

Case 2.2

If the optimal cluster has only one endpoint cell and a length less than a, and if this endpoint cell does not intersect with other optimal clusters, then OPT and $FGRID_a$ cover the same portion of this cell. If the endpoint cell intersects with other optimal clusters, then its online cost is divided between at least two optimal clusters, and we consider half of the cost. Therefore, for the GRIDa algorithm, the cost of this optimal cluster is at most $k(1+a^\theta) + \frac{1}{2}(1+a)^\theta = (k+\frac{1}{2})(1+a^\theta)$. The cost of the optimal cluster is at least $1+m^\theta$. Consequently, the competitive ratio of this sequence is at most $\frac{(k+\frac{1}{2})(1+a^\theta)}{m^\theta+1} < \frac{(k+\frac{1}{2})(1+a^\theta)}{1+k^\theta a^\theta} = F_2(k)$.

Case 3. Now, assuming $m < a$, this optimal cluster intersects with at most two cells. There are two cases for these cells.

Case 3.1 If this optimal cluster intersects with only one cell.

If the cell of this optimal cluster does not intersect with the cells of other optimal clusters, then OPT and $FGRID_a$ cover the same portion of the cell. However, its cost is at most $1 + a^\theta$. If the cell of this optimal cluster intersects with cells of other optimal clusters, then this cell may be completely covered by FGRIDa, but its cost is divided between two optimal clusters. Therefore, we consider half of the cell cost, denoted as $\frac{1}{2}(1+a^\theta)$. The cost of the optimal cluster is at least $1 + m^\theta$.

Therefore, the competitive ratio for this cost is at most $\frac{1+a^\theta}{1+m^\theta} \leq 1 + a^\theta$.

Case 3.2 If this optimal cluster intersects with two cells.

If the two cells of this optimal cluster do not intersect with cells of other optimal clusters, then OPT and $FGRID_a$ cover the same portion of the cells. If this optimal cluster has at least one cell intersecting with cells of other optimal clusters, then this cell may be completely covered by $FGRID_a$, but its cost is divided between two optimal clusters. Therefore, we consider half of the cell cost, denoted as $\frac{1}{2}(1+a^\theta)$. Thus, we obtain the cost of this cluster as $2 \cdot \frac{1}{2}(1+a^\theta)$. Therefore, the competitive ratio for this cost is at most $\frac{1+a^\theta}{1+m^\theta} \leq 1 + a^\theta$.

6 Conclusion

This paper primarily investigates online clustering on the line with variable sized clustering. In previous clustering problems, the cost of opening a cluster was 1 plus the square of the diameter. In this study, we extend the cost of opening a single cluster to 1 plus the diameter raised to the power of θ, thereby generalizing the results of previous papers. We mainly analyze the competitive ratios of online algorithms for strict, semi-online, and flexible models. Furthermore, our generalized results align with those presented in [21] when $\theta = 2$.

References

1. Leiserson, C.E., et al.: Introduction to Algorithms, 3rd edn. MIT press, Cambridge (1994)
2. Lev-Tov, N., Peleg, D.: Polynomial time approximation schemes for base station coverage with minimum total radii. Comput. Netw. **47**(4), 489–501 (2005)
3. Dai, H., Deng, B., Li, W., et al.: A note on the minimum power partial cover problem on the plane. J. Comb. Optim. **44**(2), 970–978 (2022)
4. Alt, H., Arkin, E.M., Brönnimann, H., et al.: Minimum-cost coverage of point sets by disks. In: Proceedings of the Twenty-Second Annual Symposium on Computational Geometry, pp. 449–458 (2006)
5. Bilo, V., Caragiannis, I., Kaklamanis, C., et al.: Geometric clustering to minimize the sum of cluster sizes. In: Proceedings of the European Symposium on Algorithm, pp. 460–471 (2005)
6. Liu, X., Li, W., Xie, R.: A primal-dual approximation algorithm for the k-prize-collecting minimum power cover problem. Optim. Lett. **16**(8), 2373–2385 (2022)
7. Zhang, Q., Li, W., Su, Q., et al.: A primal-dual-based power control approach for capacitated edge servers. Sensors **22**(19), 7582 (2022)
8. Sharma, Y., Swamy, C., Williamson, D.P.: Approximation algorithms for prize collecting forest problems with submodular penalty functions. In: Proceedings of the Eighteenth Annual ACM-SIAM Symposium on Discrete Algorithms, pp. 1275–1284 (2007)
9. Xu, D., Wang, F., Du, D., et al.: Approximation algorithms for submodular vertex cover problems with linear/submodular penalties using primal-dual technique. Theor. Comput. Sci. **630**, 117–125 (2016)

10. Liu, X., Dai, H., Li, W., et al.: The k-prize-collecting minimum power cover problem with submodular penalties on a plane. SCIENTIA SINICA Informationis **52**(6), 947–959 (2022)
11. Liu, X., Li, W., Dai, H.: Approximation algorithms for the minimum power cover problem with submodular/linear penalties. Theor. Comput. Sci. **923**, 256–270 (2022)
12. Charikar, M., Panigrahy, R.: Clustering to minimize the sum of cluster diameters. In: Proceedings of the Thirty-Third Annual ACM Symposium on Theory of Computing, pp. 1–10 (2001)
13. Chan, T.M., Zarrabi-Zadeh, H.: A randomized algorithm for online unit clustering. Theory Comput. Syst. **45**, 486–496 (2009)
14. Zarrabi-Zadeh, H., Chan, T.M.: An improved algorithm for online unit clustering. Algorithmica **54**, 490–500 (2009)
15. Epstein, L., Stee, R.V.: On the online unit clustering problem. ACM Trans. Algor. (TALG) **7**(1), 1–18 (2010)
16. Ehmsen, M.R., Larsen, K.S.: Better bounds on online unit clustering. Theor. Comput. Sci. **500**, 1–24 (2013)
17. Dai, Y., Duan, Y., Liu, L., et al.: Randomized approximation algorithms for a class of one-dimensional online unit clustering problem. Oper. Res. Trans. **26**(3), 143–150 (2022)
18. Csirik, J., Epstein, L., Imreh, C., et al.: Online clustering with variable sized clusters. Algorithmica **65**(2), 251–274 (2013)
19. Divéki, G., Imreh, C.: Online algorithms for clustering problems [Ph.D. thesis] (2014)
20. Araki, T., Kobayashi, K.M.: Online unit clustering with capacity constraints. IEICE Trans. Fundam. Electron. Commun. Comput. Sci. **100**(1), 301–303 (2017)
21. Divéki, G.: Online clustering on the line with square cost variable sized clusters. Acta Cybern. **21**(1), 75–88 (2013)
22. Henzinger, M., Leniowski, D., Mathieu, C.: Dynamic clustering to minimize the sum of radii. Algorithmica **82**, 3183–3194 (2020)

1-Line Minimum λ-Steiner Tree Problem

Yinhua Chen[1], Jianglin Li[1], Wencheng Wang[1], and Tongquan Zhang[2](✉)

[1] School of Mathematics and Computer Science, Yunnan Minzu University, Yuehua Street No.2929, Kunming 650504, Yunnan, China
wencheng@ymu.edu.cn

[2] School of Applied Technology, Yunnan Minzu University, Yuehua Street No.2929, Kunming 650504, Yunnan, China
tqzh1979@yeah.net

Abstract. In this paper, we consider the problem of 1-line minimum λ-Steiner tree problem , denoted as the 1L-M$_\lambda$StT problem. Given a set $X = \{r_1, r_2, \ldots, r_n\}$ of n points in the λ-plane and a straight line l in $\mathbb{R}^2$, we need to construct a Steiner tree T_l connecting the n points in X and the straight line l. The objective is to minimize the total cost of such a Steiner tree T_l, $i.e.$,min$\{\sum_{e \in T_l} w(e) \mid T_l$ is the mentioned Steiner tree $\}$, and if an edge $e = uv \in T_l$ has both endpoints u and v lying on the line l, the weight is defined as $w(e) = 0$; Otherwise, it is defined as the distance of the two endpoints u and v in the λ-plane. In particular, if all Steiner points in T_l are constrained to lie on the line l, the problem is denoted as the 1-line minimum λ-spanning tree (1L-M$_\lambda$ST) problem. We present two main results. (1) By using the strategies of the sweep-line algorithm, we can design an exact algorithm in time $O(\lambda n \log n)$ to solve the 1L-M$_\lambda$ST problem; (2) Using some properties of λ-plane, we showed that our algorithm is a ρ_λ-approximation algorithm for the 1L-M$_\lambda$StT problem, where ρ_λ is inverse of the Steiner ratio in the λ-plane.

Keywords: Sweep-line algorithm · Approximation algorithm · 1-line λ-spanning tree · 1-line λ-Steiner tree

1 Introduction

Let P be a centrally symmetric regular 2λ ($\lambda \geq 2, \lambda \in \mathbb{N}^*$) polygon with a diameter of 2 in $\mathbb{R}^2$ and $\|p - q\|_\lambda$ be the distance between two points $p, q \in \mathbb{R}^2$ in the normed plane whose unit disk is P with one of its diagonals parallel to the x-axis (as shown in Fig. 1). In general, a centrally symmetric regular 2λ ($\lambda \geq 2, \lambda \in \mathbb{N}^*$) polygon normed plane is called a λ-plane [5,9].When $\lambda = \infty$, the λ-plane becomes the Euclidean plane; when $\lambda = 2$, the λ-plane becomes the Manhattan plane.

This paper is supported by the Youth Project of the Department of Science and Technology of Yunnan Province [No. 202401AU070027], and Wencheng Wang is also supported by the Basic Research Project of the Department of Education of Yunnan Province [No. 2024J0573].

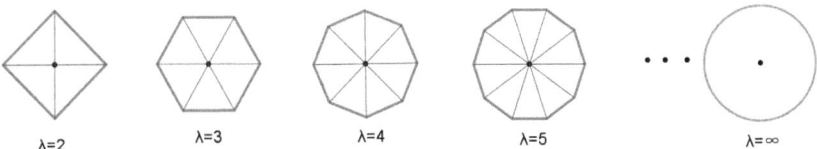

Fig. 1. The unit disk of different λ-planes.

For a given integer λ, a straight line or line segment parallel to one of the diagonals of the unit disk P is defined as being in a legal orientation in the λ-plane. The j-th orientation is denoted by the angle $j\omega(j = 1, 2, \ldots, \lambda)$, which is formed by the corresponding straight line with the x-axis, where $\omega = \pi/\lambda$ is called as a unit angle. For any two points p, q in the λ-plane, a legal path between p and q is defined as a collection of finite sequence segments with legal directions that alternate, connecting the two points p and q, where the coordinates of p and q are given by (x_p, y_p) and (x_q, y_q) respectively. The shortest legal path between p and q is also referred to as a line segment (or edge) between p and q, denoted by $\widehat{pq}$ (or pq). Note that the set of line segment between p and q may consist of an infinite number of elements, each having the same length. Here, $\widehat{pq}$ is used to represent a specific line segment between p and q, not the entire set. Furthermore, the length of the line segment $\widehat{pq}$ is denoted by $|\widehat{pq}|_\lambda$, that is, $|\widehat{pq}|_\lambda = \|p - q\|_\lambda$. Specifically, in the Euclidean plane, the line segment between p and q is denoted by $\overline{pq}$, and its length is denoted by $|\overline{pq}|$.

The minimum spanning trees and related problems [24] are very important in the field of combinatorial optimization. Some efficient exact algorithms, such as the Kruskal algorithm [16] and Prim algorithm [19], have been designed to solve the minimum spanning tree problem. The Euclidean minimum spanning tree problem is a special version of the minimum spanning tree problem. Obviously, the algorithms mentioned above can be used to solve the Euclidean minimum spanning tree problem with a running time of $O(n^2)$, where n is the number of terminal points in the Euclidean plane $\mathbb{R}^2$. However, Shamos and Hoey [21] proposed a geometric structure called the Voronoi diagram, which can solve this problem with a running time of $O(n \log n)$.

The minimum Steiner tree problem is a generalization of the minimum spanning tree problem which has wide applications in practice, such as in the design of very large scale integrated circuits, optical networks, and wireless communication systems. This problem is *NP*-hard [8] and various approximation algorithms have been proposed in the literature [1,6,14,23]. The Euclidean minimum Steiner tree problem is a new form of the minimum Steiner tree in the Euclidean plane, which is defined as follows. Given a set $X = \{r_1, r_2, \ldots, r_n\}$ of n terminal points in the Euclidean plane, it is asked to construct a Steiner tree T interconnecting these n terminal points in the Euclidean plane, the objective is to minimize the sum of the length of the edges in tree T. This problem is also *NP*-hard [11], and some approximation algorithms can be found in [2,14,23].

The minimum λ-Steiner tree problem [8] is a new form of the Steiner tree problem confined in the λ-plane, and it is modeled as follows. Given a set of n terminal points $X = \{r_1, r_2, \ldots, r_n\}$ in the λ-plane, it is asked to construct a Steiner tree T interconnecting all the terminals in X, the objective is to minimize the total length of all edges in T, where each edge in T is a legal line segment. By constructing a minimum spanning tree on the terminal point set X is an efficient heuristic for the minimum λ-Steiner tree problem. We introduce the Steiner ratio as $\frac{1}{\rho_\lambda} = \inf_X \{\frac{w_S^\lambda(X)}{w_M^\lambda(X)}\}$, where $w_S^\lambda(X)$ and $w_M^\lambda(X)$ is the length of the minimum Steiner tree and the minimum spanning tree on the terminal point set X in the λ-plane, respectively. Then, we have $w_M^\lambda(X) \leq \rho_\lambda w_S^\lambda(X)$. In the different λ-planes, the inverse ρ_λ of the Steiner ratio is shown in the Table 1.

Table 1. The inverse of the Steiner ratio in the different λ-planes.

λ	steiner ratio($\frac{1}{\rho_\lambda}$)	ρ_λ	literature
$\lambda = \infty$ (Euclidean)	$\frac{\sqrt{3}}{2}$ (conjecture)	$\frac{2}{\sqrt{3}}$	[15]
$\lambda = 2$ (Rectilinear)	$\frac{2}{3}$	$\frac{3}{2}$	[13]
$\lambda = 3$ (Hexagonal)	$\frac{3}{4}$	$\frac{4}{3}$	[17]
$\lambda = 4$ (Octilinear)	$\frac{2+\sqrt{2}}{4}$	$\frac{4}{2+\sqrt{2}}$	[22]
$\lambda > 4$	$[\frac{2}{3}, \frac{\sqrt{13}-1}{3}]$	$[\frac{3}{\sqrt{13}-1}, \frac{3}{2}]$	[4, 10, 20]

Chen and Zhang [7] in 2000 considered a variation of the Euclidean minimum Steiner tree problem. They introduced a straight line in $\mathbb{R}^2$, referring to this problem as the constrained minimum spanning tree problem, defined as follows. Given a set $X = \{r_1, r_2, \ldots, r_n\}$ of n terminals located on the same side of a straight line l in $\mathbb{R}^2$, it is asked to determine a new point s on l and a tree T to span the points in the set $X \cup \{s\}$. The objective is to minimize the weight $w(T) = \sum_{e \in T} w(e)$ of the tree T. By introducing a partition of the line l using the divide-and-conquer technique and presenting an efficient method for updating a minimum spanning tree, Chen and Zhang [7] designed an exact algorithm that operates in $O(n^2)$ time to solve this problem.

Holby [12] in 2017 considered the 1-line Euclidean minimum Steiner tree problem as a variation of the constrained minimum spanning tree problem. Given a set $X = \{r_1, r_2, \ldots, r_n\}$ of n terminals and a straight line l in $\mathbb{R}^2$, it is asked to find a Steiner tree T interconnecting these n terminals, ensuring that at least one Steiner point lies on the line l. The objective is to minimize the weight $w(T) = \sum_{e \in T} w(e)$ of the Steiner tree T, where $w(e) = 0$ if both endpoints of an edge $e \in T$ are situated on l, and otherwise $w(e)$ is the Euclidean distance between the two endpoints of $e \in T$. In 2020, Li et al. [18] reconsidered the 1-line Euclidean minimum Steiner tree problem and presented a 1.214-approximation algorithm.

Motivated by previous works mentioned-above, we address the following 1-line minimum λ-Stenier tree problem (for short, 1L-M$_\lambda$StT), which is a generalization of the 1-line Euclidean minimum Steiner tree problem. Given a set $X = \{r_1, r_2, \ldots, r_n\}$ of n terminal points in the λ-plane and a straight line l in $\mathbb{R}^2$, it is asked to construct a Steiner tree T_l connecting the terminal points in X and the straight line l. The objective is to minimize the total cost of such a Steiner tree T_l, i.e., $\min\{\sum_{e \in T_l} w(e) \mid T_l$ is the mentioned Steiner tree $\}$, where, for each edge $e = uv$ (or $\widehat{uv}) \in T_l$, if u and v lie on the line l, then $w(e) = 0$; otherwise, $w(e) = |\widehat{uv}|_\lambda$. Specifically, if all Steiner points in T_l are constrained to lie on l, the problem is referred to as the 1-line minimum λ-spanning tree(for short, 1L-M$_\lambda$ST) problem.

This paper is structured as follows. In Sect. 2, we introduce some fundamental terms and lemmas crucial for ensuring the accuracy of the approximation algorithm. In Sect. 3, by using the strategies of the sweep-line algorithm [26], we present an exact algorithm in time $O(\lambda n \log n)$ for the 1L-M$_\lambda$ST problem. Moreover, using some properties of λ-plane, we demonstrate that our algorithm is a ρ_λ-approximation algorithm for the 1L-M$_\lambda$StT problem, where ρ_λ is inverse of the Steiner ratio in the λ-plane, n is the number of terminal points. In Sect. 4, we give our conclusions and further research.

2 Terminologies and Fundamental Lemmas

In this section, we present some key terminologies and foundational lemmas essential for ensuring the validity of our algorithm.

Definition 1 [25]. *Given a weighted connected graph $G = (V, E, w)$, where $w : E \to R^+$, a subgraph G' is called a spanning graph of the vertex set V if the subgraph G' contains a minimum spanning tree of graph G.*

Definition 2. *Given a straight line l in $\mathbb{R}^2$ and a point p located on one side of the line l in the λ-plane, we define the foot of the perpendicular from p to the line l, denoted as l_p, as any point $l_p \in \arg\min\{|\widehat{pv}|_\lambda | v \in l\}$.*

We may note that any disk with an arbitrary radius in the λ-plane is a convex set, and the line l is also a convex set. Therefore, for any point p not on l, there exists at least one foot of the perpendicular from p to the line l, i.e., $|\arg\min\{|\widehat{pv}|_\lambda | v \in l\}| \geq 1$. Specifically, by fixing the position of the line l first, and then gradually expanding the radius of the disk with p as the center, we can obtain this conclusion. Since both geometric objects are convex sets, there exists at least one point on the line l such that the disk expanded with center p intersects the line for the first time and this point is a position of some foot of the perpendicular from p to the line l.

Lemma 1. *Given a straight line l in $\mathbb{R}^2$ and a point p located on one side of the line l in the λ-plane, there must exist at least one point $l_p \in \arg\min\{|\widehat{pv}|_\lambda | v \in l\}$ such that $\widehat{pl_p} = \overline{pl_p}$, as shown in Fig. 2.*

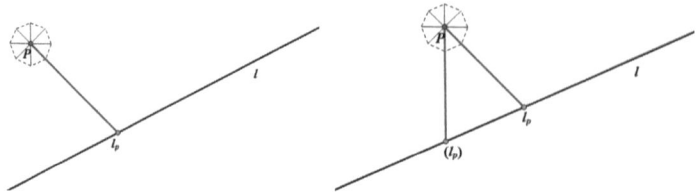

Fig. 2. A foot of the perpendicular from p to the line l in the λ-plane, where $\lambda = 4$

Proof. Let l be a straight line in $\mathbb{R}^2$, and let p be a point located on one side of the line l in the λ-plane. Now we demonstrate that there must exist a point $l_p \in \arg\min\{|\widehat{pv}|_\lambda | v \in l\}$ such that the line segment $\overline{pl_p}$ in a legal direction, as shown in Fig. 2.

In fact, if $|\arg\min\{|\widehat{pv}|_\lambda | v \in l\}| = 1$, it implies that the point $l_p \in \arg\min\{|\widehat{pv}|_\lambda | v \in l\}$ is the unique foot of the perpendicular from p to the line l. This point l_p coincides with the sole intersection point between the line l and the boundary of a disk centered at p. As the disk in the λ-plane forms a regular polygon, $\widehat{pl_p}$ necessarily coincides with one of the diagonals of the disk. Therefore, $\widehat{pl_p} = \overline{pl_p}$.

If $|\arg\min\{|\widehat{pv}|_\lambda | v \in l\}| > 1$, it implies that there exists an edge of a disk centered at p that is parallel to the line l. Following similar arguments above, there exists a point $l_p \in \arg\min\{|\widehat{pv}|_\lambda | v \in l\}$ such that the line segment $\overline{pl_p}$ in a legal direction.

This completes a proof of the lemma.

Lemma 2. *Let $X = \{r_1, r_2, \ldots, r_n\}$ be a set of n terminal points in the λ-plane. Consider a straight line l defined by the equation $\alpha_0 x + \beta_0 y + \gamma_0 = 0$ in $\mathbb{R}^2$. Then, for any two terminal points $r_i, r_j \in X$, there exist two points $l_{r_i} \in \arg\min\{|\widehat{r_i v}|_\lambda | v \in l\}$ and $l_{r_j} \in \arg\min\{|\widehat{r_j u}|_\lambda | u \in l\}$ such that the line segments $\overline{r_i l_{r_i}}$ and $\overline{r_j l_{r_j}}$ are parallel to each other, as shown in Fig. 3.*

Proof. Let $X = \{r_1, r_2, \ldots, r_n\}$ be a set of n terminal points in the λ-plane and l be a straight line with equation $\alpha_0 x + \beta_0 y + \gamma_0 = 0$ in $\mathbb{R}^2$. For each terminal point $r \in X$, consider the t-th angle, denoted by $\theta_t(r)$, formed by the t-th diagonal of a disk centered at r, where $t = 1, 2, \cdots, \lambda$. Clearly, for any two terminal point $r_i, r_j \in X$, we have $\theta_t(r_i) = \theta_t(r_j), t = 1, 2, \cdots, \lambda$.

Suppose, to a contrary, that we may assume $l_{r_i} \in \arg\min\{|\widehat{r_i v}|_\lambda | v \in l\}$, $\overline{r_i l_{r_i}} = \widehat{r_i l_{r_i}}$ and $\angle(\overline{r_i l_{r_i}}, l) = \theta_k(r_i), k \in \{1, 2, \cdots, \lambda\}$. Let p is the point of intersection of l and the k-th diagonal of a disk centered at r_j. We now show that $p \in \arg\min\{|\widehat{r_j u}|_\lambda | u \in l\}$.

In fact, suppose that p' is the point of intersection of l and the k'-th diagonal of a disk centered at r_j and $|\overline{r_j p'}| < |\overline{r_j p}|$. It follows that, in the $\triangle r_j pp'$, we have $\angle r_j pp' < \angle r_j p'p$. Let p'' be the point of intersection of l and the k'-th diagonal of a disk centered at r_i. Due to $\theta_{k'}(r_i) = \theta_{k'}(r_j)$, we have $|\overline{r_i p''}| < |\overline{r_i l_{r_i}}|$, which contradicts the fact $l_{r_i} \in \arg\min\{|\widehat{pv}|_\lambda | v \in l\}$.

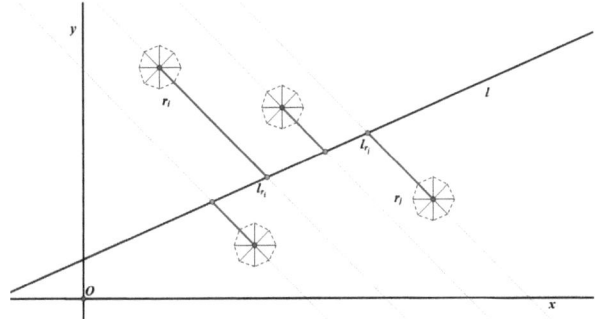

Fig. 3. An instance of Lemma 2, where $\lambda = 4$

Hence, we reach the conclusion of this lemma.

The following corollary can be obtained from the above lemma.

Corollary 1. *Let r_0 be a specified point not lying on a straight line l in $\mathbb{R}^2$, and denote $\theta(l) = \angle(\overline{r_0 l_{r_0}}, l)$ as the angle between the line segment $\overline{r_0 l_{r_0}}$ and l. Suppose $X = \{r_1, r_2, \ldots, r_n\}$ is a set containing n terminal points in the λ-plane. Then, for each terminal point $r_i \in X$, there exists a point $l_{r_i} \in \arg\min\{|\widehat{r_i v}|_\lambda | v \in l\}$ such that $\angle(\overline{r_i l_{r_i}}, l) = \theta(l)$.*

Lemma 3 [3]. *Given a weighted connected graph $G = (V, E; w)$, where $w : E \to R^+$ is the weight function, $T = (V, E_T)$ is the minimum spanning tree of G if and only if, for each edge $e \in E_T$, this edge e is the minimum weight edge of $\delta(V(C))$, where C is a connected component of $T - e$, $V(C)$ is a set of all vertices in C, and $\delta(V(C)) = \{xy \in E \mid x \in V(C), y \notin V(C)\}$.*

Lemma 4 [3,16]. *Given weighted connected graph $G = (V, E; w)$, where $w : E \to R^+$ is the weight function, a minimum spanning tree of graph G can be obtained by Kruskal's algorithm in time $O(m \log n)$, where n is the number of vertices and m is the number of edges of graph G.*

Using similar arguments as presented in [18], we have the following results, the proofs of which are omitted here.

Lemma 5. *Let $X = \{r_1, r_2, \ldots, r_n\}$ be a set of n points as an instance of the minimum λ-spanning tree problem and $T = (X, E_T)$ be an minimum λ-spanning tree to span these n points in X. For any bipartition $\{X_1, X_2\}$ of X, it follows that at least one shortest line segment $\widehat{pq}$ in the set $\delta(X_1)$ belongs to E_T, where $\delta(X_1) = \{\widehat{uv} \mid u \in X_1 \text{ and } v \in X_2\}$.*

Zhou et al. [26] in 2005 designed a polynomial-time exact algorithm, denoted by sweep-line algorithm, to solve the minimum λ-spanning tree problem. For convenience, we restate the sweep-line algorithm as the following lemma.

Lemma 6 [26]. *A spanning graph with $O(n)$ edges for the set $X = \{r_1, r_2, \ldots, r_n\}$ of n terminal points in the λ-plane can be constructed by the sweep-line algorithm in time $O(\lambda n \log n)$.*

For convenience, we denote an instance of either the 1L-M$_\lambda$ST problem or the 1L-M$_\lambda$StT problem by $I = (X, l, \lambda)$, as determined by the context. Here, $X = \{r_1, r_2, \ldots, r_n\}$ represents a set of n terminal points in the λ-plane, l denotes a straight line with equation $\alpha_0 x + \beta_0 y + \gamma_0 = 0$ in $\mathbb{R}^2$, and $\lambda \geq 2$. Given an instance $I = (X, l, \lambda)$ of either the 1L-M$_\lambda$ST problem or the 1L-M$_\lambda$StT problem, we denote T as a 1-line λ-spanning tree or a 1-line λ-Steiner tree. Without loss of generality, we assume that each terminal point $r \in X$ is located on the same side of the line l. For any subset $X' \subseteq X$, let $\delta(X') = E_1(X') \cup E_2(X')$, where $E_1(X') = \{\widehat{r_i r_j} | r_i \in X', r_j \in X \setminus X'\}$, and $E_2(X') = \{\widehat{r_i l_{r_i}} | r_i \in X'\}$.

Lemma 7. *Let $I = (X, l, \lambda)$ be an instance of the 1L-M$_\lambda$ST problem. Then T^* is a 1-line minimum λ-spanning tree if and only if, for every edge $e = uv \in E_{T^*}$ with $w(uv) \neq 0$, i.e., $u, v \notin l$, there exists a subset $X_1 (\subseteq X)$ consisting of all points in a connected component of $T^* \setminus \{uv\}$ such that the line segment $\widehat{uv}$ is a shortest line segment of $\delta(X_1)$.*

Proof. (Necessity) Let T^* be a 1-line minimum λ-spanning tree, then for any edge $uv \in E_{T^*}$ that does not lie on the line l, we can choose a subset X_1 containing all vertices of a connected component of $T^* \setminus \{uv\}$ that does not include any point of the line l, it implies that X_1 exists. Conversely, suppose that for the edge $uv \in E_{T^*}$, there exists a line segment $\widehat{pq} \in \delta(X_1)$ such that $0 < |\widehat{pq}|_\lambda < |\widehat{uv}|_\lambda$, where X_1 is the set of point mentioned above, and $\widehat{pq}$ connects two connected components of $T^* \setminus \{uv\}$. This implies that the line segment $\widehat{pq}$ is not an edge of the 1-line λ-spanning tree T^* and does not lie on the line l. Then $T^* + pq$ contains a cycle through two line segments $\widehat{pq}$ and $\widehat{uv}$, and we can obtain another 1-line λ-spanning tree $T' = (T^* - uv) + pq$, such that $w(T') = w(T^*) + w(pq) - w(uv) = w(T^*) + |\widehat{pq}|_\lambda - |\widehat{uv}|_\lambda < w(T^*)$, which contradicts our assumption that T^* is the minimum λ-spanning tree .

(Sufficiency) Let T denote a 1-line λ-spanning tree satisfying the condition that for every edge $uv \in E_T$, $w(uv) \neq 0$, and uv is the shortest line segment in $\delta(X_1)$, where X_1 is the set of points belonging to a connected component of $T - uv$ that does not contain any points of the line l. Let T^* denote a 1-line minimum λ-spanning tree that maximizes the number of $|E_T \cap E_{T^*}|$. We shall now demonstrate that $T^* = T$.

If $E_T = E_{T^*}$, the proof is complete. Let's consider the case where $E_T \neq E_{T^*}$. For each edge $e \in E_T \setminus E_{T^*}$ with $w(e) \neq 0$. As T^* is a tree, there exists only one cycle C in $T^* + e$, and at least one edge in this cycle C also belongs to $\delta(X_1)$, denoted as e'. Since $e \in E_T$, we have $w(e) \leq w(e')$.

Due to T^* is an optimal solution and $e' \in E_{T^*}$, it follows that $w(e') \leq w(e)$, implying $w(e) = w(e')$. Therefore, we can obtain another 1-line minimum λ-spanning tree, denoted as $T - e + e'$, which contains more one edge of E_T than E_{T^*}. This contradicts the assumption of the maximality of $|E_T \cap E_{T^*}|$.

This completes the proof of the lemma.

3 The 1-Line Minimum λ-Steiner Tree Problem

In this section, we consider the 1-line minimum λ-Steiner tree (1L-M$_\lambda$StT) problem. In order to solve this problem, we should first consider solving the problem of the 1-line minimum λ-spanning tree(1L-M$_\lambda$ST), which is a special case of the 1L-M$_\lambda$StT problem, where all Steiner points in the 1-line minimum λ-spanning tree are located on the straight line l.

Using the sweep-line algorithm [26] to construct the spanning graph on a subset of X and Lemma 7, we design our algorithm, denoted by A_{sl}, to solve the 1-line minimum λ-spanning tree problem in the following strategies.

(1) Using the sweep-line algorithm [26] to construct the spanning graphs $G_s^+ = (X^+, E_s^+)$ and $G_s^- = (X^-, E_s^-)$, set $E_s = E_s^+ \cup E_s^-$, where X^+ (X^-) is the set of the points that are located at the one (another) side of l.
(2) Construct a weighted graph $G = (X \cup \{r_0\}, E_s \cup E_X, w)$, where $E_X = \{r_i r_0 | r_i \in X\}$, for each $e = r_i r_j \in E_s$, $w(e) = |\widehat{r_i r_j}|_\lambda$, and for each $e = r_i r_0 \in E_X$, $w(e) = |\overline{r_i l_{r_i}}|$.
(3) Using the kruskal algorithm [16] to find a minimum spanning tree T_G of graph G, and then construct a 1-line λ-spanning tree T.

Algorithm : A_{sl}

Input: A straight line l and a set $X = \{r_1, r_2, \ldots r_n\}$ of n terminal points in the λ-plane.
Output: A 1-line minimum λ-spanning tree T.
 Begin
 Step 1 Set $T = (V, E)$ where $V = X$ and $E = \emptyset$.
 Step 2 Construct the spanning graphs $G_s^+ = (X^+, E_s^+)$ and $G_s^- = (X^-, E_s^-)$ by the sweep-line algorithm [26], set $G_s = (X, E_s)$, where $E_s = E_s^+ \cup E_s^-$.
 Step 3 Construct a weighted graph $G = (X \cup \{r_0\}, E_s \cup E_X, w)$ as mentioned-above.
 Step 4 Construct a minimum spanning tree T_G of graph G by the kruskal algorithm [16].
 Step 5 For each edge $e \in E_{T_G}$ do
  (1) If $(e = r_i r_j \in E_s)$ then
    Set $E = E \cup \{\widehat{r_i r_j}\}$;
  (2) If $(e = r_i r_0 \in E_X)$ then
    Set $E = E \cup \{\overline{r_i l_{r_i}}\}$ and $V = V \cup \{l_{r_i}\}$;
 Step 6 Output $T = (V, E)$.
 End

Theorem 1. *The algorithm A_{sl} is an exact algorithm to solve the 1L-M$_\lambda$ST problem, and it runs in time $O(\lambda n \log n)$, where n is the number of terminal points in X.*

Proof. Given a set $X = \{r_1, r_2, \ldots, r_n\}$ of n terminal points in the λ-plane and a straight line l with equation $\alpha_0 x + \beta_0 y + \gamma_0 = 0$ in $\mathbb{R}^2$ as an instance I of the 1L-M$_\lambda$ST problem. We denote by T the 1-line λ-spanning tree produced by the algorithm A_{sl} for the instance I. By Lemma 7, T is an optimal solution if and only if, for each edge $uv \in E_T$ with $w(uv) \neq 0$, there exists a subset $X_1 (\subseteq X)$ that consists of all terminal points of a connected component of $T - uv$, such that the line segment $\widehat{uv}$ is the shortest segment in $\delta(X_1)$, where X_1 is the set of terminal points of a connected component of $T - uv$.

Suppose, to the contrary, that uv is not the shortest line segment in $\delta(X_1)$, where $uv \in E_T$ with $w(uv) \neq 0$. By the definition of $\delta(X_1)$ and Lemma 6, we can choose a shortest line segment $e = pq \in E_1(X_1) \cap G_s$ or $E_2(X_1)$ such that $|\widehat{pq}|_\lambda < |\widehat{uv}|_\lambda$. Since $T + pq$ contains a circle through two line segments $\widehat{pq}$ and $\widehat{uv}$, and we can obtain another 1-line λ-spanning tree $T' = (T - uv) + pq$, such that $w(T') = w(T) + w(pq) - w(uv) = w(T) + |\widehat{pq}|_\lambda - |\widehat{uv}|_\lambda < w(T)$. Then we can construct another spanning tree T'_G of graph G with $w(T'_G) = w(T') < w(T) = w(T_G)$, which contradicts our assumption that T_G is a minimum spanning tree of G.

Therefore, the tree T produced by the algorithm A_{sl} for the instance I is a 1-line minimum λ-spanning tree.

The time complexity of the algorithm A_{sl} is determined as follows: (1) By Lemma 6, the time complexity of Step 2 to construct the spanning graph on the λ-plane using the sweep-line algorithm is $O(\lambda n \log n)$, and (2) The Kruskal algorithm can determine the minimum spanning tree of the graph G in time $O(n \log n)$. (3) Step 5 can be done in time $O(n)$. Thus, the time complexity of the entire A_{sl} algorithm is $O(\lambda n \log n)$.

This completes the proof of the theorem.

Theorem 2. *The algorithm A_{sl} is a ρ_λ approximation algorithm for solving the 1L-M$_\lambda$StT problem, and it runs in time $O(\lambda n \log n)$, where n is the number of terminal points in X, ρ_λ is inverse of the Steiner ratio in the λ-plane.*

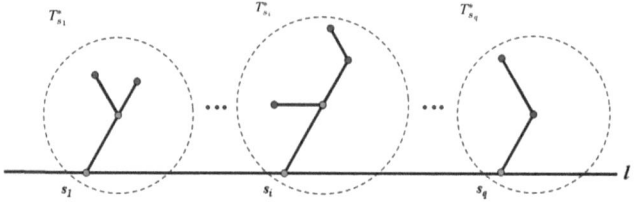

Fig. 4. The process of proof for Theorem 2.

Proof. Given a set $X = \{r_1, r_2, \ldots, r_n\}$ of n terminal points in the λ-plane and a straight line l with equation $\alpha_0 x + \beta_0 y + \gamma_0 = 0$ in $\mathbb{R}^2$ as an instance I of the 1L-M$_\lambda$StT problem. We may assume that T_S^* is an optimal 1-line minimum

λ-Steiner tree with exactly q Steiner points consecutively lying on the straight line l, saying $s_1, s_2, \ldots, s_q$ (as shown in Fig. 4) and we denote by T the 1-line minimum λ-spanning tree produced by the algorithm A_{sl} for the instance I.

For each $i \in \{1, 2, \ldots, q\}$, we denote by $T^*_{s_i}$ to represent a maximal Steiner subtree of T^*_S which contains the only point s_i on the line l, i.e., no other point on the line. We can use T'_{s_i} to denote a minimum λ-spanning tree on the set $X_{s_i} \cup \{s_i\}$, where $X_{s_i} = V(T^*_{s_i}) \cap X$. Then, for each $i \in \{1, 2, \ldots, q\}$, we have $w(T'_{s_i}) \leq \rho_\lambda w(T^*_{s_i})$, where ρ_λ is inverse of the Steiner ratio in the λ-plane. Clearly, $T' = \bigcup_{i=1}^{q} T'_{s_i} \cup l$ is a 1-line λ-spanning tree for the instance I. It implies that $w(T) \leq w(T')$. Then, we have

$$w(T) \leq w(T') = \sum_{i=1}^{q} w(T'_{s_i})$$

$$\leq \rho_\lambda \cdot \sum_{i=1}^{q} w(T^*_{s_i}) = \rho_\lambda \cdot w(T^*_S)$$

This completes the proof of this theorem.

4 Conclusions and Further Research

In this paper, we consider the 1-line minimum λ-Steiner tree problem (1L-M$_\lambda$StT). By using the strategies of the sweep-line algorithm, we can design a polynomial time exact algorithm in time $O(\lambda n \log n)$ to solve the 1-line minimum λ-spanning tree (1L-M$_\lambda$ST) problem. Additionally, we showed that our algorithm is a ρ_λ-approximation algorithm for the 1L-M$_\lambda$StT problem, where ρ_λ is inverse of the Steiner ratio in the λ-plane.

A challenging task for further research is to design some approximation algorithms with improved performance ratios and reduced running times for solving the 1L-M$_\lambda$StT problem.

References

1. Aazami, A., Cheriyan, J., Jampani, K.R.: Approximation algorithms and hardness results for packing element-disjoint Steiner trees in planar graphs. Algorithmica **63**(1), 425–456 (2012)
2. Arora, S.: Polynomial time approximation schemes for Euclidean traveling salesman and other geometric problems. J. ACM **45**(5), 753–782 (1998)
3. Bernhard, K., Vygen, J.: Combinatorial optimization: theory and algorithms (2008)
4. Blum, J., Ding, M., Thaeler, A., Cheng, X.: Connected dominating set in sensor networks and manets. In: Handbook of Combinatorial Optimization: Supplement Volume B, pp. 329–369 (2005)
5. Brazil, M., Zachariasen, M.: Optimal interconnection trees in the plane. Algor. Comb. **29** (2015)
6. Byrka, J., Grandoni, F., Rothvoß, T., Sanita, L.: An improved LP-based approximation for Steiner tree. In: Proceedings of the Forty-Second ACM Symposium on Theory of Computing, pp. 583–592 (2010)

7. Chen, G., Zhang, G.: A constrained minimum spanning tree problem. Comput. Oper. Res. **27**(9), 867–875 (2000)
8. Cheng, X., Du, D.Z.: Steiner Trees in Industry. Springer, Heidelberg (2013)
9. Das, A., Fleszar, K., Kobourov, S., Spoerhase, J., Veeramoni, S., Wolff, A.: Approximating the generalized minimum Manhattan network problem. Algorithmica **80**, 1170–1190 (2018)
10. Du, D.Z., Gao, B., Graham, R.L., Liu, Z.C., Wan, P.J.: Minimum Steiner trees in normed planes. Disc. Comput. Geom. **9**, 351–370 (1993)
11. Garey, M.R., Graham, R.L., Johnson, D.S.: The complexity of computing Steiner minimal trees. SIAM J. Appl. Math. **32**(4), 835–859 (1977)
12. Holby, J.: Variations on the Euclidean Steiner tree problem and algorithms. Rose-Hulman Undergrad. Math. J. **18**(1), 7 (2017)
13. Hwang, F.K.: On Steiner minimal trees with rectilinear distance. SIAM J. Appl. Math. **30**(1), 104–114 (1976)
14. Hwang, F.K., Richards, D.S.: Steiner tree problems. Networks **22**(1), 55–89 (1992)
15. Ivanov, A.O., Tuzhilin, A.A.: The Steiner ratio Gilbert-Pollak conjecture is still open: clarification statement. Algorithmica **62**, 630–632 (2012)
16. Kruskal, J.B.: On the shortest spanning subtree of a graph and the traveling salesman problem. Proc. Am. Math. Soc. **7**(1), 48–50 (1956)
17. Lee, D., Shen, C.: The Steiner minimal tree problem in the λ-geometry plane. Lect. Notes Comput. Sci. **1178**, 247–255 (1996)
18. Li, J., Liu, S., Lichen, J., Wang, W., Zheng, Y.: Approximation algorithms for solving the 1-line Euclidean minimum Steiner tree problem. J. Comb. Optim. **39**(2), 492–508 (2020)
19. Prim, R.C.: Shortest connection networks and some generalizations. Bell Syst. Tech. J. **36**(6), 1389–1401 (1957)
20. Sarrafzadeh, M., Wong, C.K.: Hierarchical Steiner tree construction in uniform orientations. IEEE Trans. Comput. Aided Des. Integr. Circuits Syst. **11**(9), 1095–1103 (1992)
21. Shamos, M.I., Hoey, D.: Closest-point problems. In: 16th Annual Symposium on Foundations of Computer Science (sfcs 1975), pp. 151–162. IEEE (1975)
22. Shen, C.F.C.: The λ-geometry Steiner minimal tree problem and visualization (1997)
23. Williamson, D.P., Shmoys, D.B.: The Design of Approximation Algorithms. Cambridge University Press, Cambridge (2011)
24. Wu, B.Y., Chao, K.M.: Spanning Trees and Optimization Problems. Chapman and Hall/CRC, Boca Raton (2004)
25. Zhou, H., Shenoy, N., Nicholls, W.: Efficient minimum spanning tree construction without Delaunay triangulation. In: Proceedings of the 2001 Asia and South Pacific Design Automation Conference, pp. 192–197 (2001)
26. Zhu, Q., Zhou, H., Jing, T., Hong, X.L., Yang, Y.: Spanning graph-based nonrectilinear Steiner tree algorithms. IEEE Trans. Comput. Aided Des. Integr. Circuits Syst. **24**(7), 1066–1075 (2005)

Logic

Generalized Possibilistic CTL* Model Checking with Fuzzy Temporal Logic Operators

Chuanjiang Mu[1], Wuniu Liu[2], and Yongming Li[1,2(✉)]

[1] School of Computer Science, Shaanxi Normal University, Xi'an, Shaanxi, China
{muchuanjiang,liyongm}@snnu.edu.cn
[2] School of Mathematics and Statistics, Shaanxi Normal University, Xi'an, Shaanxi, China
liuwuniu@snnu.edu.cn

Abstract. Based on the generalized possibilistic Kripke structure, possibilistic fuzzy linear temporal logic, GPoCTL* and generalized possibility measure, this article studies the model-checking problems of generalized possibilistic fuzzy CTL* (GPoFCTL*). GPoFCTL* includes fuzzy temporal logic operators such as "soon", "presently", "gradually", "last", "within", "finally", "nearly always", "almost always", "in the distant future", "in the middle", "almost until", "nearly until". This paper studies the syntax of GPoFCTL* and its semantics based on generalized possibility measures. In addition, we present an model checking algorithm for GPoFCTL* using fuzzy matrix operations. Finally, we present an example to illustrate the computational process of the model checking algorithm.

Keywords: Generalized possibility theory · fuzzy temporal operator · GPoFCTL* · model checking

1 Introduction

Model checking [1,2] is an efficient technique for automatically verifying the behavior of hardware and software systems. Its core process consists of three key steps: system modeling, specification definition, and verification process. In the system modeling step, state transition models such as Kripke structure are constructed. Then the properties or specifications that the system should satisfy need to be specified. In the verification proxess, model checker checks whether these properties hold for this model. The model checker outputs the boolean answer and generates a counterexample if the system violates this property. The classical model checking technique, returning only 0 or 1, making it inadequate for analyzing models with uncertainty. To address this limitation, probabilistic model checking [2], based on probability measure theory is suitable for systems with uncertainty caused by randomness. However, those involving human judgments and fuzzy systems, are often characterized by non-additive events. To deal with the uncertainty caused by vagueness and incompleteness in the system mentioned above, Li et al. [3–11,18–24] have further developed a model-checking methods based on possibility measures and their generalized forms. This possibilistic model checking approach finds application in verifying nondeterministic and non-additive systems. Compared to classical temporal logic, the representational power of temporal logic under the possibility theory surpasses that of the classical temporal logic [1,2]. However, possibilistic temporal logic does not allow us to represent fuzzy (linguistic) temporal properties with vagueness on time. For example, when attempting to describe the precise arrival time of a bus, we encounter the reality that due to unpredictable factors during its journey, the bus may arrive a few minutes earlier or later. Consequently, we can only observe that the bus "almost always" arrives punctually. This scenario cannot be adequately captured using classical temporal operators. Since the occurrence of the event may slightly precede or follow the expected time, the property is fulfilled except for a brief time interval. To represent this fuzzy temporal attribute, [13] introduces short-term fuzzy temporal logic operators and realizes their semantics through the inclusion of an evasion function. [17] further extends this foundation by adding long-term and medium-term temporal terms and integrating these fuzzy temporal logic operators into a generalized possibility linear temporal logic, which then defines generalized possibility fuzzy temporal logic.

Our work is to introduce fuzzy temporal logic operators, such as "soon", "presently", "gradually", "last", "within", "nearly always", "almost always", "in a long distant future", "in the middle", "nearly until", or "almost until", and then proposed an extension of GPoCTL*, called GPoFCTL*. In this fuzzy temporal logic, semantics are achieved through the introduction of weight functions. Finally, a fuzzy matrix approach for GPoFCTL* model checking is presented.

The main contributions of this article are:

a. We introduced fuzzy temporal logic operators into GPoCTL*, extended it accordingly, and ultimately obtained GPoFCTL*.
b. We studied the model checking problem of GPoFCTL* and proposed a fuzzy matrix calculation method.

The content of this paper is arranged as follows. Sect. 2 is the preparatory knowledge. In Sect. 3 we introduce the syntax and semantics of GPoFCTL*, In particular, we discuss in detail the weighting functions used for the semantics of fuzzy time operators. In Sect. 4 we introduce the GPKS-based model checking method for GPoFCTL* and discuss the fuzzy matrix computation method for several properties of GPoFCTL*, Sect. 5 gives an illustrative example. Finally, Sect. 6 concludes this paper.

2 Some Preliminaries

In this section, we give some basic knowledge about model checking, including generalized possibilistic theory [3,7,11,14–16], GPKS [8], and GPoCTL* [12].

2.1 Generalized Possibility Theory

Let universe of discourse U be a nonempty set, and assume that all subsets are measurable. A possibility measure is a function Π from the powerset 2^U to $[0, 1]$ such that: (1) $\Pi(\emptyset) = 0$, (2) $\Pi(U) = 1$, (3) $\Pi(\bigcup E_i) = \bigvee \Pi(E_i)$ for any subset family $\{E_i\}_{i \in I}$ of the universe set U, where we use the symbol $\bigvee$ to denote the supremum operation of real numbers. If Π only satisfies the conditions (1) and (4), then we call Π a generalized possibility measure.

It follows that the generalized possibility measure on a nonempty set is determined by its behavior on singletons:

$$\Pi(E) = \bigvee_{x \in E} \Pi(\{x\}). \tag{1}$$

The function $\pi : U \to [0, 1]$ defined by $\pi(x) = \Pi(\{x\})$ is called the possibility distribution of Π, and the measure Π is uniquely defined by (1).

Dually, the necessity measure is a function N from the powerset 2^U to $[0, 1]$ such that (1) $N(\emptyset) = 0$, (2) $N(U) = 1$ and (3) $N(\bigcap E_i) = \bigwedge N(E_i)$ for any subset family $\{E_i\}_{i \in I}$ of the universe set U, where we use the symbol $\bigwedge$ to denote the infimum operation of real numbers. If N only satisfies the conditions (2) and (3), then we call N a generalized necessity measure.

2.2 Generalized Possibilistic Kripke Structure

The models of uncertainty systems we used in this article are as follows.

Definition 1. *(see [8]) A GPKS is a tuple $M = (S, P, I, AP, L)$, where*

1) *S is a countable, nonempty set of states;*
2) *$P : S \times S \to [0, 1]$ is a function, called possibilistic transition distribution function;*
3) *$I : S \to [0, 1]$ is a function, called possibilistic initial distribution function;*
4) *AP is a set of atomic propositions;*
5) *$L : S \times AP \to [0, 1]$ is a possibilistic labeling function, which can be viewed as function mapping a state s to the fuzzy set of atomic propositions, which are possible in the state s, i.e., $L(s, a)$ denotes the possibility or truth value of atomic proposition a that is supposed to hold in s.*

If the set S, AP are finite sets, then $M = (S, P, I, AP, L)$ is called a finite GPKS. A sequence of states $s_0 s_1 s_2 \cdots \in S^\omega$ is called an (infinite) path in M if for any i there is $P(s_i, s_{i+1}) > 0$. Let $Paths(M)$ denote the set of all paths in M and $Paths_M(s_0)$ denote the set of all paths in M starting from the state s_0.

For a path $\pi = s_0 s_1 s_2 \cdots$ in M, its *trace* is defined as $L(\pi) = L(s_0)L(s_1)L(s_2)\cdots$, which is an infinite string over $[0,1]^{AP}$. Here, $[0,1]^{AP}$ denotes the set of all fuzzy sets over AP.

Remark 1. For a fuzzy matrix P on a state set S, P is the distribution function of possible state transitions of GPKS M, the transitive closure of the fuzzy matrix

P is denoted by P^+. If S is a finite set, then $P^+ = P \vee P^2 \vee P^3 \vee \ldots \vee P^{|S|}$, where $P^{k+1} = P^k \circ P$ is any positive integer k and $|S|$ denotes the number of elements in S. In this article, we use the symbol o to denote the max-min composition operation of a fuzzy matrix. The reflexive and transitive closure of a fuzzy matrix P is denoted by P^*, which is defined as $P^* = P^0 \vee P^+$, where P^0 denotes the identity matrix.

Definition 2. *(see [8]) In a finite GPKS $M = (S, P, I, AP, L)$, we define a function $Po_M : Paths(M) \longrightarrow [0,1]$ as follows:*

$$Po_M = I(s_0) \wedge \bigwedge_{i \geq 0} P(s_i, s_{i+1}), \tag{2}$$

for any $\pi = s_0 s_1 s_2 \cdots \in Paths(M)$. If M is konwn by context, we could omit the superscript M and write Po_M as Po.

Furthermore, for $E \subseteq Paths(M)$, define $Po(E) = \bigvee \{Po(\pi) \mid \pi \in E\}$, then we have $Po : 2^{Paths(M)} \longrightarrow [0,1]$ as the generalized possibility measure over $\Omega = 2^{Paths(M)}$.

Let $M = (S, P, I, AP, L)$ be a finite GPKS, we define $r_M : S \longrightarrow [0,1]$. For any $s \in S$ as:

$$r_M(s) = \bigvee \left\{ \bigwedge_{i \geq 0} P(s_i, s_{i+1}) \mid s_0 = s, s_i \in S, \text{for any } i \geq 0 \right\}, \tag{3}$$

then $r_M(s)$ denotes the maximum possibility of the paths starting from the state s. The calculation of r_M is given as follows.

Theorem 1. *(see [8]) For a finite GPKS $M = (S, P, I, AP, L)$, then for all $s \in S$:*

$$r_M(s) = \bigvee_{t \in S} \left(P^+(s,t) \wedge P^+(t,t) \right). \tag{4}$$

2.3 Generalized Possibilistic CTL*(GPoCTL*)

Definition 3. *(see [12]) (Syntax of GPoCTL*) GPoCTL* state formulas over the set AP of atomic propositions are formed according to the following grammar:*

$$\Phi ::= true \mid a \mid \Phi_1 \wedge \Phi_2 \mid \neg \Phi \mid Po(\varphi)$$

where $a \in AP$, φ is a GPoCTL path formula. GPoCTL* path formulas are formed according to the following grammar:*

$$\varphi ::= \Phi \mid \varphi_1 \wedge \varphi_2 \mid \neg \varphi \mid \bigcirc \varphi \mid \varphi \sqcup \varphi$$

Definition 4. *(see [12]) (Semantics of GPoCTL*): Let $a \in AP$ be an atomic proposition, $M = (S, P, I, AP, L)$ be a GPKS, $s \in S$ be a state, Φ be GPoCTL* state formulas, and φ be a GPoCTL* path formula. For state formula Φ, its semantics is a fuzzy set $\|\Phi\| : S \longrightarrow [0,1]$, which is defined recursively as follows, for any $s \in S$:*

$$\|true\|(s) = 1$$
$$\|a\|(s) = L(s, a)$$
$$\|\Phi_1 \wedge \Phi_2\|(s) = \|\Phi_1\|(s) \wedge \|\Phi_2\|(s)$$
$$\|\neg\Phi\|(s) = 1 - \|\Phi\|(s)$$
$$\|Po(\varphi)\|(s) = Po(s \models \varphi).$$

$Po(s \models \varphi)$ is defined as follows:

$$Po(s \models \varphi) = \bigvee_{\pi \in Paths(s)} Po^{M_s}(\pi) \wedge \|\varphi\|(\pi).$$

For a path formula φ, $\pi = s_0 s_1 s_2 \cdots$, $\pi_i = s_i s_{i+1} \cdots$, $\pi[i] = s_i$, its semantics is a fuzzy set $\|\varphi\| : Paths(M) \longrightarrow [0, 1]$, which is defined recursively as follows:

$$\|\Phi\|(\pi) = \|\Phi\|(s_0)$$
$$\|\varphi_1 \wedge \varphi_2\|(\pi) = \|\varphi_1\|(\pi) \wedge \|\varphi_2\|(\pi)$$
$$\|\neg\varphi\|(\pi) = 1 - \|\varphi\|(\pi)$$
$$\|\bigcirc\varphi\|(\pi) = \|\varphi\|(\pi_1)$$
$$\|\varphi_1 \sqcup \varphi_2\|(\pi) = \bigvee_{j \geq 0} \|\varphi_2\|(\pi_j) \wedge \bigwedge_{0 \leq i < j} \|\varphi_1\|(\pi_i).$$

3 Generalized Possibilistic Fuzzy CTL*(GPoFCTL*)

GPoCTL* cannot describe fuzzy temporal attributes like "soon", "presently", "gradually", "last", "within", "nearly always", etc. In order to extend the expression ability of GPoCTL*, this section introduces some fuzzy temporal operators and provides the syntax and semantic interpretation of GPoFCTL*.

Definition 5. *(Syntax of GPoFCTL*)* *GPoFCTL* state formulas over the set AP of atomic propositions are formed according to the following grammar:*

$$\Phi ::= true \mid a \mid \Phi_1 \wedge \Phi_2 \mid \neg \Phi \mid Po(\varphi)$$

where $a \in AP$, φ is a GPoFCTL* path formula. GPoFCTL* path formulas are formed according to the following grammar:

$$\varphi ::= \Phi \mid \varphi_1 \wedge \varphi_2 \mid \neg \varphi \mid \mathcal{O}\varphi \mid \varphi \mathcal{T} \varphi$$

where Φ are state formulas, $\mathcal{O} \in O$ and $\mathcal{T} \in T$, O and T are the set of unary and binary (fuzzy) temporal modalities.

In this article we consider only some specific unitary and binary (fuzzy) temporal patterns. We consider the unary operator $\bigcirc$ (next), $Soon$(soon), $Presently$ (presently), $\Diamond$(eventually), $Gradu$ (gradually), $\square$ (forever, always), ILD (in the long distant future), W (within), L (last), $N\Box$ (nearly always), IM (in the middle of), $A\Box$ (almost always), and their bounded versions $\Diamond^{\leq n}, \Box^{\leq n}, L_n, N\Box^{\leq n}, W_n$. Binary operations, are $\sqcup$(until), $N \sqcup$ (nearly until), $A \sqcup$ (always until) and their bounded versions $\sqcup^{\leq n}, N\sqcup^{\leq n}, A\sqcup^{\leq n}$. The term "fuzzy" here refers to the uncertainty in the number of delayed or ignored events. In order to quantify the effect of this uncertainty on the formula, a weight function η is introduced. This function is used to quantify the impact due to the number of delayed or ignored events. Specifically, for any given i (representing the number of delays or omissions), $\eta(i)$ denotes the weight of the corresponding fuzzy modality at time i. This weight can be thought of as the weight of the fuzzy modality.

The weight function η is defined as: $\eta : \mathbf{Z} \rightarrow [0,1]$, where $\mathbf{Z}$ is the set of integers to denote the (discrete) time. If the fuzzy modalities are in short term, such as "soon, last, within", the corresponding η is a decreasing function such that $\eta(i) = 1$ when $i \leq t$ for some integer $t \geq 0$ for some integer $t \geq 0$ and $\lim_{i \rightarrow +\infty} \eta(i) = 0$. Contrarily, if the fuzzy modalities are in long term, such as "gradually," the corresponding η is an increasing function, such as $\eta(i) = 0$ when $i \leq t$ for some positive integer t and $\lim_{i \rightarrow +\infty} \eta(i) = 1$.

We can describe the weighted function with a unique decreasing function in some cases. Given a decreasing function $\eta : \mathbf{Z} \rightarrow [0,1]$ such that $\eta(i) = 1$ when $i \leq 0$ and there exists a positive integer n_η such that $\eta(i) = 0$ whenever $i \geq n_\eta$. Then, the above-mentioned fuzzy modalities can be defined using η as follows:

$$\eta_{Soon}(i) = \eta(i) \text{ for any } i \quad (5)$$

$$\eta_{Presently}(i) = (\eta(i))^2 \text{ for any } i \quad (6)$$

$$\eta_{Gradu}(i) = \eta(n_\eta - i) \text{ for any } i \quad (7)$$

$$\eta_L(i) = \eta(i) \text{ for any } i \quad (8)$$

$$\eta_{W_t}(i) = \eta(i - t) \text{ for any } i \quad (9)$$

$$\eta_{N_t}(i) = \eta(t - i) \text{ for any } i \quad (10)$$

$$\eta_{A_t}(i) = \eta(t - i)^2 \text{ for any } i \quad (11)$$

$$\eta_{ILD}(i) = \eta(n_2 - i) \text{ for any } i, \text{ with } n_\eta = n_2 - n_1 \quad (12)$$

$$\eta_{IM}(i) = \begin{cases} \eta(\frac{n_1+n_2}{2} - i), i \leq \frac{n_1+n_2}{2} \\ \eta(i - \frac{n_1+n_2}{2}), i > \frac{n_1+n_2}{2} \end{cases}, \text{here } n_\eta = \frac{n_2 - n_1}{2}. \quad (13)$$

To give a precise semantics of GPoFCTL*, we assume that D is a nonempty set of weighted functions η as described by (5)–(13), such that the above defined weighted functions all belong to D. The following is a semantic interpretation of the GPoFCTL* formula under D.

Definition 6. *(Semantics of GPoFCTL* under D): Let $a \in AP$ be an atomic proposition, $M =$(S,P, I, AP, L) be a GPKS, $s \in S$ be a state, Φ be GPoFCTL* state formulas, and φ be a GPoFCTL* path formula. For state formula Φ, its semantics is a fuzzy set $\|\Phi\| : S \longrightarrow [0,1]$, which is defined recursively as follows, for any $s \in S$:*

$$||true||(s) = 1$$
$$||a||(s) = L(s, a)$$
$$||\Phi_1 \wedge \Phi_2||(s) = ||\Phi_1||(s) \wedge ||\Phi_2||(s)$$
$$||\neg \Phi||(s) = 1 - ||\Phi||(s)$$
$$||Po(\varphi)||(s) = Po(s \models \varphi).$$

For a path formula φ, $\pi_i = \pi[i]\pi[i+1]\cdots$, $\pi[i] = s_i$, its semantics is a fuzzy set $||\varphi|| : Paths(M) \longrightarrow [0,1]$, which is defined recursively for $\pi \in Paths(M)$ as follows:

$$||\Phi||(\pi) = ||\Phi||(\pi[0])$$
$$||\varphi_1 \wedge \varphi_2||(\pi) = ||\varphi_1||(\pi) \wedge ||\varphi_2||(\pi)$$
$$||\neg \varphi||(\pi) = 1 - ||\varphi||(\pi)$$
$$||\bigcirc \varphi||(\pi) = ||\varphi||(\pi_1)$$
$$||\text{Soon}\varphi||(\pi) = \bigvee_{i=1}^{n_\eta} ||\varphi||(\pi_i) \cdot \eta_{\text{Soon}}(i-1)$$
$$||\text{Gradu}\varphi||(\pi) = \bigvee_{i=1}^{n_\eta - 1} ||\varphi||(\pi_i) \cdot \eta_{\text{Gradu}}(i) \vee \bigvee_{i=n_\eta}^{+\infty} ||\varphi||(\pi_i)$$
$$||\text{ILD}\varphi||(\pi) = \bigvee_{i=n_1}^{n_2 - 1} ||\varphi||(\pi_i) \cdot \eta_{\text{ILD}}(i) \vee \bigvee_{i=n_2}^{+\infty} ||\varphi||(\pi_i)$$
$$||\text{IM}\varphi||(\pi) = \bigvee_{i=n_1}^{n_2} ||\varphi||(\pi_i) \cdot \eta_{\text{IM}}(i)$$
$$||\Diamond^{\leq t}\varphi||(\pi) = \bigvee_{i=0}^{t} ||\varphi||(\pi_i)$$
$$||\Diamond \varphi||(\pi) = \bigvee_{i \geq 0} ||\varphi||(\pi_i)$$
$$||W_t \varphi||(\pi) = \bigvee_{i=0}^{t+n_\eta - 1} ||\varphi||(\pi_i) \cdot \eta_{W_t}(i)$$
$$||\Box^{\leq t}\varphi||(\pi) = \bigwedge_{i=0}^{t} ||\varphi||(\pi_i)$$
$$||\Box \varphi||(\pi) = \bigwedge_{i \geq 0} ||\varphi||(\pi_i)$$
$$||L_t \varphi||(\pi) = \bigvee_{i=0}^{\min\{n_\eta - 1, t\}} ||\Box \varphi||(\pi) \cdot \eta_{L_t}(i)$$
$$||N\Box^{\leq t}\varphi||(\pi) = \bigvee_{i \in I_t} \bigvee_{H \subseteq I_t, |H|=i} \bigwedge_{h \in H} ||\varphi||(\pi_h) \cdot \eta_{N_t}(i)$$

$$\|A\Box^{\leq t}\varphi\|(\pi) = \bigvee_{i \in I_t} \bigvee_{H \subseteq I_t, |H|=i} \bigwedge_{h \in H} \|\varphi\|(\pi_h) \cdot \eta_{A_t}(i)$$

$$\|N\Box\varphi\|(\pi) = \lim_{t \to \infty} \|N\Box^{\leq t}\varphi\|(\pi)$$

$$\|A\Box\varphi\|(\pi) = \lim_{t \to \infty} \|A\Box^{\leq t}\varphi\|(\pi)$$

$$\|\varphi_1 \sqcup^{\leq t} \varphi_2\|(\pi) = \bigvee_{j=0}^{t} \|\varphi_2\|(\pi_j) \wedge \bigwedge_{0 \leq i < j} \|\varphi_1\|(\pi_i)$$

$$\|\varphi_1 \sqcup \varphi_2\|(\pi) = \bigvee_{j \geq 0} \|\varphi_2\|(\pi_j) \wedge \bigwedge_{0 \leq i < j} \|\varphi_1\|(\pi_i)$$

$$\|\varphi_1 N \sqcup^{\leq t} \varphi_2\|(\pi) = \bigvee_{j=0}^{t} (\|\varphi_2\|(\pi_j) \wedge \|N\Box^{\leq j-1}\varphi_1\|(\pi))$$

$$\|\varphi_1 A \sqcup^{\leq t} \varphi_2\|(\pi) = \bigvee_{j=0}^{t} (\|\varphi_2\|(\pi_j) \wedge \|A\Box^{\leq j-1}\varphi_1\|(\pi))$$

$$\|\varphi_1 N \sqcup \varphi_2\|(\pi) = \lim_{t \to \infty} \|\varphi_1 N \sqcup^{\leq t} \varphi_2\|(\pi)$$

$$\|\varphi_1 A \sqcup \varphi_2\|(\pi) = \lim_{t \to \infty} \|\varphi_1 A \sqcup^{\leq t} \varphi_2\|(\pi),$$

where "$\cdot$" denotes the multiplication operation of real numbers, $\pi_i = \pi[i]\pi[i+1]\cdots$, $\pi[i] = s_i$, $I_t = \{0, 1, \ldots, t\}$, η_- in each equation is the corresponding weight function from D.

Other formulas can be induced according to the above mentioned semantic definition.

$\lim_{t \to \infty} \|N\Box^{\leq t}\varphi\|(\pi)$ has the following form:

$$\bigvee_{i=0}^{n_\eta - 1} \bigvee_{H \subseteq \mathbf{N}, |H|=i} \bigwedge_{j \in \mathbf{N} - H} \|\varphi\|(\pi_j) \cdot \eta(i),$$

where $\mathbf{N}$ is the set of non-negative integers. This is just the value of $\|N\Box\varphi\|(\pi)$. Hence, $\|N\Box\varphi\|(\pi)$ is well defined. Similarly, $\|A\Box\varphi\|(\pi)$ is also well defined.

For $Po(s \models \varphi_1 \wedge \varphi_2)$ and $Po(s \models \neg\varphi)$, the semantics is as follows:

$$Po(s \models \varphi_1 \wedge \varphi_2)$$
$$= \bigvee_{\pi \in Paths(s)} Po^{M_s}(\pi) \wedge \|\varphi_1 \wedge \varphi_2\|(\pi)$$
$$= \bigvee_{\pi \in Paths(s)} [Po^{M_s}(\pi) \wedge \|\varphi_1\|(\pi) \wedge \|\varphi_2\|(\pi)].$$

$$Po(s \models \neg\varphi)$$
$$= \bigvee_{\pi \in Paths(s)} Po^{M_s}(\pi) \wedge ||\neg\varphi||(\pi)$$
$$= \bigvee_{\pi \in Paths(s)} Po^{M_s}(\pi) \wedge (1 - ||\varphi||(\pi)).$$

We give some explanation of the introduced fuzzy modalities as follows, *Soon*, representing a time at or after the next time, allowing delay for a period of time (up to n_η) at the next moment. *Presently*, can be seen as "very soon". W_t(eventually within t time instants later), denotes the event is supposed to occur in at least one of the next t moments, or possibly, in the next $t + n_\eta$ moments. Here, the moment after t is the delay moment, we apply a weight for each moment after the tth. The possibility of $W_t\varphi$ is calculated from the current moment; however, the possibility of $Soon\varphi$ is calculated from the next time. $W_t\varphi$ can be considered as a generalized interpretation of $Soon\varphi$ in time.

L_t (last for t consecutive time instants at most) indicates that it has always occurred from the start moment to t moment or at a time before t moment, allowing it to be completed in advance at a time prior to t moment (up to n_η moment).

Gradu (gradually within n_η time) indicates an event will occur after n_η time, but may occur before n_η time.

ILD (in the long distant future) indicates an event will occur after a long time, for example, after n_2 time, and allowing advance for a period of time up to $n_2 - n_1$ times, and for each time before n_2th, the weight function is applied. *IM* (in the middle of) indicates an event will occur in a middle of the time interval $[n_1, n_2]$, it emphasizes the middle point $\frac{n_1+n_2}{2}$ of the interval $[n_1, n_2]$, allowing delay or advance for a period of time up to $\frac{n_1-n_2}{2}$, and for each time delay or advance the middle point $\frac{n_1 \pm n_2}{2}$, the weighted function η_{IM} is applied.

$N\square^{\leq t}$(nearly always within t time instants) indicates that an event nearly always occurs within t time, but allows it not to occur at some point. $N\square$(nearly always) is the ultimate form of $N\square^{\leq t}$, where $||N\square^{\leq t}\varphi||_M(\pi)$ indicates the extent to which φ "nearly always" occurs.

$N\sqcup^{\leq t}$ (nearly always ... until within t time instants), $||\varphi_1 N \sqcup^{\leq t} \varphi_2||(\pi)$ indicates that π nearly always satisfies the property φ_1 before it satisfies the property φ_2.

4 Model Checking of GPoFCTL*

The GPoFCTL* model-checking problem can be formulated as follows: for a given finite GPKS $M = (S, P, I, AP, L)$, a state in M, and a GPoFCTL* state formula Φ, compute the value $||\Phi||(s)$. If $\Phi = a \in AP, \neg\Phi, \Phi_1 \wedge \Phi_2$, then we can computing $||\Phi||$ inductively using semantic formula for the state of GPoFCTL*. For the formula $Po(\varphi)$, where φ is a path formula, according to its semantics, we get $||Po(\varphi)||(s) = Po(s \models \varphi)$, the key point is to calculate $Po(s \models \varphi)$ for any state s. We now discuss the possibility of temporal operators with fuzzy temporal properties. For a given GPKS M, $\mathcal{O}b$ and $a\mathcal{T}b$ can be viewed as two GPoFCTL* formulas on the set AP of atomic propositions, where a and b are atomic propositions, $\mathcal{O}$ is the unary temporal operator, and $\mathcal{T}$ is the binary time operator.

Theorem 2. *Let M be a finite GPKS, let b a atomic propositions, we have:*

$$Po_M(s_0 \models \text{Soon } b) = \bigvee_{i=1}^{n_\eta} (P^i \circ \eta(i-1) \cdot D_b) \circ r_M(s_0). \tag{14}$$

$$Po_M(s_0 \models \text{Gradu } b) = \left(\bigvee_{i=1}^{n_\eta} (P^i \circ \eta(i) \cdot D_b) \vee P^{n_\eta - 1} \circ P^* \circ D_b \right) \circ r_M(s_0). \tag{15}$$

$$Po_M(s_0 \models ILD \ b) = \left(\bigvee_{i=n_1}^{n_2 - 1} (P^i \circ \eta(i) \cdot D_b) \vee Po_M^{n_2 - 1} \circ P^* \circ D_b \right) \circ r_M(s_0). \tag{16}$$

$$Po_M(s_0 \models IM \ b) = \bigvee_{i=n_1}^{n_2} (P^i \circ \eta(i) \cdot D_b) \circ r_M(s_0). \tag{17}$$

$$Po_M(s_0 \models \diamond^{\leq t} b) = \left(\bigvee_{i=0}^{t} P^i \right) \circ D_b \circ r_M(s_0). \tag{18}$$

$$Po_M(s_0 \models W_t \ b) = \bigvee_{i=0}^{t+n_\eta - 1} (P^i \circ \eta(i) \cdot D_b) \circ r_M(s_0). \tag{19}$$

$$Po_M(s_0 \models \Box^{\leq t} b) = (D_b \circ P)^{t+1} \circ r_M(s_0). \tag{20}$$

$$Po_M(s_0 \models L_t b) = \bigvee_{i=0}^{\min\{n_\eta - 1, t\}} (\eta(i) \cdot D_b \circ P)^{t-i+1} \circ r_M(s_0), \tag{21}$$

where $D_b = diag(b(s))_{s \in S}$ is a diagonal matrix, η is the weighted function for the corresponding fuzzy temporal operator, $\eta(i-1) \cdot D_b$ or $\eta(i) \cdot D_b$ is the scale product of $\eta(i-1)$ or $\eta(i)$ with matrix D_b as a real matrix. Here, we require the scale product operation to have a higher priority than the max-min composite operation $\circ$. Specially when $n_\eta = 1$

$Po_M(s_0 \models \text{Soon} b) = Po_M(s_0 \models \bigcirc b) = P \circ D_b \circ r_M(s_0).$

$Po_M(s_0 \models W_t b) = Po_M(s_0 \models \diamond^{\leq t} b) = (\bigvee_{i=0}^{t} P^i) \circ D_b \circ r_M(s_0).$

$Po_M(s_0 \models L_t b) = Po_M(s_0 \models \Box^{\leq t} b) = (D_b \circ P)^{t+1} \circ D_b \circ r_M(s_0).$

When $t \to \infty$, $\eta(i-t) = 1$

$Po_M(s_0 \models \lim_{t \to \infty} W_t b) = P^* \circ D_b \circ r_M(s_0) = Po_M(s_0 \models \diamond b).$

When $t \to \infty$,

$Po_M(s_0 \models \lim_{t \to \infty} L_t b) = Po_M(s_0 \models \lim_{t \to \infty} \Box^{\leq t} b) = Po_M(s_0 \models \Box b).$

Since $Po_M(s_0 \models \Box b) = \lim_{t \to +\infty} Po_M(s_0 \models \Box^{\leq t} b)$, we can use Eq. (21) to calculate $Po_M(s_0 \models \Box b)$. In [4], we give another approach to calculate $Po_M(s_0 \models \Box b)$ using the greatest fixed point algorithm.

Taking the limit of (19), we then get the following result which has been shown in [5].

Theorem 3. *Let M be a finite GPKS, b is a atomic proposition,*

$$Po_M(s_0 \models \Diamond b) = P^* \circ D_b \circ r_M(s_0), \qquad (22)$$

where $D_b = diag(b(s_i))_{s_i \in S}$ is a diagonal matrix.

Theorem 4. *Let M be a finite GPKS, b is a atomic proposition, then*

$$Po_M(s_0 \models N \Box^{\leq t} b) = \bigvee_{j=0}^{t} \bigvee_{H \subseteq I_t, |H|=j} b_{j,H}^P \circ r_M(s_0). \qquad (23)$$

Specially where $n_\eta = 1$
$Po_M(s_0 \models N \Box^{\leq t} b) = Po_M(s_0 \models \Box^{\leq t} b) = (D_b \circ P)^{t+1} \circ r_M(s_0)$.

Theorem 5. *Let M be a finite GPKS, c and b are two atomic propositions, then*

$$Po_M(s_0 \models cN \sqcup^{\leq t} b) = \bigvee_{i=0}^{t} \bigvee_{j=0}^{i} \bigvee_{H \subseteq I_i, |H|=j} C_{i,j,H}^P \circ D_b \circ r_M(s_0). \qquad (24)$$

Specially, when $n_\eta = 1$,
$Po_M(s_0 \models cN \sqcup^{\leq t} b) = Po_M(s_0 \models c \sqcup^{\leq t} b) = (\bigvee_{i=0}^{t}(D_c \circ P)^i \circ D_b \circ r_M)(s_0)$,
as shown in [4]. it follows that
$Po_M(s_0 \models c \sqcup b) = \lim_{t \to +\infty} Po_M(s_0 \models c \sqcup^{\leq t} b) = (D_c \circ P)^* \circ D_b \circ r_M(s_0)$.

Remark 2. If we replace the weight function η by η^2 in (14), (23), and (24), then we get the formulas to calculate $Po_M(s_0 \models Presently\ b), Po_M(s_0 \models a \Box^{\leq t} b)$ and $Po_M(s_0 \models cA \sqcup b^{\leq t})$ and by the semantics of *Presently*, $A\Box$ and $A\sqcup$, respectively.

5 Illustrative Example

Let us give an example to illustrate the application of GPoFCTL* model-checking technique. Here, we give a finite GPKS $M = (S, P, I, AP, L)$ shown in Fig. 1. It has given three atomic propositions a, b, c. For these three atomic propositions, we assign them a fuzzy value with a range of [0,1]. We have $L(s_1, a) = 0.6$. The value of the weighted function we use is: $\eta(0) = 1$, $\eta(1) = 0.9$, $\eta(2) = 0.7$, $\eta(3) = 0$.

According to Fig. 1, the following matrices are obtained: $D_a = diag(1, 0.6, 0, 0.4)$, $D_b = diag(0.8, 1, 0, 0.5)$, $D_c = diag(0, 0, 0.7, 1)$.

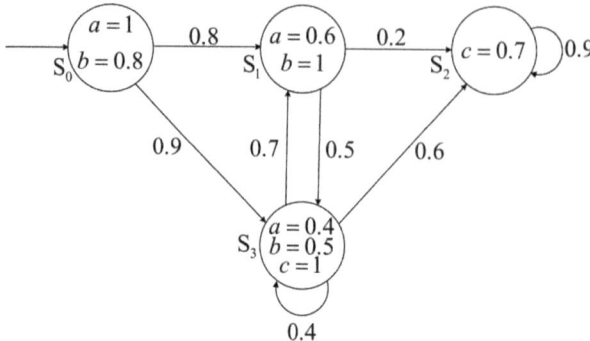

Fig. 1. GPKS.

$$P = \begin{pmatrix} 0 & 0.8 & 0 & 0.9 \\ 0 & 0 & 0.2 & 0.5 \\ 0 & 0 & 0.9 & 0 \\ 0 & 0.7 & 0.6 & 0.4 \end{pmatrix}, P^* = \begin{pmatrix} 1 & 0.8 & 0.6 & 0.9 \\ 0 & 1 & 0.5 & 0.5 \\ 0 & 0 & 1 & 0 \\ 0 & 0.7 & 0.6 & 1 \end{pmatrix}$$

For this model, let us check some properties as follows.

1) $Po(s_0 \models \bigcirc a) = 0.6$, means that from s_0, after one transition, the possibility of the a is 0.6.
2) $Po(s_0 \models Soon\ a) = 0.5$, means that from s_0, after some transitions, the possibility of the a is 0.5.
3) $Po(s_0 \models \Diamond a) = 0.5$, means that from s_0, after the transitions, the possibility of the a is 0.5.
4) $Po(s_0 \models W_3 a) = 0.5$, means that from s_0, within 3 times of the combined transitions, the possibility of the a is 0.5.
5) $Po(s_0 \models Gradu\ a) = 0.5$, means that from s_0, after the transitions, the possibility of the a is 0.5.

6 Conclusions

The problem of GPoFCTL* model checking is investigated. The syntax, semantics of GPoFCTL* under generalized possibility measure is given. Then, several fuzzy time operators are discussed using matrix operations and a GPoFCTL* model checking algorithm is given. Finally an example is given and specifically analysed.

Acknowledgment. This work was partially supported by National Science Foundation of China (Grant Nos: 12071271,11671244) and the Shaanxi Fundamental Science Research Project for Mathematics and Physics (Grant Number: 23JSZ011). The author would like to thank Prof. Li for his guidance and help. Useful suggestions given by Dr. Qing He and Dr. Wuniu Liu are also acknowledged.

References

1. Grumberg, Orna, Clarke, E. M., and Peled, D. A.: Model checking. In: International Conference on Foundations of Software Technology and Theoretical Computer Science, Springer, Heidelberg (1999)
2. Baier, C., Joost-Pieter, K.: Principles of Model Checking. MIT Press, Cambridge (2008)
3. Li, Y., Manfred, D., Lihui, L.: Model checking of linear-time properties in multi-valued systems. Inf. Sci. **377**, 51–74 (2017)
4. Li, Y., Lihui, L., Sanjiang, L.: Multi-valued computation tree logic model checking based on multi-valued possibility measures. Inf. Sci. **485**, 87–113 (2019)
5. Li, Y.: Quantitative model checking of linear-time properties based on generalized possibility measures. Fuzzy Sets Syst. **320**, 17–39 (2017)
6. Li, Y., Yali, L., Zhanyou, M.: Computation tree logic model checking based on possibility measures. Fuzzy Sets Syst. **262**, 44–59 (2015)
7. Li, Y., Li, L.: Model checking of linear-time properties based on possibility measure. IEEE Trans. Fuzzy Syst. **21**(5), 842–854 (2013)
8. Li, Y., Ma, Z.: Quantitative computation tree logic model checking based on generalized possibility measures. IEEE Trans. Fuzzy Syst. **23**(6), 2034–2047 (2015)
9. Liang, C., Yongming, L.: Model checking of fuzzy linear temporal logic based on generalized possibility measures. Acta Electron. Sin. **45**(12), 2971–2977 (2017)
10. Pan, H., Yongming, L., Yongzhi, C., Zhanyou, M.: Model checking fuzzy computation tree logic. Fuzzy Sets Syst. **262**, 60–77 (2015)
11. Ma, Z., Li, Y.: Model checking generalized possibilistic computation tree logic based on decision processes. Sci. China Inf. Sci. **46**(11), 1591–1607 (2016)
12. Xingxing, Z., Nanyi, D., Zhanyou, M., Yongming, L.: Possibilistic bisimulation based on generalized possibility measures and its logical characterizations. Comput. Eng. Sci. **37**(05), 951 (2015)
13. Frigeri, A., Liliana, P., Paola, S.: Fuzzy time in linear temporal logic. ACM Trans. Comput. Logic (TOCL) **15**(4), 1–22 (2014)
14. Dubois, D., Prade, H.: Possibility Theory. Plenum, New York (1988)
15. Didier, D., Henri, P.: Qualitative possibility theory and its applications to constraint satisfaction and decision under Intelligence, pp. 31–60. Springer, Berlin (2015)
16. Dubois, Didier and Prade, Henry: Possibility theory and its applications: Where do we stand? In Springer handbook of computational intelligence, pp. 31–60. Springer (2015)
17. Li, Y., Wei, J.: Possibilistic fuzzy linear temporal logic and its model checking. IEEE Trans. Fuzzy Syst. **29**(7), 1899–1913 (2021)
18. Liu, W., Wang, J., He, Q., Li, Y.: Model checking computation tree logic over multi-valued decision processes and its reduction techniques. Chin. J. Electron. **34**, 1–13 (2024)
19. Liu, W., He, Q., Li, Z., Li, Y.: Self-learning modeling in possibilistic model checking. IEEE Trans. Emerg. Top. Comput. Intell. (2023)
20. Liu, W., He, Q., Li, Y.: Computation tree logic model checking over possibilistic decision processes under finite-memory scheduler. In: National Conference of Theoretical Computer Science, pp. 75–88 (2021). Organization:
21. Li, Y., Liu, W., Wang, J., Yu, X., Li, C.: Model checking of possibilistic linear-time properties based on generalized possibilistic decision processes. IEEE Trans. Fuzzy Syst. (2023)

22. Liu, W., Li, Y.: optimal strategy model checking in possibilistic decision processes. IEEE Trans. Syst. Man, Cybern. Syst. (2023)
23. Liu, W.: Li, Z., Li, Y.: Quantum reachability games. IEEE Trans. Emerg. Top. Comput. Intell. (2024)
24. Liu, W., Li, Z., Li, Y.: Complex objective optimization in fuzzy environments. J. Intell. Fuzzy Syst. **45**(2), 3539–3553 (2023)

Medical Procedures Based on Bayesian Network and Possibilistic Model Checking

Ying Wen[2], Qing He[2], and Yongming Li[1,2(✉)]

[1] School of Mathematics and Statistics, Shaanxi Normal University, Xi'an, Shaanxi, China
[2] School of Computer Science, Shaanxi Normal University, Xi'an, Shaanxi, China
{codingw,heqing,liyongm}@snnu.edu.cn

Abstract. In this paper, we present a method that integrates Bayesian network and generalized possibilistic model checking to improve the accuracy of initial diagnostics and quantify uncertainties in the rehabilitation process. Bayesian network provides probabilistic decision support using data-driven statistical information from various sources. Computational tree logic, combined with generalized possibility measures, effectively manages the uncertainties associated with patient rehabilitation.

Keywords: Model checking · Bayesian network · Generalized possibilistic computation tree logic (GPoCTL) · Generalized possibilistic Kripke structure (GPKS)

1 Introduction

Physicians often face ambiguous information during medical procedures [1]. Many factors influence disease occurrence, making it challenging to quantify treatment outcomes during rehabilitation precisely. These challenges make it difficult to precisely quantify treatment outcomes during rehabilitation and require new methods to address the inherent uncertainties. Bayesian network (BN) [2] provides a probabilistic framework that utilizes Bayes' theorem to integrate and analyze diverse data, enhancing diagnostic accuracy. Similarly, possibilistic model checking introduces fuzzy logic to handle the uncertainties of treatment responses, improving the management and assessment of rehabilitation processes.

BN is an advanced probabilistic model in medical diagnostics. It predicts unknown variables by combining expert knowledge with empirical data. This ability to integrate various data sources enables BN to tackle the critical uncertainties that often arise in medical settings, such as symptoms and disease interactions [3,4]. The advantages of BN lie in its capacity to provide a sophisticated analysis of the probabilities associated with different diagnoses, enhancing the accuracy and reliability of medical decision-making. BN supports physicians in making decisions by evaluating the likelihood of various diseases based on observed symptoms and test results. BN can also be used in various fields, including fire prediction [5], climate change [6], groundwater management [7], green energy production [8], engineering fault diagnosis [9], and metro tunnel construction risk assessment [10].

Since the introduction of fuzzy set theory [11,12], researchers have explored applications in modeling systems with fuzzy uncertainties. Possibilistic model checking [13,14] uses possibility measures to handle uncertainties, particularly effective in medical contexts where data and responses are often imprecise or incomplete. The use of generalized possibilistic Kripke structures (GPKS) [15–17] enables the formal verification of fuzzy system properties through generalized possibilistic Computational Tree Logic (GPoCTL) [17–20]. This allows physicians to evaluate different treatment outcomes under uncertain conditions systematically.

This research method presents a new approach to improving the predictability and effectiveness of medical processes. Probabilistic uncertainty arises from random phenomena, and possibility can address the uncertainty resulting from incomplete and ambiguous information [21–23]. We use BN to help doctors determine disease decisions and use GPoCTL to model recovery, improving assessment and management of uncertainties related to recovery [24–28].

The main contributions of this article are as follows:

a. Combining BN with model checking to evaluate medical diagnosis and treatment, improving medical decision-making by identifying disease causes and evaluating treatment effectiveness.
b. Utilizing GPoCTL to consider the interactions and cumulative effects of treatments, aiding in the development of comprehensive treatment plans and enhancing the feasibility of treatment assessment.

The rest of the paper is structured as follows: Sect. 2 provides background and related work. Sect. 3 explains the basics of BN and its use in medical diagnosis. Section 4 discusses generalized possibilistic model checking and its application in medical treatment. Lastly, the paper concludes with a summary.

2 Preliminaries

2.1 Bayesian Network

Definition 1. *BN [5] integrates expert knowledge, historical data, and uncertain information to represent, infer, and predict outcomes in uncertain environments. BN comprises a directed acyclic graph (DAG) and a conditional probability table (CPT). The DAG uses nodes to represent variables and directed edges to show causal relationships. Each node's CPT defines its probability distribution based on the states of its parent nodes. The essence of BNs lies in utilizing Bayes' theorem to update probabilities, considering dependencies only between a node and its immediate predecessors.*

Prior probability reflects the likelihood of events based on historical data or subjective assessments. Conditional probability, represented as $P(A|B)$, measures the probability of event A occurring if B has already happened [10]. It is calculated by the formula $P(A|B) = \frac{P(A \cap B)}{P(B)}$. Marginal probability, which is derived from joint probabilities, simplifies distributions by aggregating over non-essential variables. This can be achieved through summation for discrete variables or integration for continuous ones. For example, the marginal probabilities of events A and B are denoted as $P(A)$ and $P(B)$. The joint probability of multiple independent variables is given by:

$$P(x_1, x_2, ..., x_n) = p(x_1)p(x_2|x_1)p(x_3|x_1, x_2)...p(x_n|x_n - 1...x_1). \quad (1)$$

$Parents(X_i)$ denotes the set of parents of X_i, then it can be expressed as,

$$P(x_1, x_2, ..., x_n) = P(x_i | \prod_{i=1}^{n} Parents(X_i)). \quad (2)$$

2.2 Generalized Possibilistic Kripke Structures

Definition 2. *(see [16,29]) A GPKS is a tuple $M = (S, P, I, AP, L)$, where*

1) *S is a countable, nonempty set of states;*
2) *$P : S \times S \to [0, 1]$ is a function, called possibilistic transition distribution function;*
3) *$I : S \to [0, 1]$ is a function, called possibilistic initial distribution function;*
4) *AP is a set of atomic propositions;*
5) *$L : S \times AP \to [0, 1]$ is a possibilistic labeling function, which can be viewed as a function mapping a state s to the fuzzy set of atomic propositions, which are possible in the state s, i.e., $L(s, a)$ denotes the possibility or truth value of atomic proposition a that is supposed to hold in s.*
   Furthermore, if the set S and AP are finite sets, then $M = (S, P, I, AP, L)$ is called a finite GPKS.

2.3 Generalized Possibilistic Computation Tree Logic

Definition 3. *(Syntax of GPoCTL) [17] GPoCTL state formulas over the set AP of atomic propositions are formed according to the following grammar,*

$$\Phi ::= true | a | \Phi_1 \wedge \Phi_2 | \neg \Phi | Po(\varphi).$$

Where $a \in AP$, φ is a GPoCTL path formula. GPoCTL path formulas are formed according to the following grammar:

$$\varphi ::= \bigcirc \Phi | \Phi_1 \sqcup \Phi_2 | \Phi_1 \sqcup^{\leq n} \Phi_2 | \square \Phi.$$

Where Φ, Φ_1 and Φ_2 are state formulas, and $n \in \mathbb{N}$.

Definition 4. *(Semantics of GPoCTL) [17] Let $a \in AP$ be an atomic proposition, $M = (S, P, I, AP, L)$ be a GPKS, state $s \in S$, Φ, Ψ be GPoCTL state formulas, and φ be a GPoCTL path formula. Let $Paths(M)$ denote the set of all paths in M, for $\pi \in Paths(M)$ as follows:*

$$\|\bigcirc \Phi\|(\pi) = \|\Phi\|(\pi[1]). \tag{3}$$

$$\|\Phi \sqcup \Psi\|(\pi) = \bigvee_{j \geq 0}((\bigwedge_{k<j} \|\Phi\|(\pi[k])) \wedge \|\Psi\|(\pi[j]))). \tag{4}$$

$$\|\Box \Phi\|(\pi) = \bigwedge_{i=0}^{\infty} \|\Phi\|(\pi([i]). \tag{5}$$

Alternatively, $\Diamond \Phi = true \sqcup \Phi$.

$$\|\Diamond \Phi\|(\pi) = \bigvee_{j=0}^{\infty} \bigwedge_{k \leq j} P(\pi[k-1], \pi[k]) \wedge \|\Phi\|(\pi[j]). \tag{6}$$

3 Pathological Diagnosis Based on Bayesian Network

In this section, we discuss the use of BN to create a broadly applicable etiological diagnostic model for identifying causes, from foundational theory to practical applications. BN provides a structure for handling uncertainty in clinical medicine, improving the accuracy of medical decisions amid complex data.

3.1 Bayesian Network Design

In developing an etiological diagnostic model, the process starts with designing a network structure that connects symptoms to their causes. This involves:

1. Define Variables: Select and define the variables, including potential causes (diseases) and observable symptoms.
2. Identify Nodes: Each variable becomes a node in the Bayesian network, with cause nodes as parents to symptom nodes, illustrating cause-effect relationships.
3. Create Directed Edges: Connect nodes with directed edges to represent dependencies, and use arrows from causes to symptoms to indicate potential effects.
4. Determine Prior Probabilities: Establish initial probabilities for each disease based on its prevalence or specific risk factors, regardless of symptoms.
5. Establishing Variable Dependencies and CPT: To build an etiological diagnostic model, start by identifying the connections between diseases and symptoms. Then, create CPTs to display the probability distributions for these relationships, based on historical data, clinical insights, or expert opinions.
6. Compute the Posterior Probability:
   (a) Observed Symptoms: based on the actual symptom profile of the patient, the status of the observed symptoms is determined, i.e., the values of the individual symptom nodes are determined.

(b) Calculate the posterior probability of each etiology: For each possible etiology, the posterior probability is calculated using Bayes' theorem. For each etiological node B_i, its posterior probability $P(B_i|E)$ can be calculated by the following formula, where E is the set of events for the symptom:

$$P(B_i|E) = \frac{P(B_i) \times P(E|B_i)}{\Sigma_j P(B_j) \times P(E|B_j)}.$$

$P(B_i)$ is the prior probability of the etiological node B_i; $P(E|B_i)$ is the conditional probability of observing symptom E given etiological agent B_i, which can be obtained from a conditional probability table. The denominator is the joint probability of all possible etiological agents, and it is used to normalize the posterior probability.

(c) Based on the calculated posterior probabilities, the etiology with the highest posterior probability is selected as the final diagnosis.

3.2 Practical Application

First, we define the nodes in the Bayesian network, i.e., the etiological and symptomatic nodes. Disease (D) nodes are Stroke (St), Myasthenia Gravis (M), and Bell's Palsy (B). Symptoms nodes (N) are Facial muscle dysfunction (n_1), Speech difficulties (n_2), and Dry eyes (n_3). As shown in Fig. 2, we need to set the prior probabilities for each etiology. In this context, we adopt the Bayesian BDeu scoring criterion [30], which incorporates a uniform prior distribution. Choosing a uniform prior, also known as an uninformative prior, ensures that the structure learning process begins without any inherent biases towards specific network structures. Next, as part of our analysis, we calculate the posterior probability of observing a particular symptom for each etiology considered in the model. Moreover, we assume that each etiology affects each symptom independently of others, which is a simplifying assumption commonly adopted to facilitate the computational tractability of the BN (Fig. 1).

$$P(St) = P(M) = P(B) = \frac{1}{3}.$$

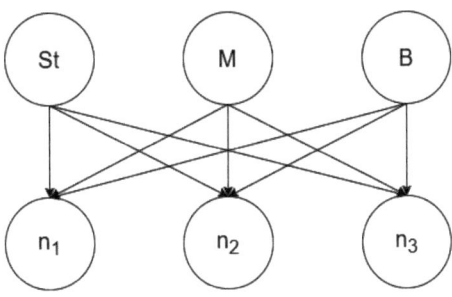

Fig. 1. Bayesian Network Diagram.

The conditional probability table is shown in Table 1.

Table 1. Conditional probability table

etiology	Probability of n_1	Probability of n_2	Probability of n_3
M	60%	20%	70%
St	70%	80%	30%
B	90%	30%	50%

The CPT listed above probability values are based on simulated data.

Calculate the complete joint probability that facial muscle dysfunction and dry eyes occur together for given etiologies:

1. For Myasthenia Gravis, $P(n_1, n_3, M) = P(n_1|M) \times P(n_2|M) \times P(M) = 0.14$.
2. For Stroke, $P(n_1, n_3, St) = P(n_1|St) \times P(n_3|St) \times P(St) = 0.07$.
3. For Bell's Palsy, $P(n_1, n_3, B) = P(n_1|B) \times P(n_3|B) \times P(B) = 0.15$.

Calculate the marginal probability that facial muscle dysfunction and ocular dryness co-occur in all possible etiologies:

$$P(n_1, n_3) = 0.14 + 0.07 + 0.15 = 0.36.$$

Calculate the posterior probability of each particular etiology in the presence of known symptoms:

$$P(M|n_1, n_3) = \frac{P(n_1, n_3, M)}{P(n_1, n_3)} \approx 0.39.$$

$$P(St|n_1, n_3) = \frac{P(n_1, n_3, St)}{P(n_1, n_3)} \approx 0.19.$$

$$P(B|n_1, n_3) = \frac{P(n_1, n_3, B)}{P(n_1, n_3)} \approx 0.42.$$

The results of these calculations suggest that Bell's palsy emerges as the leading candidate when confronted with a patient exhibiting facial muscle dysfunction and experiencing symptoms such as dry eyes. Therefore, we initially considered Bell's palsy as a potential cause of the patient's condition. When combined with the doctor's empirical knowledge, the judgment of the cause of the disease will be more precise.

Algorithm 1: Bayesian Network

Input: The network and evidence E
Output: Posterior probabilities for query variables

1 **for** *each node X in the network* **do**
2   **if** *X has evidence in E* **then**
3   Set $P(X)$ to the observed evidence value
4   **else**
5   Compute initial probability distribution from CPT

6 **for** *each query variable Q* **do**
7   Initialize posterior probability $P(Q|E)$ to some value
8   **while** *not converged* **do**
9   **for** *each node X in the network* **do**
10   Calculate the posterior distribution using CPTs and evidence
11   Update $P(X)$
12   Return the posterior probability for Q

4 Treatment Effect Assessment Based on GPoCTL

In cases where the cause of Bell's palsy is well-understood, accurately monitoring the patient's recovery is essential for effective clinical decision-making. Traditional methods for assessing recovery, which typically rely on linear medical indexes, may not sufficiently capture the dynamic and complex physiological changes during the recovery process.

For assessing rehabilitation, CTL is used to track the patient's recovery trajectory and potential state transitions. By outlining a series of states and the relationships between these states, we develop a model that accurately represents the patient's recovery. We consider not only varying treatment approaches but also individual differences among patients and the effects of factors like treatment duration on recovery outcomes.

Possibility measures are used to quantify the uncertainties in assessing a patient's recovery during rehabilitation, taking into account factors such as the severity of Bell's palsy, treatment effectiveness, and the patient's physical condition. These measures enable a quantitative assessment of recovery, which provides a reliable basis for clinical decisions.

The data for this study, sourced from Kaggle, comprises facial function scores of Bell's palsy patients at different stages, pre-treatment, during treatment, and post-treatment. These stages are crucial for evaluating the effectiveness of the treatment. To validate the accuracy of our model, we use a visualization tool called GPoChecker. By inputting the patient's initial state and treatment plan into the tool, we calculate possibility measures, enabling doctors to make informed assessments of recovery levels based on these metrics.

4.1 Constructing States and Atomic Propositions of GPKS

To evaluate the effectiveness of treatment for Bell's palsy, we first need to construct a GPKS. GPKS can introduce possibility measures to quantify the uncertainty of these transfers, and for each of the two different medications we will construct different GPKS for each of the two different medications.

The GPKS for treatment with only prednisone medication is shown below.

1. State:$S_0 - S_{11}$. Where S_0 is before the start of treatment, S_1, S_2, S_3, S_4, S_5 is the early stage of treatment, S_6, S_7, S_8 is the middle stage of treatment and S_9, S_{10}, S_{11} is the late stage of treatment.
2. $Po{:}S \times S \to [0, 1]$.
3. $I{:}S \to [0, 1]$.
4. $AP = \{SoF, TS, RP\}$
5. $L{:}S \times AP \to [0, 1]$.

The GPKS for acyclovir-only drug therapy is shown below.

1. State:$S_0 - S_{13}$. Where S_0 is before the start of treatment, S_1, S_2, S_3, S_4, S_5 is the early stage of treatment, S_6, S_7, S_8, S_9 is the middle stage of treatment and $S_{10}, S_{11}, S_{12}, S_{13}$ is the late stage of treatment.
2. Po, I, AP, L:Consistent with the definition of prednisone.

These states delineate the different phases of the patient's treatment process, encompassing pre-treatment, early treatment, mid-treatment, and late treatment stages. In the construction of the GPKS, the atomic propositions are defined as follows: SeverityOfFacialImpairment (SoF) for facial disorder severity, TreatmentStage (TS) for the treatment timeline, and RecoveryPotential (RP) for the potential for recovery. These propositions are assigned values based on specific criteria:

1. SoF:Reflects the severity of the patient's impaired facial function.
2. TS:The early, intermediate to late stages of treatment are rationally classified, reflecting the time dimension of treatment progression.
3. RP:The potential for a patient's recovery is influenced by the severity of facial impairment and the length of treatment. The possibility of returning to a healthy state is higher early in treatment, even with less severe impairment, and decreases over time, regardless of whether the impairment worsens. This highlights the importance of early treatment and ongoing assessment.

These atomic propositions form a quantitative framework for analyzing the patient's treatment and recovery processes. Each proposition is clearly defined, enhancing its relevance and usefulness in both medical research and clinical practice. The atomic proposition RP is especially crucial as it directly correlates with the overall effectiveness of the treatment and serves as a vital metric for evaluating the success of long-term treatment strategies. Consequently, physicians can more precisely monitor and forecast the treatment's specific impact on the patient's recovery trajectory (Tables 2 and 3).

Table 2. The significance represented by the possibility values of SoF.

Possibility values	Significance
SoF=0	House-Brackmann scale is 1
SoF=0.2	House-Brackmann scale is 2
SoF=0.4	House-Brackmann scale is 3
SoF=0.6	House-Brackmann scale is 4
SoF=0.8	House-Brackmann scale is 5
SoF=1	House-Brackmann scale is 6

Table 3. The significance represented by the possibility values of TS.

Possibility values	Significance
TS=0.1	Before the start of treatment
TS=0.2	Beginning of treatment, at the first rating
TS=0.5	Mid-treatment, at the second rating
TS=1	Late in treatment, at the third rating

4.2 Calculating GPKS

By calculating the proportions of associations between states, combined with the application of a logarithmic mapping method, these proportions are transformed into the possibility of transfer between states. This step helps us to more accurately capture trends in patient state changes and provides strong data support for subsequent research and medical decision-making.

The logarithmic mapping formula $\pi = log_{10}(1+9 \times p)$ is used to enhance the impact of low proportions of events in the model. This approach is particularly important for dealing with events with low proportions and high variability that are common in medical data, where patients have a high possibility of recovery even if the current proportion is small.

This mapping not only amplifies the impact of these events but also improves the model's sensitivity to subtle differences in treatment effects, allowing it to more accurately capture changes in the treatment process. This rule is more sensitive as the ratio approaches 0 and 1, as it amplifies changes around these extreme values.

The mapping ensures that when the ratio is 1, the possibility also maps exactly to 1, allowing for more accurate treatment of extreme cases. At the same time, this mapping strictly limits the possibility to the range of 0 to 1, making the mapping results more consistent with the range of possibility measures.

In the next step, we calculate the logarithmic mapping result corresponding to the prednisone drug, illustrated only by the state to which S_0 is transferred,

$$Pr(S_0, S_1) = \frac{24}{123} \approx 0.195,$$

$$Po(S_0, S_1) = log_{10}(1 + 9 \times 0.195) \approx 0.440.$$
$$Pr(S_0, S_2) = \frac{35}{123} \approx 0.285,$$
$$Po(S_0, S_2) = log_{10}(1 + 9 \times 0.285) \approx 0.552.$$
$$Pr(S_0, S_3) = \frac{40}{123} \approx 0.325,$$
$$Po(S_0, S_3) = log_{10}(1 + 9 \times 0.325) \approx 0.594.$$

These calculations allow us to quantify the possibilities of transiting each state and thus assess the effects of different treatment stages. For the atomic propositions associated with each state, we define the possibilities labeling function L, which provides the possibilities of a particular state on a given atomic proposition.

For example, state S_1 ($SoF = 0.2$, $TS = 0.2$) means that $L(S_1, SoF) = 0.2, L(S_1, TS) = 0.2$.

4.3 Model Checking and Validation of Propositions

With Sect. 4.2, we have obtained the transition possibilities for both GPKS models. Using the results of these calculations, propositions about treatment effects can be further validated. Knowing the possibilities that a particular adverse outcome will not eventually occur is crucial for developing strategies and contingencies in the medical decision-making process.

Proposition $Po(\Diamond RP)$: Calculate the possibilities that a patient's facial function will return to an unimpaired state at the next time point from the current state.

We have obtained the GPKS model and associated proposition, which will now be validated using the GPoChecker model checking instrument (Figs. 2, 3, 4, 5 and Tables 4, 5).

For ease of calculation, the transfer matrix is kept to a maximum of two decimals, and a measure of future possibilities for each state is calculated using GPoChecker. In the case of prednisone-only medication, the possibilities of eventual recovery, $Po(\Diamond RP)$, is high in stages S_1 to S_5, ranging from 0.91 to 0.95, indicating that at the beginning of the treatment period, the patient's possibilities of recovery is high. The possibilities of recovery in stage S_6 is 1.00, indicating that the patient's possibilities of a full recovery is extremely high at this stage. In stages S_7 to S_{11}, excluding S_9, which is a full recovery, the possibilities of recovery decrease from 0.87 to 0.70, suggesting that the possibilities of recovery decrease as the treatment enters the later stages. From a long-term perspective, prednisone medication is superior to acyclovir and in the middle and late stages of treatment, acyclovir medication does not have an excellent effect in patients with a relatively severe degree of facial impairment. However, in the short term, acyclovir medication is more effective than prednisone and the possibility of the final recovery potential for mildly ill patients using acyclovir medication is better than that of prednisone. In fact, according to the literature [31] we can tell

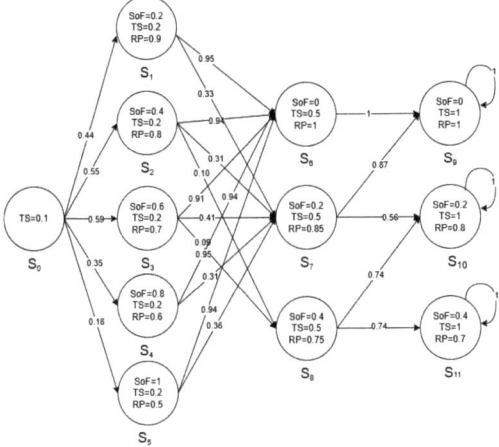

Fig. 2. Patients' GPKS (Prednisone).

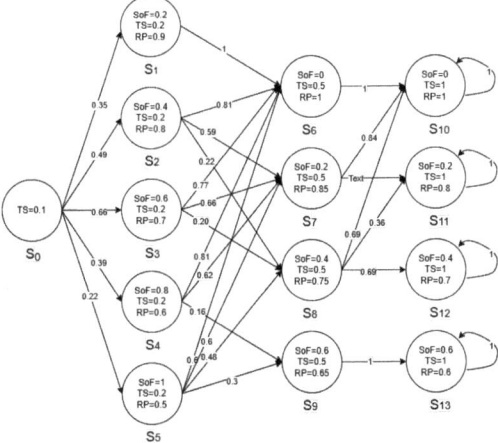

Fig. 3. Patients' GPKS (Acyclovir).

that prednisone is indeed superior to acyclovir in the treatment of Bell's palsy and prednisone has better long-term effects, which is consistent with the results obtained from the possibility model checking, so the model can be considered valid.

Through possibility model checking, we can see that the combination of the two is more effective in patients with less severe facial disorders, and it is the use of acyclovir in the first period and prednisone in the second period. Treatment plans can be customized based on each patient's possibility measures at different points in time, ensuring that each patient receives the most appropriate treatment for their condition. In addition, systematic comparisons of the effectiveness

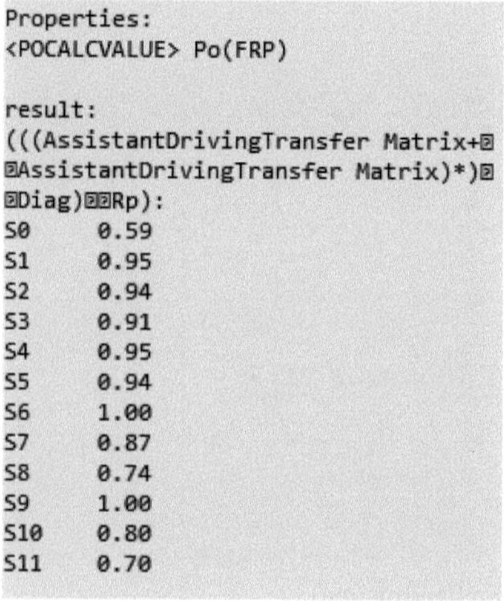

```
Properties:
<POCALCVALUE> Po(FRP)

result:
(((AssistantDrivingTransfer Matrix+?
?AssistantDrivingTransfer Matrix)*)?
?Diag)??Rp):
S0      0.59
S1      0.95
S2      0.94
S3      0.91
S4      0.95
S5      0.94
S6      1.00
S7      0.87
S8      0.74
S9      1.00
S10     0.80
S11     0.70
```

Fig. 4. Output result 1 (Prednisone).

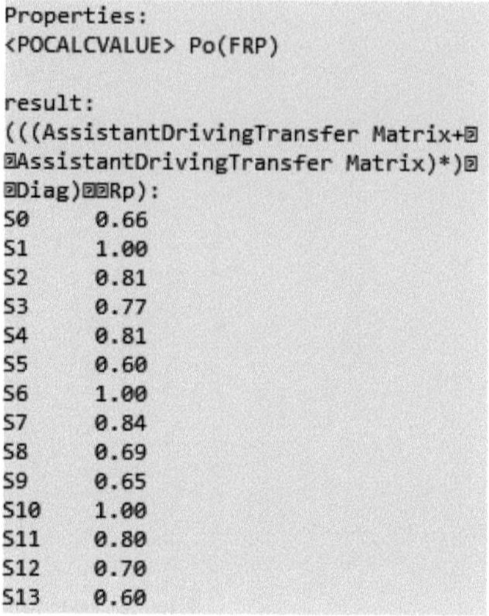

```
Properties:
<POCALCVALUE> Po(FRP)

result:
(((AssistantDrivingTransfer Matrix+?
?AssistantDrivingTransfer Matrix)*)?
?Diag)??Rp):
S0      0.66
S1      1.00
S2      0.81
S3      0.77
S4      0.81
S5      0.60
S6      1.00
S7      0.84
S8      0.69
S9      0.65
S10     1.00
S11     0.80
S12     0.70
S13     0.60
```

Fig. 5. Output result 2 (Acyclovir).

Table 4. Output results(Prednisolone).

	S_0	S_1	S_2	S_3	S_4	S_5	S_6	S_7	S_8	S_9	S_{10}	S_{11}
$Po(\Diamond RP)$	0.59	0.95	0.94	0.91	0.95	0.94	1.00	0.87	0.74	1.00	0.80	0.70

Table 5. Output results(Acyclovir).

	S_0	S_1	S_2	S_3	S_4	S_5	S_6	S_7	S_8	S_9	S_{10}	S_{11}	S_{12}	S_{13}
$Po(\Diamond RP)$	0.66	1.00	0.81	0.77	0.81	0.60	1.00	0.84	0.69	0.65	1.00	0.80	0.70	0.60

of different treatments can help medical researchers and drug developers understand the long-term effects and potential directions for improvement of various treatments.

5 Conclusions

This study successfully applies Bayesian networks to the medical diagnostic process to achieve an accurate determination of the cause of the disease. It demonstrates the excellent ability of Bayesian network to handle complex medical data. Based on the determined etiology, this study introduces the concept of possibility measures in model checking into the treatment process to support the real-time adjustment of clinical decision-making and meticulously assess the effects of drugs in treatment.

Acknowledgments. This work was partially supported by National Science Foundation of China (Grant Nos: 12071271,11671244) and the Shaanxi Fundamental Science Research Project for Mathematics and Physics (Grant Number: 23JSZ011). The author would like to thank Prof. Li for his guidance and help. Useful suggestions given by Dr. Qing He and Dr. Wuniu Liu are also acknowledged.

References

1. Debbi, H., Bourahla, M., Debbi, A.: Medical treatment analysis using probabilistic model checking. Int. J. Biomed. Eng. Technol. **12**(4), 346–359 (2013)
2. Robert, C.P.: The Bayesian Choice: From Decision-theoretic Foundations to Computational Implementation, 2nd edn. Springer, New York (2007)
3. Fenton, N., Neil, M.: Risk Assessment and Decision Analysis with Bayesian Networks. CRC Press, Taylor & Francis Group, Boca Raton, FL (2013)
4. Marcot, B.G., Penman, T.D.: Advances in Bayesian network modelling: integration of modelling technologies. Environ. Model. Softw. **111**, 386–393 (2019)
5. Dlamini, W.M.: A Bayesian belief network analysis of factors influencing wildfire occurrence in Swaziland. Environ. Model. Softw. **25**(2), 199–208 (2010)
6. Sperotto, A., Molina, J.-L., Torresan, S., Critto, A., Marcomini, A.: Reviewing Bayesian networks potentials for climate change impacts assessment and management: a multi-risk perspective. J. Environ. Manage. **202**, 320–331 (2017)
7. Giordano, R., D'Agostino, D., Apollonio, C., Lamaddalena, N., Vurro, M.: Bayesian belief network to support conflict analysis for groundwater protection: the case of the Apulia region. J. Environ. Manage. **115**, 136–146 (2013)
8. Carta, J.A., Velázquez, S., Matías, J.M.: Use of Bayesian networks classifiers for long-term mean wind turbine energy output estimation at a potential wind energy conversion site. Energy Convers. Manage. **52**(2), 1137–1149 (2011)
9. Cai, B., Huang, L., Xie, M.: Bayesian networks in fault diagnosis. IEEE Trans. Industr. Inf. **13**(5), 2227–2240 (2017)
10. Lu, X., Xu, C., Hou, B., Du, X., Li, L.: Risk assessment of metro construction based on dynamic Bayesian network. Chin. J. Geotech. Eng. **44**(3), 492–501 (2022)
11. Zadeh, L.A.: Fuzzy sets. Inf. Control **8**(3), 338–353 (1965)
12. Zadeh, L.A.: Fuzzy sets as a basis for a theory of possibility. Fuzzy Sets Syst. **1**(1), 3–28 (1978)
13. Baier, C., Katoen, J.-P.: Principles of Model Checking. The MIT Press, Cambridge (2008)
14. Grumberg, O., Clarke, E.M., Peled, D.A.: Model checking. In: International Conference on Foundations of Software Technology and Theoretical Computer Science. Springer, Berlin (1999)
15. Li, Y.: Analysis of Fuzzy Systems (in Chinese). Science Press, Beijing (2005)
16. Li, Y., Li, L.: Model checking of linear-time properties based on possibility measure. IEEE Trans. Fuzzy Syst. **21**(5), 842–854 (2013)
17. Li, Y., Ma, Z.: Quantitative computation tree logic model checking based on generalized possibility measures. IEEE Trans. Fuzzy Syst. **23**(6), 2034–2047 (2015)
18. Li, Y.: Quantitative model checking of linear-time properties based on generalized possibility measures. Fuzzy Sets Syst. **320**, 17–39 (2017)
19. Li, Y., Droste, M., Lei, L.: Model checking of linear-time properties in multi-valued systems. Inf. Sci. **377**, 51–74 (2017)
20. Ma, Z., Li, Y.: Model checking generalized possibilistic computation tree logic based on decision processes. Sci. China Inf. Sci. **46**(11), 1591–1607 (2016)

21. Pan, H., Li, Y., Cao, Y., Ma, Z.: Model checking fuzzy computation tree logic. Fuzzy Sets Syst. **262**, 60–77 (2015)
22. Liu, W., Li, Z., Li, Y.: Complex objective optimization in fuzzy environments. J. Intell. Fuzzy Syst. **45**(2), 3539–3553 (2023)
23. Liu, W., Li, Z., Li, Y.: "Quantum reachability games." IEEE Trans. Emerg. Top. Comput. Intell. (2024). https://doi.org/10.1109/TETCI.2024.3419704
24. Li, Y., Liu, W., Wang, J., Yu, X., Li, C.: Model checking of possibilistic linear-time properties based on generalized possibilistic decision processes. IEEE Trans. Fuzzy Syst. **31**(10), 3495–3506 (2023)
25. Liu, W., He, Q., Li, Y.: Computation tree logic model checking over possibilistic decision processes under finite-memory scheduler. In: National Conference of Theoretical Computer Science, Springer, pp. 75–88 (2021)
26. Liu, W., He, Q., Li, Z., Li, Y.: Self-learning modeling in possibilistic model checking. IEEE Trans. Emerg. Top. Comput. Intell. **8**(1), 264–278 (2024)
27. Liu, W., Li, Y.: Optimal strategy model checking in possibilistic decision processes. IEEE Trans. Syst. Man, Cybern. Syst. **53**(10), 6620–6632 (2023)
28. Liu, W., Wang, J., He, Q., Li, Y.: Model checking computation tree logic over multi-valued decision processes and its reduction techniques. Chin. J. Electron. **34**, 1–13 (2024)
29. Kripke, S.A.: Semantical considerations on modal logic. Acta Philosophica Fennica **16** (1963)
30. Chickering, D.M.: Optimal structure identification with greedy search. J. Mach. Learn. Res. **3**(Nov), 507–554 (2002)
31. Quant, E.C., Jeste, S.S., Muni, R.H., Cape, A.V., Bhussar, M.K., Peleg, A.Y.: The benefits of steroids versus steroids plus antivirals for treatment of Bell's palsy: a meta-analysis. BMJ **339**, b3354 (2009). https://doi.org/10.1136/bmj.b3354

Artificial Intelligence Theory and Algorithm

A Triple-Branch Frequency-Aware Network for Image Manipulation Detection

Wenyan Pan[1], Zhihua Xia[2(✉)], and Jiaohua Qin[3]

[1] School of Computer Science, Nanjing University of Information Science and Technology, Nanjing 210044, China
[2] College of Cyber Security, Jinan University, Guangzhou 510632, China
xia_zhihua@163.com
[3] College of Computer Science and Information Technology, Central South University of Forestry and Technology, Changsha 410004, China

Abstract. The goal of Image Manipulation Detection (IMD) is to identify and locate manipulated regions within images. Recent approaches have primarily designed sophisticated neural networks to capture high-frequency information for IMD tasks. However, these methods often overemphasize high-frequency information while overlooking the important role of low-frequency information in IMD tasks. To address this issue, we propose a Triple-Branch Frequency-Aware Network (TFNet), which includes an Information Separation Module (ISM), a Main Steam Branch (MSB), a Low-Frequency Learning Branch (LFL), a High-Frequency Learning Branch (HFL), and an Adaptive Aggregate Module (AAM) within a unified framework. Specifically, TFNet initially employs FSM to separate the manipulated image into RGB, high-frequency, and low-frequency components. Then, MSB, LFB, and HFB take the above components as input to learn the distinct features. Furthermore, the HFB is supervised with the boundary information to encourage the network to focus on the high-frequency information. Finally, the outputs of MSB, LFB, and HFB are sent to the ABM to adaptively aggregate features learned from the MSB, LFB, and HFB. Experiments on the CASIA, NIST, and Coverage datasets demonstrate the effectiveness of our TFNet.

Keywords: Image manipulation detection · frequency information

1 Introduction

Recently, determining the authenticity of images has become increasingly challenging. With the availability of powerful image editing tools, malicious users can easily manipulate digital images without leaving obvious traces. Common image manipulation operations usually modify the image content by adopting several operations, *i.e.*, copy-move, splicing, and removal. As a result, IMD has received considerable attention as an effective way to determine image authenticity.

Traditional IMD methods primarily extract handcrafted features to locate manipulated regions, including Color Filter Array (CFA) [1], Discrete Cosine Transform (DCT) [2], and Color Features [3]. While these approaches have achieved impressive performance, they are limited by their manually designed feature extraction algorithms. Consequently, these methods are effective for specific types of manipulation operations.

To address the limitations of traditional IMD methods [1–5], recent efforts have focused on designing sophisticated neural networks to automatically learn features for IMD. These approaches can be broadly divided into two categories. For the first category, some methods have demonstrated that exploring the high-frequency information is effective for IMD, therefore, they usually design a unique module to encourage the model to focus on the high-frequency information. Another category uses the manipulated image from different spaces, such as RGB, YCbCr, or other domains, allowing the network to learn the features of different domains to accurately locate the manipulated regions. However, these methods tend to be high-frequency sensitive and often overlook low-frequency information, which may contain crucial clues for identifying manipulated regions.

To address this problem, we propose a Triple-Branch Frequency-Aware Network (TFNet) for image manipulation detection, which consists of three parallel branches: the Main Steam Branch (MSB), the Low-Frequency Learning Branch (LFL), and the High-Frequency Learning Branch (HFL), along with Information Separation Module (ISM) and Adaptive Aggregate Module (AAM). Specifically, to fully exploit the different information of the manipulated image, we first sent the image into FSM to separate the image into RGB, high-frequency, and low-frequency components, which are then fed into MSB, HFL, and LFL, respectively. Moreover, the HFL is supervised by the boundary information of the manipulated regions to ensure high-frequency learning. Moreover, to effectively aggregate the different information learned from the MSB, HFL, and LFL, the ABM is proposed to adaptively aggregate information from different spaces to obtain power features. Experiments on the CASIA, NIST, and Coverage datasets demonstrate that our TFNet achieves performance comparable to existing methods. The contributions of this work can be outlined as follows:

- We develop a novel TFNet for IMD tasks, which learns the information from the RGB, high-frequency, and low-frequency information by the MSB, HFL, and LFL. This design effectively alleviates the problem of overlooking low-frequency information in previous methods and achieves accurate performance in locating manipulated regions.
- We design an Information Separation Module (ISM) and Adaptive Aggregate Module (AAM) to encourage the network to learn different features respectively, and adaptively aggregate different information to learn powerful features.
- By training our model on the training set of various used CASIA, NIST, and Coverage, and evaluating the performance on the test set, we achieve better performance compared to previous methods.

2 Related Work

2.1 Image Manipulation Detection

In early work, the image manipulation detection approaches usually extract handcraft-ed features, such as Color Filter Array (CFA) [1], Discrete Cosine Transform (DCT) [2], and Color Features [3], to capture the tampering traces left in the images for localizing the manipulated regions.

Specifically, Jaiprakash et al. [4] proposed an approach to extract the features from image statistics and the correlation of image pixels in DCT and DWT domains for image manipulation detection. Popescu et al. [5] proposed the CFA-based model to analyze the statistical characteristics introduced by the filter array patterns of different cameras for identifying manipulated images. Hadwiger et al. [3] proposed a novel type of cue based on the color information of an image for image splicing detection.

However, the handcrafted features can only capture the traces caused by one or several certain tampering operations, leading to the limited generalization ability of these approaches.

To improve the accuracy and generalization ability of handcrafted feature-based approaches, a research area currently receiving substantial interest across image manipulation detection is deep learning. Some approaches explore sophisticated CNNs to automatically learn the tampering trace features for image manipulation detection. Some other approaches suppress the image content to facilitate the extraction of tampering trace features.

Specifically, Salloum et al. [6] utilized a fully convolutional network (FCN) to localize manipulated regions. Zhou et al. [7] proposed a two-stream network called RGB-N, which pays more attention to the noise feature, to locate the manipulated regions. Li et al. [8] extended the RGB-N, which combines the Convolutional Block Attention Module (CBAM) and SRM to learn the manipulation trace features for image manipulation detection. Hu et al. [9] used self-attention to explore the long-range relation to locate manipulated regions. Liu et al. [10] proposed a densely connected network to fully explore the multi-scale feature for IMD tasks.

Although these approaches generally outperform the handcrafted feature-based approaches, they tend to be high-frequency sensitive and often overlook low-frequency information, which may contain crucial clues for identifying manipulated regions. Thus, there is still a large room for performance improvement.

3 Proposed Method

This section introduces the proposed network architecture for IMD, called TFNet, which consists of three parallel branches: the Main Steam Branch (MSB), the Low-Frequency Learning Branch (LFL), and the High-Frequency Learning Branch (HFL), along with the Information Separation Module (ISM) and the Adaptive Aggregate Module (AAM). The overall architecture of TFNet is shown in Fig. 1. Each branch is described in detail below.

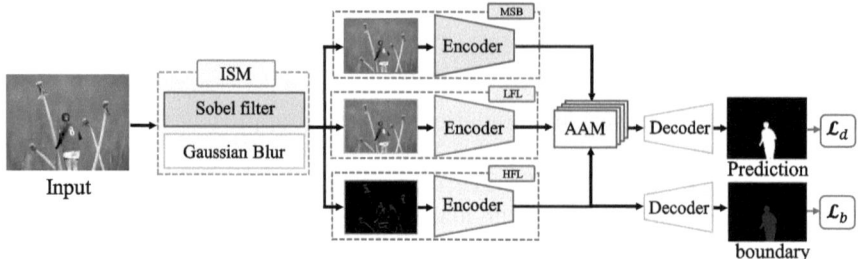

Fig. 1. The architecture of proposed TFNet.

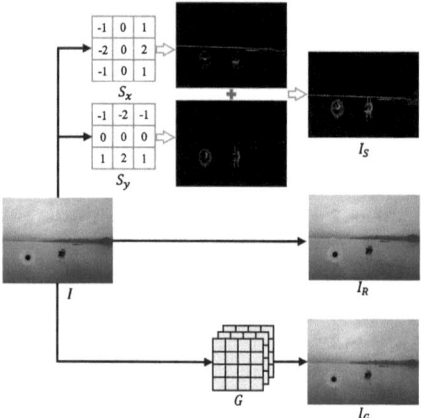

Fig. 2. The architecture of proposed ISM.

3.1 Information Separation Module (ISM)

The goal of the Information Separation Module (ISM) is to separate the information from the manipulated image into different components, including RGB, high-frequency, and low-frequency components. To achieve this goal, given I as the input image, we first apply the Sobel filter to filter out the low-frequency component of the image as shown in Fig. 2. This is achieved by separately detecting the horizontal and vertical boundaries along an image. The Sobel filter adopts two 3 × 3 convolution kernels (S_x and S_y) in both the horizontal and vertical directions by measuring the two-dimensional spatial gradient on an image. The S_x calculates the spatial gradient in the horizontal direction while the S_y calculates the spatial gradient in the vertical direction. Finally, the information of two directions is added together to generate I_s, which can be formulated as

$$I_s = I \cdot S_x + I \cdot S_y, \tag{1}$$

where · is the two-dimensional signal processing convolution operation.

Moreover, in order to preserve the low-frequency information of the image, we further adopt the Gaussian blur to filter the high-frequency information as

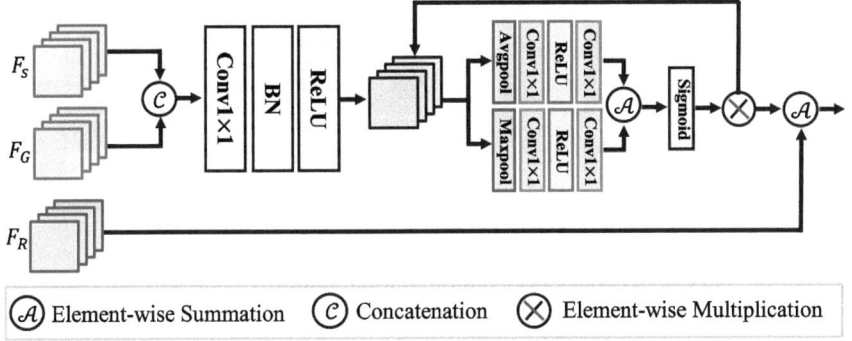

Fig. 3. The architecture of proposed AAM.

shown in Fig. 2. Formally, we adopt a Gaussian filter G with 3×3 kernels to process the image I, and obtain the I_G. To this end, the ISM is able to separate the image I into I_S, I_G, and I_R (the image I in the RGB domain), which are sent to the HFL, LFL, and MSB, respectively.

3.2 Triple Branches Architecture

The triple branches, *i.e.*, Main Steam Branch (MSB), Low-Frequency Learning Branch (LFL), and the High-Frequency Learning Branch (HFL), aim to learn the distinct feature from different aspects. As shown in Fig. 1. the triple parallel branches take the I_S, I_G, and I_R as input, and learn the different features F_s, F_G, and F_R. Here, $F_S = \{f_{S1}, f_{S2}, f_{S3}, f_{S4}\}$, $F_G = \{f_{G1}, f_{G2}, f_{G3}, f_{G4}\}$, and $F_R = \{f_{R1}, f_{R2}, f_{R3}, f_{R4}\}$ are the multi-scale features with a size of $\{1/4, 1/8, 1/16, 1/32\}$ of the original image resolution. Then the F_S, F_G, and F_R are sent to the AAM for further processing. Moreover, to supervise the F_s learning, the F_s is sent to another encoder to calculate loss with boundary information.

3.3 Adaptive Aggregate Module (AAM)

Since features F_S, F_G, and F_R represent different information of the manipulated image. To better use the above information as effectively as possible, we design an Adaptive Aggregate Module (AAM) to aggregate F_S, F_G, and F_R adaptively. The architecture of AAM is shown in Fig. 3. For the input F_S, F_G, and F_R, we first fuse the F_S, F_G by the concatenation operation along the channel dimension. Then, the concatenated feature is sent to a convolutional layer with 1×1 kernel, a batch normalization layer, and a ReLU activation function. The above operation can be formulated as

$$X = \text{Conv}_{1\times1}(\text{BN}(\text{ReLU}(\text{cat}\,(F_S; F_G)))), \tag{2}$$

Fig. 4. Some toy examples of manipulated images.

where $\text{Conv}_{1\times 1}$ is a convolution with 1×1 kernel. BN is the batch normalization layer. ReLU is the ReLU activation function. Then, X is sent to the two branches to generate the weighted matrix M, which can be calculated by

$$M = \text{Sum}\left(\text{Conv}_{1\times 1}(\text{BN}(\text{ReLU}(\text{Avg}(X)))); \text{Conv}_{1\times 1}(\text{BN}(\text{ReLU}(\text{Max}(X)))))\right), \quad (3)$$

where Avg and Max denote the Average pooling and Max pooling layer. The Sum denotes the element-wise summation, and the Sigmoid is the Sigmoid activation function. After obtaining the weighted matrix M, the output of AAM can be calculated by

$$F = \text{Sigmoid}(M) \otimes X \oplus F_R, \quad (4)$$

where the F is the output of the AAM, $\otimes$ denotes element-wise multiplication and the $\oplus$ denotes element-wise summation.

3.4 Training Objectives

The learned F is sent to the decoder to generate the final prediction P. Meanwhile, to supervise F_S, the F_S is sent to the decoder to generate the boundary prediction P_b. Hence, the overall loss function of our model consists of two parts: the boundary loss $\mathcal{L}_b$ and the detection loss $\mathcal{L}_d$, where the $\mathcal{L}_b$ is used to supervise the F_S, and the $\mathcal{L}_d$ is used to supervise the entire model training. The overall loss function can be defined as follows:

$$\mathcal{L}_{all} = \mathcal{L}_b(P_b, GT_b) + \mathcal{L}_d(P, GT), \quad (5)$$

where the $\mathcal{L}_d$ and $\mathcal{L}_b$ hybrid loss [11]. GT is the ground-truth mask, GT_b is the boundary ground-truth.

Table 1. F1 score performance comparison of TFNet with other methods.

Methods	Venue	CASIA	NIST	Coverage
RGB-N	CVPR'18	40.8	72.2	43.7
SPAN	ECCV'20	38.2	58.2	55.8
PSCCNet	TCSVT'22	55.4	81.9	72.3
TFNet (ours)	-	**56.3**	**85.0**	**73.5**

Table 2. The ablation study of TFNet.

Methods	F1	mIoU
TFNet	**85.0**	**77.0**
TFNet w/o LFL	84.1	75.8
TFNet w/o HFL	83.8	75.3

4 Experimental Settings

4.1 Datasets

CASIA [12] is a widely used dataset for IMD. It comprises two versions: CASIA1.0 and CASIA2.0. CASIA1.0 contains 921 manipulated images, encompassing splicing and copy-move manipulation operation. CASIA2.0 is a more comprehensive dataset, consisting of 5,123 images, including splicing and copy-move, along with post-processing methods like filtering and blurring. In the training, we utilize CASIA2.0 for training and evaluate the performance of CASIA1.0.

NIST [13] comprises 564 manipulated images with high-resolution, each of which has undergone one of three common manipulation operations: copy-move, splicing, and removal. We chose 404 images for training, and 160 for testing.

Coverage [14] is a small dataset that only contains copy-move manipulated images, and comprises 100 images. We chose 75 images for training, and 25 for testing.

We present some toy examples of different manipulated operations from CASIA, NIST, and Coverage datasets. As can be seen from Fig. 4, the manipulated image is extremely deceptive, which makes it difficult for a model to accurately locate the manipulated regions.

4.2 Competitors

Our model is compared with various methods, including J-LSTM and H-LSTM, RGB-N, SPAN, and PSCCNet, which are introduced below:

RGB-N [7] designs a two-branch network that extracts the feature from the noise in-formation and RGB images to locate the manipulated regions.

SPAN [9] adopts self-attention to capture the long-range relationship within the manipulated image.

Table 3. The robustness performance of TFNet.

Attack	CASIA		NIST		Coverage	
	F1-score	mIoU	F1-score	mIoU	F1-score	mIoU
w/o Attack	56.3	49.5	85.0	77.0	73.5	63.2
Gaussian Blur ($k=3$)	54.0	47.1	84.7	76.7	54.2	43.8
Gaussian Blur ($k=5$)	50.7	43.8	84.1	75.8	45.5	35.5
Gaussian Blur ($k=7$)	46.1	39.3	83.7	75.2	36.9	27.4
Gaussian Noise ($\sigma=3$)	32.4	25.8	78.4	68.7	48.0	37.9
Gaussian Noise ($\sigma=5$)	26.9	20.7	74.3	64.5	46.1	35.8
Gaussian Noise ($\sigma=7$)	26.1	19.6	71.7	61.6	42.1	32.4
JPEG Compression ($q=60$)	23.8	18.4	84.8	76.7	61.5	50.5
JPEG Compression ($q=80$)	34.7	28.3	85.0	77.0	71.7	61.3
JPEG Compression ($q=100$)	52.5	45.8	85.0	77.0	74.4	64.2
Resize ($22\times$)	33.3	26.3	82.5	74.4	33.0	24.2
Resize ($50\times$)	51.3	44.3	84.7	76.6	45.3	35.8
Resize ($78\times$)	53.0	46.1	84.9	76.9	64.1	53.9

PSCCNet [10] designs a dense connection method to fuse different scale features for IMD tasks.

4.3 Implementation Details and Evaluation Metrics

The model is implemented using Pytorch 2.0 with Python 3.8.0 in the Ubuntu 22.04. The training ended after 60K iterations in the CASIA dataset, and was solved after 8K iterations on the NIST and Coverage dataset. The batch size is set to 16. The AdamW optimizer is used in training and the initial learning rate is set to 6×10^{-5} and the weight decay to 10^{-2} following the SegformerB0 [15]. The encoder is chosen as SegformerB0 [15] and the decoder is set to FPN. The training set is processed with data augmentation by the toolbox Albumentation, including flipping, rotating, filling, cropping, and adding Gaussian noise. The input image is 512×512.

Following previous works, we use the F1 score and mIoU (Mean Intersection over Union) for evaluation metrics.

5 Experimental Results and Analysis

5.1 Comparison with Methods

In this section, we conducted a comparison between our TFNet and existing methods on the CASIA, NIST, and Coverage benchmarks. As shown in Table 1, our TFNet exceeds these methods by large margins. For the CASIA dataset,

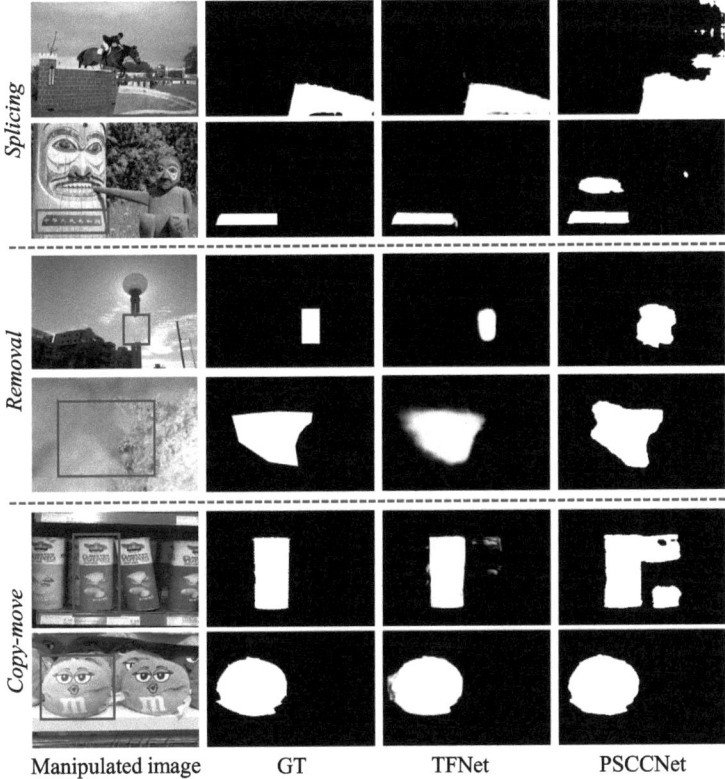

Fig. 5. Qualitative results compare to PSCCNet.

TFNet achieves an impressive F1 of **56.3%**, which is **0.9%** higher than the PSCCNet. In addition, for the NIST dataset, our model outperforms the best PSCCNet with **3.1%** F1. For the Coverage dataset, our model obtains an impressive performance of **73.5%** F1, surpassing PSCCNet **1.2%** F1. These results demonstrate that TFNet is capable of achieving satisfactory results for IMD tasks.

5.2 Ablation Study

In this section, we conduct ablation experiments to verify the effectiveness of each model in the proposed TFNet. Here, we use the NIST dataset to train and evaluate the performance.

As shown in Table 2, we verify the effectiveness of LFL and HFL by removing the modules. It is clearly shown that without LFL, the performance decreases by 0.9%/1.2%. While the model without the HFL, the performance decreases by 1.2%/1.7% in terms of F1 and mIoU, which shows that the high-frequency and low-frequency information is important for IMD tasks.

5.3 Robustness

In real scenarios, images often undergo different attacks, which can cause the model's detection performance to deteriorate. Therefore, the robustness of the model is very important for the stability of the model. In this section, we investigate the robustness of our model against different attacks, including: 1) Gaussian Blurring with kernels $k = 3, 5, 7$; 2) Gaussian Noise with different $\sigma = 3, 5, 7$; 3) JPEG Compression with different quality factors $q = 60, 80, 100$; 4) Resizing of different actors of 0.22, 0.5, and 0.78.

The robustness performance is shown in Table 3. It is clear that our TFNet can handle different attacks, and achieve desirable performance.

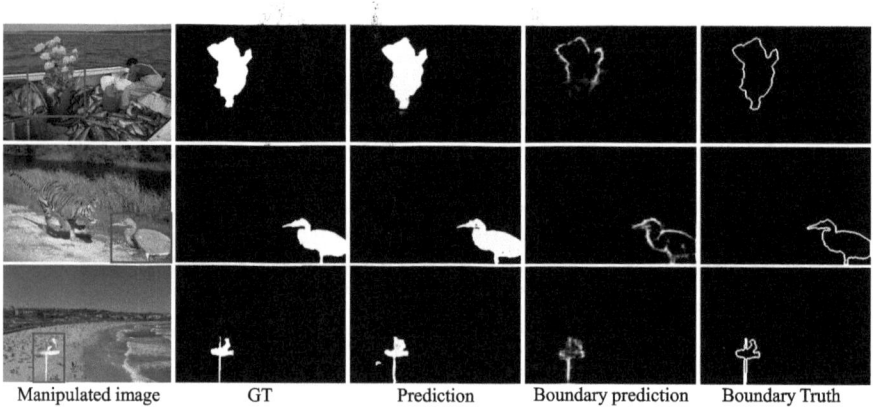

Fig. 6. Qualitative results about boundary information.

5.4 Qualitative Results

To further prove the effectiveness of our TFNet, we present some visualizations. First, we show the qualitative results compared to the PSCCNet in Fig. 5. It is observed from the figure that the prediction of our model is better than PSCCNet with rich details.

Moreover, we also show the qualitative results about the high-frequency information (boundary information) learned by the HFL in Fig. 6. It is clear that our model can detect the boundary information of manipulated regions effectively. The boundary information also benefits the locating of the manipulated regions.

6 Conclusions

In this paper, we proposed TFNet, a novel triple-branch frequency-aware network for IMD tasks. Specifically, our method comprises four models, an Information Separation Module (ISM), a Main Steam Branch (MSB), a Low-Frequency Learning Branch (LFL), a High-Frequency Learning Branch (HFL), and an

Adaptive Aggregate Module (AAM) with-in a unified framework. These models jointly provide a more robust feature, leading to better performance for IMD tasks.

References

1. Ferrara, P., Bianchi, T., De Rosa, A., Piva, A.: Image forgery localization via fine-grained analysis of CFA artifacts. IEEE Trans. Inf. Forensics Secur. **7**(5), 1566–1577 (2012)
2. Chen, B., Yu, M., Su, Q., Li, L.: Fractional quaternion cosine transform and its application in color image copy-move forgery detection. Multimed. Tools Appl. **78**(7), 8057–73 (2019)
3. Hadwiger, B., Baracchi, D., Piva, A., Riess, C.: Towards learned color representations for image splicing detection. In: IEEE International Conference on Acoustics, Speech and Signal Processing, pp. 8281–8285 (2019)
4. Jaiprakash, S.P., Desai, M.B., Prakash, C.S., Mistry, V.H., Radadiya, K.L.: Low dimensional DCT and DWT feature based model for detection of image splicing and copy-move forgery. Multimed. Tools Appl. **79**(39–40), 29977–30005 (2020)
5. Popescu, A.C., Farid, H.: Exposing digital forgeries in color filter array interpolated images. IEEE Trans. Signal Process **53**(10), 3948–3959 (2005)
6. Salloum, R., Ren, Y., Kuo, C.-C.J.: Image splicing localization using a multi-task fully convolutional network (MFCN). J. Vis. Commun. Image Represent. **51**, 201–209 (2018)
7. Zhou, P., Han, X., Morariu, V.I., Davis, L.S.: Learning rich features for image manipulation detection. In: Proceedings of the IEEE Conference on Computer Vision and Pattern Recognition, pp. 1053–1061 (2018)
8. Yang, C., Li, H., Lin, F., Jiang, B., Zhao, H.: Constrained r-CNN: a general image manipulation detection model. In: Proceedings of the IEEE International Conference on Multimedia and Expo, pp. 1–6 (2020)
9. Hu, X., Zhang, Z., Jiang, Z., Chaudhuri, S., Yang, Z., Nevatia, R.: SPAN: spatial pyramid attention network for image manipulation localization. In: Vedaldi, A., Bischof, H., Brox, T., Frahm, J.-M. (eds.) ECCV 2020. LNCS, vol. 12366, pp. 312–328. Springer, Cham (2020). https://doi.org/10.1007/978-3-030-58589-1_19
10. Liu, X., Liu, Y., Chen, J., Liu, X.: PSCC-Net: progressive spatio-channel correlation network for image manipulation detection and localization. IEEE Trans. Circ. Syst. Video Technol. **32**(11), 7505–7517 (2022)
11. Zhou, Z., Siddiquee, M.M.R., Tajbakhsh, N., Liang, J.: UNet++: redesigning skip connections to exploit multiscale features in image segmentation. IEEE Trans. Med. Imaging **39**(6), 1856–1867 (2019)
12. Dong, J., Wang, W., Tan, T.: CASIA image tampering detection evaluation database. In: Proceedings of the IEEE China Summit and International Conference on Signal and Information Processing. pp. 422–426. IEEE (2013)
13. Guan, H., et al.: MFC datasets: large-scale benchmark datasets for media forensic challenge evaluation. In: Proceedings of the IEEE Winter Applications of Computer Vision Workshops, pp. 63–72. IEEE (2019)

14. Wen, B., Zhu, Y., Subramanian, R., Ng, T.-T., Shen, X., Winkler, S.: Coverage-a novel database for copy-move forgery detection. In: Proceedings of the IEEE International Conference on Image Processing. pp. 161–165. IEEE (2016)
15. Xie, E., Wang, W., Yu, Z., Anandkumar, A., Alvarez, J.M., Luo, P.: SegFormer: simple and efficient design for semantic segmentation with transformers. Adv. Neural Inf. Process. Syst. **34**, 12077–12090 (2021)

Advances in Neural Radiance Fields for Large-Scale 3D Scene Reconstruction: A Comprehensive Review

Yu Du[1,2], Fuchun Sun[2(✉)], Xiao Lv[1], and Xian Zhang[1]

[1] School of Electronic Engineering, Naval University of Engineering, Wuhan 430033, Hubei, People's Republic of China
M22385401@nue.edu.cn
[2] Department of Computer Science and Technology, Tsinghua University, Beijing 100084, People's Republic of China
sunfcgl@163.com

Abstract. In the field of 3D reconstruction, there has been a notable shift from traditional Structure-from-Motion methods to Neural Radiance Fields (NeRF). Introduced in 2020, NeRF has quickly gained global attention for its ability to reconstruct complex 3D scenes using only posed 2D images, achieving impressive synthesis results. Its effectiveness, particularly in rendering and synthesizing large-scale scenes, underscores its growing significance. This review examines NeRF's applications and developments in large-scale scene reconstruction over recent years. We explore its specific applications, enhancements, development directions, and performance comparisons among key NeRF models. Our goal is to introduce NeRF to a broader research audience, providing a comprehensive reference for significant work in this field and inspiring future research directions.

Keywords: Neural Radiance Fields · 3D Reconstruction · Large-Scale Scene Synthesis · Novel View Synthesis

1 Introduction

In recent years, Neural Radiance Fields (NeRF) [17] have revolutionized the field of 3D reconstruction and novel view synthesis, offering a powerful method for representing complex scenes using implicit representations learned from 2D images. Since its introduction by Mildenhall et al. in 2020, NeRF has garnered significant attention for its ability to generate photorealistic renderings from sparse input images, showcasing unprecedented detail and accuracy in the reconstruction of 3D environments [17, 18, 31].

NeRF operates by learning a continuous volumetric scene function that maps spatial locations and viewing directions to emitted radiance and density. This implicit representation allows NeRF to synthesize highly realistic novel views, which is particularly advantageous in applications such as virtual reality [23], augmented reality [15], and autonomous driving [21]. However, scaling NeRF to handle large-scale scenes presents unique challenges, including managing memory consumption, computational complexity, and maintaining high fidelity in diverse and expansive environments.

To address these challenges, various innovative techniques have been developed. Hierarchical modeling, multi-resolution feature grids, and adaptive sampling strategies are among the methods proposed to enhance scalability and efficiency. These advancements aim to maintain the high quality of NeRF's reconstructions while extending its applicability to larger and more complex scenes, such as urban environments [9], extensive natural landscapes [16], and intricate indoor settings [19].

Several reviews have previously examined the evolution and applications of NeRF. In 2020, Dellaert and Yen-Chen [3] published a 5-page survey summarizing NeRF papers from 2020 and early 2021. Xie et al. [29] provided a detailed technical description of neural radiance fields for visual computing in their Eurographics 2022 preprint. Tewari et al.'s comprehensive survey on advances in neural rendering [23], published in May 2022, included many influential papers, emphasizing NeRF's role. More recently, Gao et al. [6] updated a summary on arXiv categorizing NeRF papers based on innovative techniques and applications. Zhu et al. [38] reviewed related works, focusing on the main features of NeRF.

Unlike these surveys, our paper focuses specifically on several notable issues regarding the scalability, generalizability, and applicability of NeRF in large-scale scene reconstruction. We summarize existing solutions for these challenges while emphasizing NeRF's significant role in the field of artificial intelligence-generated content (AIGC) in recent years. Our review includes important articles addressing these problems and the most recent works since 2023. Furthermore, we provide predictions about their current and potential future applications.

This review aims to offer a comprehensive overview of the advancements in NeRF technologies for large-scale scene reconstruction, identifying current capabilities, existing limitations, and future research directions. As illustrated in Fig. 1, we will mainly provide an overview from two perspectives: Scalable NeRF Frameworks and Enhancements, and Innovative Techniques and Applications. By doing so, we hope to provide a valuable resource for researchers and practitioners looking to leverage NeRF for large-scale 3D reconstruction and inspire new approaches that push the boundaries of what is possible with neural scene representations.

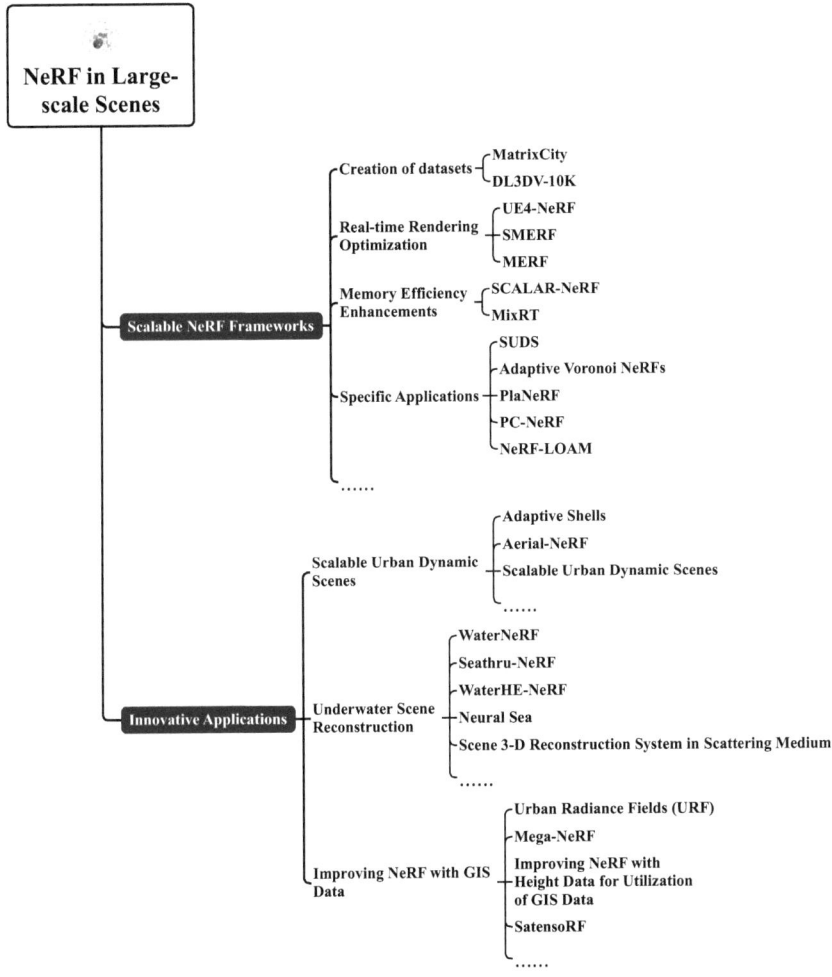

Fig. 1. Overview of NeRF Technologies for Large-Scale 3D Scene Reconstruction.

2 Background

2.1 Neural Radiance Field Theory

Neural Radiance Fields (NeRF) is a novel approach to novel view synthesis introduced by Ben Mildenhall et al. in 2020. It achieves photo-realistic view synthesis using implicit representations. Unlike previous methods, NeRF uses a volumetric approach as an intermediate representation, reconstructing an implicit volume. Its primary contributions include:

– Proposing a 5D neural radiance field method for implicit representations of complex scenes.

- Introducing a differentiable rendering pipeline based on classical volume rendering, with a coarse-to-fine sampling strategy.
- Presenting a positional encoding technique that maps 5D coordinates to high-dimensional space.

Implicit Scene Representation. NeRF represents a scene using a fully connected deep network, where the input is a single continuous 5D coordinate consisting of a spatial location (x, y, z) and viewing direction (θ, ϕ). The output is the volume density and view-dependent emitted radiance at that spatial location.

The algorithm, as illustrated in Fig. 2, can be expressed as follows:

$$F(x, y, z, \theta, \phi) \rightarrow (c, \sigma) \tag{1}$$

where (x, y, z) is the point in the scene's coordinate system, θ and ϕ denote the azimuthal and polar viewing angles, respectively. The variable $c = (r, g, b)$ represents the RGB value of a point on the rendered image, while σ signifies the volumetric density at that point.

In this model, F is an 8-layer MLP network that maps each input 5D coordinate to its corresponding volumetric density and directional emitted color by optimizing the weights of F. To ensure multi-view consistency, the network predicts volumetric density σ as a function of position X only, while allowing RGB color c to be predicted as a function of both position and viewing direction.

The network processes the input 3D coordinate $X = (x, y, z)$ using eight fully connected layers with 256 channels each, outputting σ and a 256-dimensional feature vector. This feature vector is then concatenated with the viewing direction and passed to another fully connected layer (using ReLU activation with 128 channels), which outputs the view-dependent RGB color.

Volumetric Rendering. The 5D neural radiance field represents the scene as a volume density and directional emission radiation at any point in space. After obtaining the volume density and color of the rendered scene through F, classical volume rendering is employed. The color $C(r)$ of the camera ray $r(t) = o + td$ that passes through the scene can be obtained with a camera position o and a viewing direction d. The near and far boundaries of the ray are denoted as t_n and t_f, respectively:

$$C(r) = \int_{t_n}^{t_f} T(t) \sigma(r(t)) c(r(t), d) \, dt \tag{2}$$

$$T(t) = \exp\left(-\int_{t_n}^{t} \sigma(r(s)) \, ds\right) \tag{3}$$

T denotes accumulated transmittance, which signifies the likelihood of a ray propagating from t_n to t without interception. To estimate continuous integration over $[t_n, t_f]$, the interval is divided into N evenly spaced segments, with random sampling within each segment. The equations can then be expressed as:

$$\hat{C}(r) = \sum_{i=1}^{N} T_i (1 - \exp(-\sigma_i \delta_i)) c_i \tag{4}$$

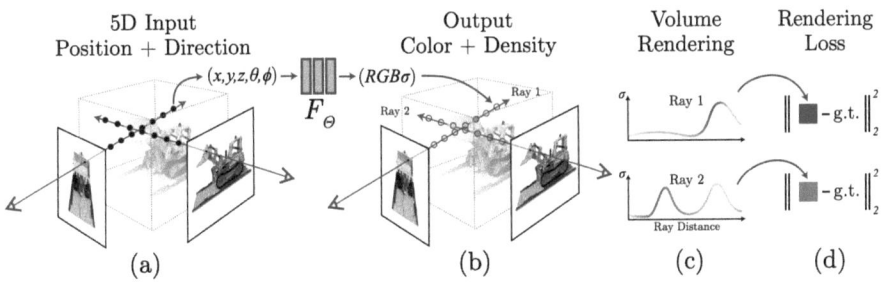

Fig. 2. NeRF volume rendering and training process. Image sourced from [17].

$$T_i = \exp\left(-\sum_{j=1}^{i-1} \sigma_j \delta_j\right) \quad (5)$$

The distance between adjacent samples, δ_i, is defined as $t_{i+1} - t_i$. This function for calculating $\hat{C}(r)$ from the set of (c_i, σ_i) values is differentiable and simplifies to traditional alpha compositing using alpha values $\alpha_i = 1 - \exp(-\sigma_i \delta_i)$.

Training Process. In the NeRF training process, both coarse and fine networks are trained simultaneously. Initially, a set of N_c positions is chosen from the scene using stratified sampling. The "coarse" network evaluates color and opacity at these positions. Based on the output of the "coarse" network, points along each ray that are more relevant to the scene are selected. The loss is the total squared error between the rendered and true pixel colors for both the coarse and fine renderings:

$$L = \sum_{r \in R} \left[\|\hat{C}_c(r) - C(r)\|_2^2 \right] + \left[\|\hat{C}_f(r) - C(r)\|_2^2 \right] \quad (6)$$

NeRF utilizes positional encoding to reconstruct high-dimensional features. The following positional encoding is applied to each component of scene coordinates x (normalized to $[-1, 1]$) and observation direction unit vector d:

$$\gamma(p) = \left(\sin(2^0 \pi p), \cos(2^0 \pi p), \ldots, \sin(2^{L-1} \pi p), \cos(2^{L-1} \pi p)\right) \quad (7)$$

By leveraging these techniques, NeRF provides a powerful framework for novel view synthesis and high-quality 3D scene reconstruction, pushing the boundaries of what is possible with neural implicit representations.

2.2 Common Quality Assessment Metrics

In computer vision, many evaluation metrics are used for image generation tasks. Currently, three main evaluation metrics are used for image generation tasks with real references: Structural Similarity Index (SSIM) [27], Peak Signal to Noise Ratio (PSNR), and Learned Perceptual Image Patch Similarity (LPIPS) [32]. NeRF utilizes these three metrics. Higher values indicate better performance for PSNR/SSIM, while lower values indicate better performance for LPIPS [32].

The Structural Similarity Index (SSIM) evaluates the quality of images by measuring their similarity, considering luminance, contrast, and structure. The SSIM values range from 0 to 1, with higher values indicating greater similarity. Given two images x and y, the formulas are:

$$l(x,y) = \frac{2\mu_x\mu_y + c_1}{\mu_x^2 + \mu_y^2 + c_1} \tag{8}$$

$$c(x,y) = \frac{2\sigma_x\sigma_y + c_2}{\sigma_x^2\sigma_y^2 + c_2} \tag{9}$$

$$s(x,y) = \frac{\sigma_{xy} + c_3}{\sigma_x\sigma_y + c_3} \tag{10}$$

SSIM is defined as:

$$SSIM(x,y) = [l(x,y)^\alpha \cdot c(x,y)^\beta \cdot s(x,y)^\gamma] \tag{11}$$

Let α, β, γ all be 1. Therefore, SSIM is:

$$SSIM(x,y) = \frac{(2\mu_x\mu_y + c_1)(2\sigma_{xy} + c_2)}{(\mu_x^2 + \mu_y^2 + c_1)(\sigma_x^2 + \sigma_y^2 + c_2)} \tag{12}$$

μ_x is the average value of x, σ_x is the variance of x, μ_y is the average value of y, σ_y is the variance of y, and σ_{xy} is the covariance between x and y. $c_1 = (k_1 L)^2$ and $c_2 = (k_2 L)^2$ are constants to maintain stability and avoid division by zero. L represents the range of pixel values. Typically, $k_1 = 0.01$ and $k_2 = 0.03$.

Peak Signal to Noise Ratio (PSNR) measures image quality, with higher values indicating less distortion. Generally, a PSNR above 40 dB indicates high image quality; between 30–40 dB is acceptable; between 20–30 dB is poor; and below 20 dB is severe distortion. PSNR is defined based on MSE (Mean Square Error):

$$MSE = \frac{1}{H \times W} \sum_{i=0}^{m-1} \sum_{j=0}^{n-1} [X(i,j) - Y(i,j)]^2 \tag{13}$$

MSE is the mean squared error between the current image X and the reference image Y, where H and W are the image height and width.

PSNR is defined as:

$$PSNR = 10 \cdot \log_{10}(\frac{MAX_x^2}{MSE}) = 10\log_{10}(\frac{(2^n - 1)^2}{MSE}) \tag{14}$$

MAX_x is the maximum pixel value of image X; n is the number of bits per pixel, usually set to 8, meaning the pixel grayscale level is 256.

In practice, there are three methods to calculate the PSNR of a color RGB image:

1. Calculate the PSNR separately for each RGB channel and then find the average.

2. Compute the mean squared error (MSE) for each channel in RGB, followed by calculating the overall PSNR.
3. Convert RGB to YCbCr color space and calculate only the PSNR for the Y (luminance) component.

The second method is commonly used.

Learned Perceptual Image Patch Similarity (LPIPS) quantifies the dissimilarity between two images using convolutional neural networks (CNNs) to learn perceptual characteristics. It partitions the input image into multiple patches and computes the representation of each patch using the neural network. LPIPS compares these representations to evaluate image similarity. A lower LPIPS value indicates higher similarity. The formula for measuring perceptual similarity given a patch x on the Ground Truth image and a patch x_0 on the noisy generated image is:

$$LPIPS(x, x_0) = \sum_l \frac{1}{H_l W_l} \sum_{h,w} \|w_l \odot (\hat{y}_{hw}^l - \hat{y}_{0hw}^l)\|_2^2 \tag{15}$$

where $\hat{y}_{hw}^l$ and $\hat{y}_{0hw}^l$ are the features of the reference and evaluation images at pixel width w, pixel height h, and layer l. W_l and H_l are the feature map height and width of the corresponding layer. The two inputs are fed into neural network F (which can be VGG, Alexnet, Squeezenet) for feature extraction. The output of each layer is activated, normalized, then multiplied by weight before calculating L_2 distance. Note that in actual implementation, the L_2 distance is not squared.

3 Scalable NeRF Frameworks and Enhancements

In recent years, to enhance the efficiency, scalability, and accuracy of large-scale 3D scene reconstruction, several scalable NeRF frameworks and enhancements have been developed. These advancements address critical challenges such as computational complexity, memory consumption, and the handling of diverse scene elements. This section outlines some of these challenges and provides an overview of prominent methods and frameworks developed to tackle them, highlighting their contributions and unique approaches. Table 1 presents a comparative summary of these innovative NeRF frameworks.

3.1 Creation of Datasets

MatrixCity [13] introduces a comprehensive and high-quality synthetic dataset, consisting of 67k aerial images and 452k street-level images from the maps of two cities, covering a total area of 28 square kilometers. This dataset addresses the lack of suitable data for city-scale neural rendering. Developed using Unreal Engine 5, it provides rich urban bird's-eye views and street perspectives, along with accurate ground-truth camera poses and various data modalities. Moreover, the dataset's flexibility in environmental control allows for data collection under dynamic conditions, such as varying lighting, weather, and levels of human and vehicle congestion. This flexibility enables the study of urban-scale neural rendering under diverse scenarios. The MatrixCity dataset makes a significant contribution to the field of urban-scale neural rendering, offering valuable opportunities for research in neural rendering and related applications.

DL3DV-10K (A Large-Scale Scene Dataset for Deep Learning-based 3D Vision) [14] is a comprehensive dataset proposed by Lu Ling et al. to support deep learning-based 3D vision. This dataset contains 10,510 4K resolution videos from 65 different locations, addressing the limitations of existing datasets in deep learning-based 3D analysis. It provides a thorough benchmark for novel view synthesis (NVS) and supports learning-based 3D representation techniques. Prior to **DL3DV-10K**, existing datasets suffered from a critical drawback: they were either synthetic or covered only a narrow range of real-world scenarios. This limitation hindered comprehensive benchmarking of NVS methods and the generalizability of deep 3D representation learning methods. To bridge this gap, **DL3DV-10K** includes a variety of real-world scenes, encompassing both bounded and unbounded environments with diverse levels of reflectivity, transparency, and lighting conditions. This dataset allows for robust evaluation of NVS methods in complex real-world scenarios, making it a significant contribution to the field of 3D vision and novel view synthesis.

3.2 Real-Time Rendering Optimization for Large-Scale Scene Reconstruction

Real-time rendering optimization is another significant challenge in large-scale scene reconstruction. This challenge is not only related to the large number of parameters involved in extensive scenes but also to the ray sampling inherent in NeRF itself. Consequently, various improvement methods have been proposed.

UE4-NeRF [7] integrates with the rasterization pipeline of Unreal Engine 4 (UE4) to achieve real-time rendering of large-scale scenes at 4K resolution, with frame rates reaching up to 43 FPS. It divides large scenes into sub-NeRFs represented by polygon meshes. These meshes are initialized with multiple regular octahedrons in the scene and their vertices are continuously optimized during training. The system employs level-of-detail (LOD) techniques, training meshes of different detail levels for varying levels of observation. Experimental results show that this method's rendering quality is comparable to state-of-the-art approaches while providing real-time performance and facilitating scene editing in UE4. This advancement is significant for applications in virtual reality, computer games, and the Metaverse.

SMERF [5] provides a streaming, memory-efficient radiance field for large-scale scenes, achieving real-time view synthesis. It addresses the challenge of balancing high-quality rendering with the computational and memory constraints of real-time applications. In large-scale scenes with a volume resolution of 3.5 cubic millimeters and an area of up to 300 square meters, SMERF achieves state-of-the-art accuracy among real-time methods. This method is based on two key contributions: a hierarchical model segmentation scheme that enhances model capacity while controlling computational and memory usage, and a distillation training strategy that ensures high fidelity and internal consistency. SMERF enables full six degrees of freedom (6DOF) navigation in web browsers and real-time rendering on various devices, including smartphones and laptops.

MERF (Memory-Efficient Radiance Fields) [20] for Real-time View Synthesis in Unbounded Scenes, introduced by Christian Reiser et al., presents a novel approach to real-time rendering of large-scale scenes with a focus on memory efficiency. MERF addresses the issue of existing radiance field representations being too compute-intensive or memory-demanding for real-time rendering, particularly in large, unbounded scenes. It achieves this by using a combination of a sparse feature grid and high-resolution 2D feature planes, significantly reducing memory consumption compared to previous methods. The core innovation lies in MERF's unique scene representation, which combines a low-resolution 3D grid with high-resolution 2D planes, allowing for efficient memory usage while maintaining high-quality rendering. Additionally, a novel contraction function efficiently maps scene coordinates into a bounded volume, facilitating effective ray-box intersection crucial for rendering. The authors also developed a lossless procedure for converting the training parameterization into a model optimized for real-time rendering, preserving the photorealistic quality of volumetric radiance fields. MERF's training and baking process optimizes a compressed representation of the grid during training using multi-resolution hash encoding for memory efficiency, along with a quantization-aware training method to minimize quality loss during the baking process for real-time rendering.

3.3 Memory Efficiency Enhancements

SCALAR-NeRF [2] introduces a coarse-to-fine strategy to enhance memory efficiency. The authors developed an encoder-decoder architecture, where the encoder processes 3D point coordinates to generate encoded features, and the decoder produces geometric values, including signed distance and volumetric density of color. Initially, a coarse global model is trained on the entire image dataset. Subsequently, the images are segmented into smaller blocks using KMeans, with each block modeled by a dedicated local model. The boundaries of each local block's bounding box are expanded to enhance the overlap between different blocks. Notably, the decoder from the global model is shared across different blocks, promoting the alignment of local encoder feature spaces. This efficient method demonstrates the scalability of large-scale scene reconstruction. This advancement is particularly crucial for applications such as augmented reality, real-world simulation, and localization, where large-scale and detailed scene reconstruction is essential.

In the work by Chaojian Li et al., **MixRT (Hybrid Neural Representation for Real-time NeRF Rendering)** [12] challenges the necessity of high-quality geometry in neural rendering. They combine low-quality meshes with a compressed NeRF model to optimize memory usage and achieve real-time rendering. MixRT leverages existing graphics hardware to enable real-time NeRF rendering on edge devices. The WebGL-optimized MixRT framework achieves over 30 frames per second on a MacBook M1 Pro laptop at a resolution of 1280×720, with higher rendering quality and smaller storage space compared to state-of-the-art methods. This advancement in NeRF rendering technology is significant for immersive interactions on edge devices, balancing rendering speed, quality, and resource efficiency.

3.4 Specific Applications

Several works are designed for specific applications. **SUDS: Scalable Urban Dynamic Scenes** [25] extends neural radiance fields to dynamic, large-scale urban environments. It uses inputs such as RGB images, sparse LiDAR, and optical flow to introduce a three-branch hash table for four-dimensional urban reconstruction. This enables efficient modeling of static, dynamic, and far-field elements, facilitating large-scale applications such as novel view synthesis, unsupervised 3D instance segmentation, and cuboid detection.

Adaptive Voronoi NeRFs [28] utilizes Voronoi diagrams for scene segmentation, accelerating the training and inference of distributed NeRFs. Each Voronoi cell contains a neural network. This method is compatible with various NeRF variants and is particularly effective for large-scale scenes or real-time applications like autonomous driving.

PlaNeRF [26] introduces a new method for enhancing the geometric reconstruction of neural radiance fields (NeRF) in large-scale outdoor urban scenes. It is an unsupervised regularization technique that does not rely on explicit 3D supervision. PlaNeRF employs a novel plane regularization technique based on singular value decomposition (SVD) and utilizes the structural similarity index measure (SSIM) in a patch-based loss design. This effectively initializes NeRF's volumetric representation, significantly improving its 3D structure and enabling more accurate geometric reconstruction in large outdoor scenes.

PC-NeRF [8] addresses the issue of partial sensor data loss in autonomous driving environments by proposing a new 3D scene reconstruction framework. This framework consists of a parent neural radiance field and child neural radiance fields, optimizing scene-level, segment-level, and point-level representations simultaneously. This allows for the rapid acquisition of approximate volumetric representations of scenes, even with limited observational data.

NeRF-LOAM [4] combines neural radiance fields with LiDAR odometry and mapping, improving the accuracy of large-scale 3D mapping and odometry in outdoor environments.

These frameworks and enhancements represent significant strides in the development of scalable NeRF technologies, enabling more efficient and accurate large-scale 3D scene reconstructions. They collectively address key challenges in memory management, computational efficiency, and the handling of complex scene elements, paving the way for broader applications and improved performance in diverse environments.

Table 1. Comparison of Innovative NeRF Frameworks

Framework	Key Features	Challenges Addressed	Unique Approaches
MatrixCity	High-quality synthetic dataset	Lack of suitable data	Developed using Unreal Engine 5, flexible environmental control
DL3DV-10K	Comprehensive real-world dataset	Limitations of existing datasets	Variety of real-world scenes, diverse reflectivity and lighting
UE4-NeRF	Real-time rendering, 4K resolution	Parameter complexity	Integration with Unreal Engine 4, LOD techniques
SMERF	Streaming, memory-efficient	Balancing quality and constraints	Hierarchical model segmentation, distillation training strategy
MERF	Memory-efficient, real-time rendering	Compute and memory demands	Sparse feature grid, high-resolution 2D planes, contraction function
SCALAR-NeRF	Coarse-to-fine strategy	Memory efficiency	Encoder-decoder architecture, shared global decoder
MixRT	Real-time rendering, edge devices	High-quality geometry necessity	Low-quality meshes with compressed NeRF, WebGL optimization
SUDS	Dynamic urban environments	Large-scale dynamic scenes	Three-branch hash table, four-dimensional urban reconstruction
Adaptive Voronoi NeRFs	Scene segmentation	Distributed NeRF training	Voronoi diagrams for segmentation, neural network in each cell
PlaNeRF	Geometric reconstruction	Lack of explicit 3D supervision	Plane regularization (SVD), SSIM in patch-based loss
PC-NeRF	Sensor data loss	Partial data loss in autonomous driving	Parent and child NeRFs, multi-level scene representation
NeRF-LOAM	3D mapping, odometry	Accuracy in outdoor environments	Combination of NeRF and LiDAR odometry

4 Innovative Techniques and Applications

Recent advancements in NeRF technologies have led to the development of innovative techniques and applications in large-scale 3D scene reconstruction. The previous chapter introduced common technical frameworks and representative works for large-scale scenes. This section focuses on specific application scenarios, highlighting notable methods and frameworks, each contributing unique solutions to complex problems in large-scale 3D scene reconstruction and rendering. The comparative summary of these innovative NeRF applications is presented in Table 2.

Scalable Urban Dynamic Scenes. Capturing and rendering large-scale urban environments with dynamic elements is a significant challenge. By leveraging scalable neural rendering techniques, researchers aim to create realistic and detailed urban scenes that can adapt to changes in lighting, weather, and movement. This task is crucial in large-scale scene reconstruction. Notable works include **Scalable Urban Dynamic Scenes (SUDS)** [25], which focuses on efficiently rendering urban environments with dynamic elements. SUDS employs strategies to handle varying lighting conditions, weather changes, and the presence of moving objects, providing a comprehensive approach to dynamic urban scene reconstruction. Another significant contribution is the **Aerial-NeRF** [35], which addresses the complexities of rendering large-scale aerial scenes by introducing adaptive spatial partitioning and sampling methods. This approach allows for the efficient rendering of complex urban environments from different flight trajectories, significantly improving both speed and accuracy. Additionally, the work on **Adaptive Shells for Efficient Neural Radiance Field Rendering** [28] presents a method that improves the efficiency of neural radiance field rendering by using adaptive sampling strategies. This technique allocates computational resources to regions of interest, enhancing rendering efficiency and making it particularly useful for interactive applications requiring real-time performance. These advancements are essential for the development of autonomous driving technologies, where accurate and real-time representation of dynamic urban environments is critical.

Underwater Scene Reconstruction. Underwater scene reconstruction presents unique challenges due to the scattering and absorption properties of water. Recent advancements in underwater neural renderers have addressed these challenges by developing specialized techniques for underwater environments. Notable works include **WaterNeRF**, developed by Sethuraman et al. [22], which estimates medium parameters from histogram-equalized images and learns color distributions to restore underwater images independently of rendering. Zhou et al. introduced **WaterHE-NeRF** [37], which estimates medium parameters and reconstructs underwater scenes by considering the scattering effects of water. Zhang et al. [33] introduced a physical model for underwater robots equipped with light sources, correcting color distortions by considering specific lighting conditions and analyzing coefficients of the underwater physical model across different distances. Another significant contribution is by Zhang et al. [36], who modularized the underwater 3D scene reconstruction system to enhance both color restoration and structural reconstruction. Additionally, **Seathru-NeRF**, demonstrated by Levy et al. [11], highlighted the significant benefits of incorporating diverse scattering media models into the rendering equation, which simultaneously reconstructs the scene and its 3D structure.

Improving NeRF with GIS Data. Integrating Geographic Information System (GIS) data with NeRF techniques opens new avenues for enhancing 3D reconstructions of large-scale outdoor environments. GIS data adds valuable context and additional layers of information, which improve the accuracy and realism of NeRF models.**Improving NeRF with Height Data for Utilization of GIS Data** [1] by Hinata Aoki and Takao Yamanaka proposes a method to enhance Neural Radiance Fields (NeRF) for large-scale scene reconstruction by effectively utilizing height data obtained from Geographic Information Systems (GIS). This method segments the scene space into multiple objects and backgrounds based on height data and represents them with independent neural networks. Additionally, an adaptive sampling method is introduced, using height data to densely set sampling points at object boundaries. This significantly

Table 2. Comparative Summary of Innovative NeRF Applications

Application	Notable Works	Key Techniques	Use Case
Scalable Urban Dynamic Scenes	SUDS [25]	Efficient rendering of dynamic elements	Autonomous driving
	Aerial-NeRF [35]	Adaptive spatial partitioning and sampling methods	Autonomous driving
	Adaptive Shells for Efficient Neural Radiance Field Rendering [28]	Allocates computational resources to regions of interest, enhancing rendering efficiency	Interactive applications
Underwater Scene Reconstruction	WaterNeRF [22]	Estimates medium parameters and restores underwater images	Marine research, underwater robotics
	WaterHE-NeRF [37]	Considers scattering effects of water for reconstruction	Marine research, underwater robotics
	Beyond Physical Models [33]	Corrects color distortions using specific lighting conditions	Marine research, underwater robotics
	Modularized Underwater 3D Scene Reconstruction [36]	Enhances color restoration and structural reconstruction	Marine research, underwater robotics
	Seathru-NeRF [11]	Incorporates scattering media models into the rendering equation	Marine research, underwater robotics
Improving NeRF with GIS Data	Improving NeRF with Height Data [1]	Utilizes height data to segment scene space and enhances image rendering accuracy	Urban planning, geography, environmental studies
	Fast Satellite Tensorial Radiance Field [34]	Addresses challenges in handling large satellite images for 3D reconstruction	Urban planning, geography, environmental studies
	Mega-NeRF [24]	Uses adaptive spatial partitioning and sampling for efficient rendering of large-scale aerial scenes	Urban planning, geography, environmental studies
	Urban Radiance Fields (URF) [21]	Leverages lidar inputs to enhance the accuracy of urban-scale environments	Urban planning, geography, environmental studies
	CityNeRF [30]	Employs multi-scale data modeling for effective handling of large urban scenes	Urban planning, geography, environmental studies

improves image rendering accuracy and accelerates the training process.**Fast Satellite Tensorial Radiance Field for Multi-date Satellite Imagery of Large Size** [34] introduces SatensoRF, a significant advancement in Neural Radiance Field (NeRF) models for satellite images. SatensoRF addresses challenges such as slow processing speeds, the need for solar information as input, and limitations in handling large satellite images. This method holds substantial potential for fields requiring extensive aerial surveys and 3D reconstruction, such as geography, environmental studies, and urban planning. It offers an efficient NeRF solution for novel view synthesis of satellite images, particularly excelling in handling single-view or few-view inputs, and generating high-quality 3D scene reconstructions and view synthesis.**Mega-NeRF** [24] addresses the complexities of large-scale aerial scene rendering by introducing adaptive spatial partitioning and sampling methods. This approach allows for efficient rendering of complex urban environments from different flight trajectories, significantly improving both speed and accuracy. Mega-NeRF employs strategies such as foreground and background decomposition to manage the extensive data involved in large-scale scene reconstruction.**Urban Radiance Fields (URF)** [21] and **CityNeRF** [30] are other notable examples. URF leverages lidar inputs to enhance the accuracy of urban-scale environments, while CityNeRF employs multi-scale data modeling to handle large urban scenes effectively. These methods can complement Mega-NeRF by adding more detailed and structured geographic data into the NeRF models.

These integrations of GIS data with NeRF technologies represent significant advancements in the field, offering more precise and contextually enriched 3D reconstructions. They are particularly beneficial for urban development, environmental monitoring, and smart city initiatives, where detailed and accurate 3D models are crucial.

5 Conclusion

This review has highlighted the significant advancements in Neural Radiance Fields (NeRF) technologies for large-scale 3D scene reconstruction. It provided an overview of the current work from two key perspectives: scalable NeRF frameworks and enhancements, and innovative environments and applications.

Beyond the use of RGB images in conventional outdoor urban and indoor scenes, the application of NeRF for large-scale scene reconstruction has extended to other data types and domains. Integrating NeRF with Geographic Information System (GIS) data, as demonstrated in Geo-NeRF, has significantly improved the accuracy and realism of 3D models, showcasing the interdisciplinary potential of NeRF technologies in urban planning and environmental monitoring. Additionally, addressing dynamic and unconstrained environments, such as underwater scenes, has expanded the applicability of NeRF to challenging conditions.

The review indicates substantial progress in handling complex environments, improving computational efficiency, and integrating diverse data sources. These advancements have important implications for industries reliant on precise 3D reconstructions, such as autonomous driving, virtual tourism, and cultural heritage preservation.

Looking forward, future research should focus on further enhancing scalability and efficiency, integrating additional data sources, and extending applications to more dynamic and diverse environments. The intersection of NeRF with emerging technologies, such as 3D Gaussian splatting (3DGS), promises further improvements in rendering quality and computational performance. The integration of NeRF with advanced AI techniques will likely drive substantial innovations in the field of artificial intelligence-generated content (AIGC), offering new possibilities for creative and practical applications.

NeRF technologies are poised to drive significant innovations in large-scale 3D scene reconstruction, transforming both academic research and practical applications across various fields. The ongoing advancements in NeRF, combined with new approaches like 3D Gaussian Splatting [10], will continue to push the boundaries of what is achievable in 3D rendering and scene reconstruction, fostering new developments in AIGC and beyond.

References

1. Aoki, H., Yamanaka, T.: Improving nerf with height data for utilization of GIS data. In: 2023 IEEE International Conference on Image Processing (ICIP), pp. 935–939. IEEE (2023)
2. Chen, Y., Lee, G.H.: Scalar-nerf: scalable large-scale neural radiance fields for scene reconstruction. arXiv preprint arXiv:2311.16657 (2023)
3. Dellaert, F., Lin, Y.C.: Neural volume rendering: nerf and beyond. ArXiv **abs/2101.05204** (2020). https://api.semanticscholar.org/CorpusID:231592673
4. Deng, J., et al.: Nerf-loam: neural implicit representation for large-scale incremental lidar odometry and mapping. In: Proceedings of the IEEE/CVF International Conference on Computer Vision, pp. 8218–8227 (2023)
5. Duckworth, D., et al.: Smerf: streamable memory efficient radiance fields for real-time large-scene exploration. arXiv preprint arXiv:2312.07541 (2023)
6. Gao, K., Gao, Y., He, H., Lu, D., Xu, L., Li, J.: Nerf: neural radiance field in 3d vision, a comprehensive review. ArXiv **abs/2210.00379** (2022). https://api.semanticscholar.org/CorpusID:252683586
7. Gu, J., et al.: Ue4-nerf: neural radiance field for real-time rendering of large-scale scene. In: Advances in Neural Information Processing Systems, vol. 36 (2024)
8. Hu, X., Xiong, G., Zang, Z., Jia, P., Han, Y., Ma, J.: Pc-nerf: parent-child neural radiance fields under partial sensor data loss in autonomous driving environments. arXiv preprint arXiv:2310.00874 (2023)
9. Johari, M.M., Lepoittevin, Y., Fleuret, F.: Geonerf: generalizing nerf with geometry priors. In: Proceedings of the IEEE/CVF Conference on Computer Vision and Pattern Recognition, pp. 18365–18375 (2022)
10. Kerbl, B., Kopanas, G., Leimkühler, T., Drettakis, G.: 3d gaussian splatting for real-time radiance field rendering. ACM Trans. Graph. **42**(4), 1–14 (2023)
11. Levy, D., et al.: SeaThru-nerf: neural radiance fields in scattering media. In: Proceedings of the IEEE/CVF Conference on Computer Vision and Pattern Recognition, pp. 56–65 (2023)
12. Li, C., Wu, B., Vajda, P., Lin, Y.: Mixrt: mixed neural representations for real-time nerf rendering. In: 2024 International Conference on 3D Vision (3DV), pp. 1115–1124. IEEE (2024)
13. Li, Y., et al.: Matrixcity: a large-scale city dataset for city-scale neural rendering and beyond. In: Proceedings of the IEEE/CVF International Conference on Computer Vision, pp. 3205–3215 (2023)
14. Ling, L., et al.: Dl3dv-10k: a large-scale scene dataset for deep learning-based 3d vision. In: Proceedings of the IEEE/CVF Conference on Computer Vision and Pattern Recognition, pp. 22160–22169 (2024)

15. Martin-Brualla, R., Radwan, N., Sajjadi, M.S.M., Barron, J.T., Dosovitskiy, A., Duckworth, D.: Nerf in the wild: neural radiance fields for unconstrained photo collections. In: 2021 IEEE/CVF Conference on Computer Vision and Pattern Recognition (CVPR), pp. 7206–7215 (2020). https://api.semanticscholar.org/CorpusID:220968781
16. Mildenhall, B., Hedman, P., Martin-Brualla, R., Srinivasan, P.P., Barron, J.T.: Nerf in the dark: high dynamic range view synthesis from noisy raw images. In: Proceedings of the IEEE/CVF Conference on Computer Vision and Pattern Recognition, pp. 16190–16199 (2022)
17. Mildenhall, B., Srinivasan, P.P., Tancik, M., Barron, J.T., Ramamoorthi, R., Ng, R.: Nerf: representing scenes as neural radiance fields for view synthesis. Commun. ACM **65**(1), 99–106 (2021)
18. Park, K., et al.: Nerfies: deformable neural radiance fields. In: Proceedings of the IEEE/CVF International Conference on Computer Vision, pp. 5865–5874 (2021)
19. Reiser, C., Peng, S., Liao, Y., Geiger, A.: Kilonerf: speeding up neural radiance fields with thousands of tiny MLPs. In: Proceedings of the IEEE/CVF International Conference on Computer Vision, pp. 14335–14345 (2021)
20. Reiser, C., et al.: MERF: memory-efficient radiance fields for real-time view synthesis in unbounded scenes. ACM Trans. Graph. (TOG) **42**(4), 1–12 (2023)
21. Rematas, K., et al.: Urban radiance fields. In: Proceedings of the IEEE/CVF Conference on Computer Vision and Pattern Recognition, pp. 12932–12942 (2022)
22. Sethuraman, A.V., Ramanagopal, M.S., Skinner, K.A.: Waternerf: neural radiance fields for underwater scenes. In: OCEANS 2023-MTS/IEEE US Gulf Coast, pp. 1–7. IEEE (2023)
23. Tewari, A., et al.: Advances in neural rendering. Comput. Graph. Forum **41** (2021). https://api.semanticscholar.org/CorpusID:236162433
24. Turki, H., Ramanan, D., Satyanarayanan, M.: Mega-nerf: scalable construction of large-scale nerfs for virtual fly-throughs. In: Proceedings of the IEEE/CVF Conference on Computer Vision and Pattern Recognition, pp. 12922–12931 (2022)
25. Turki, H., Zhang, J.Y., Ferroni, F., Ramanan, D.: Suds: scalable urban dynamic scenes. In: Proceedings of the IEEE/CVF Conference on Computer Vision and Pattern Recognition, pp. 12375–12385 (2023)
26. Wang, F., Louys, A., Piasco, N., Bennehar, M., Roldão, L., Tsishkou, D.: Planerf: SVD unsupervised 3d plane regularization for nerf large-scale scene reconstruction. arXiv preprint arXiv:2305.16914 (2023)
27. Wang, Z., Bovik, A.C., Sheikh, H.R., Simoncelli, E.P.: Image quality assessment: from error visibility to structural similarity. IEEE Trans. Image Process. **13**, 600–612 (2004)
28. Wang, Z., et al.: Adaptive shells for efficient neural radiance field rendering. arXiv preprint arXiv:2311.10091 (2023)
29. Xie, Y., et al.: Neural fields in visual computing and beyond. Comput. Graph. Forum **41** (2021). https://api.semanticscholar.org/CorpusID:244478496
30. Xu, L., et al.: Grid-guided neural radiance fields for large urban scenes. In: Proceedings of the IEEE/CVF Conference on Computer Vision and Pattern Recognition, pp. 8296–8306 (2023)
31. Zhang, K., Riegler, G., Snavely, N., Koltun, V.: Nerf++: analyzing and improving neural radiance fields. arXiv preprint arXiv:2010.07492 (2020)
32. Zhang, R., Isola, P., Efros, A.A., Shechtman, E., Wang, O.: The unreasonable effectiveness of deep features as a perceptual metric. 2018 IEEE/CVF Conference on Computer Vision and Pattern Recognition, pp. 586–595 (2018)

33. Zhang, T., Johnson-Roberson, M.: Beyond nerf underwater: learning neural reflectance fields for true color correction of marine imagery. IEEE Robot. Autom. Lett. (2023)
34. Zhang, T., Li, Y.: Fast satellite tensorial radiance field for multi-date satellite imagery of large size. arXiv preprint arXiv:2309.11767 (2023)
35. Zhang, X., Qiu, Y., Sun, Z., Liu, Q.: Aerial-nerf: adaptive spatial partitioning and sampling for large-scale aerial rendering. arXiv preprint arXiv:2405.06214 (2024)
36. Zhang, Z., Zhang, L., Wang, L., Wu, H.: Scene 3-d reconstruction system in scattering medium. arXiv preprint arXiv:2312.09005 (2023)
37. Zhou, J., et al.: Waterhe-nerf: water-ray tracing neural radiance fields for underwater scene reconstruction. arXiv preprint arXiv:2312.06946 (2023)
38. Zhu, F., Guo, S., Song, L., Xu, K., Hu, J.: Deep review and analysis of recent nerfs. APSIPA Trans. Sig. Inf. Process. (2023). https://api.semanticscholar.org/CorpusID:257420578

Chinese Medical Spoken Language Understanding Based on Prototypical Modification Network and Contrastive Learning

Guofeng Zheng[1,2], Na Liu[1,2(✉)], Chen Li[1,2], Jie Yang[1,2], and Lu Dao[1,2]

[1] North Minzu University, Yinchuan 750021, China
liuna@nun.edu.cn
[2] The Key Laboratory of Images and Graphics Intelligent Processing of State Ethnic Affairs Commission, North Minzu University, Yinchuan 750021, China

Abstract. Intent classification and slot filling are critical tasks in Spoken Language Understanding (SLU). Currently, prototypical networks are used as the primary method to solve the problems of few-shot learning. However, directly applying prototypical networks to few-shot Chinese medical SLU tasks can lead to issues such as the prototypes being susceptible to noise interference in samples and non-medical entities introducing irrelevant features, which hinder the performance of prototypical networks. To address these problems, we propose a Chinese medical SLU model based on Prototypical Modification Network and Contrastive Learning (PMNCL). Its highlights are as follows: (1) To improve the efficiency of distance measurement, the distance weights between support set samples are calculated and used to modify the prototypes. (2) To obtain better class discriminative representations, the contrastive learning loss function is designed so that similar and dissimilar samples can be separated. (3) We conduct sufficient experiments on the benchmark Chinese medical intent classification datasets such as IMCS-V2, KUAKE-QIC, and CMID. Results demonstrate that our proposed model outperforms previous methods and achieves state-of-the-art performance.

Keywords: Spoken Language Understanding · Prototypical Networks · Few-Shot Learning · Contrastive Learning

1 Introduction

In recent years, Dialogue Artificial Intelligence (DAI) has been receiving wide attention in many fields, e.g., industry, biomedical, finance, and education. DAI is an artificial intelligent technology that enables human-computer interaction by applying natural language processing (NLP), automatic speech recognition (ASR), and dialogue understanding to intelligent speech dialogue systems [1]. The development of pre-trained language models in the biomedical fields has led to an increasing number of people seeking healthcare consultations online to understand their health status. Therefore, researching models suitable for medical SLU is significant for improving the system's ability to understand the content of users' medical inquiries correctly.

Spoken Language Understanding (SLU) is crucial for medical DAI systems. Its target is to extract the intents contained in the utterances and provide feedback. Current research commonly divides SLU into two subtasks: intent classification and slot filling [2]. Intent classification aims to identify specific behaviors, while the slot filling task involves sequentially annotating input utterances [3]. This division of SLU is illustrated in Table 1.

Table 1. Example of Chinese Medical SLU tasks.

Task	Example				
	治	疗	高	血	压
Slot filling	O	O	B-illness	I-illness	I-illness
Intent classification	疾病治疗 (treatment of diseases)				

Recent processes of pre-trained language models based on big data have yielded remarkable results on traditional SLU datasets. However, unlike the data-rich setting, SLU often suffers from data scarcity in real-world applications. Especially in the field of Chinese medical SLU, the medical corpus is characterized by high professionalism and complex entity structure, and large-scale annotation corpus requires a vast workforce and financial resources, which leads to the problem of annotation corpus scarcity. To address the issues mentioned above, Li et al. [4] proposed the concept of few-shot learning, which enables models to achieve performance comparable to or surpass that of big data deep learning by training on a minimal number of samples.

There are three main different lines of research dedicated to few-shot learning: (1) Model fine-tuning-based methods aim to migrate models trained on large-scale datasets to the target task for fine-tuning. (2) Data augmentation-based methods improve the model's generalization ability by augmenting the samples' spatial features. (3) Metric learning-based methods focus on designing a metric function to calculate sample similarity.

Among them, the metric learning-based method is currently the mainstream method for solving few-shot SLU tasks. Geng et al. [5] were inspired by capsule networks and proposed the architecture of Induction Networks (IN). A key challenge for IN is the frequent loss of essential information when switching between meta-tasks. Geng et al. [6] addressed this problem through further research based on IN and proposed Dynamic Memory Induction Networks (DMIN). After the dynamic memory module, the sample vectors are better separated, and it can effectively utilize the experience of supervised learning to encode the semantic relationship between the low-level and the high-level sample features. Prototypical Networks (PN) [7] is another similarity measure. Dopierre et al. [8] based on the PN and proposed PROTAUGMENT, a meta-learning algorithm is applied in intent classification. To improve the efficiency of the distance metric of the prototypical networks, Wen et al. [9] proposed a clustering-based prototypical networks (CBPM) in a few-shot relationship classification task, which uses the category information hidden in the query set to generate more accurate relationship prototypes. The drawback of this method is that the clustering process is time-consuming and increases the training overhead of the model.

Although the above prototypical-network-based approaches have achieved excel-lent performance, they ignore the adverse effects of various noises in the data, particularly in the domain of Chinese medical SLU. Therefore, using only the average vector as the computing method of the prototype is always unreliable owing to the limited instances in the support set. Moreover, slot information contains numerous non-medical entities with no semantic relationship. If all the entities participate equally in the prototype calculation, the constructed entity prototype refers to many irrelevant features, which weakens the discrimination and expressiveness of the prototype.

To solve these two problems simultaneously, we proposed a Chinese medical SLU model based on the Prototypical Modification Network and Contrastive Learning (PMNCL). When calculating the class prototype, weights are assigned to each sample based on the distance between the samples to reduce the influence of abnormal intention samples and non-entities on the class prototype. At the same time, the contrastive learning loss function is designed to optimize the model to obtain a better representation of the categories. Finally, a random training strategy is introduced to simulate the problem of imbalance between the classes of medical intentions and entities in a real scenario. The contributions of this paper are summarized as follows:

- To alleviate the problem that traditional prototypical networks cannot effectively perform distance metrics, we designed the Prototypical Modification Network to correct the generated class prototypes by distance weights.
- To obtain better class discriminative representations, we integrated the supervised contrastive learning method to construct positive-negative sample pairs by selecting samples in the support set using the query set samples as anchors.
- To illustrate and validate the effectiveness of the proposed model, we conducted extensive experiments and visualization analysis on the Chinese medical SLU datasets. The experimental results demonstrated that our proposed model outperforms other baseline methods and achieves state-of-the-art performance.

2 Related Work

2.1 Pre-trained Language Models in Biomedical Domain

With the development of pre-trained language models, pre-trained language models represented by BERT and its variants have become a new paradigm for solving problems in medical natural language understanding. Lee et al. [10] used large-scale biomedical corpora such as PubMed Abstracts to retrain and fine-tune the BERT model to obtain the BioBERT model, vastly outperforming BERT and previous models in various biomedical text mining tasks. Different from most previous studies, Gu et al. [11] observed that fine-tuning the pre-trained models with biomedical corpora is not applicable in the biomedical field. Pre-training directly on biomedical corpora could achieve more significant gains in specific areas. Similarly, Kamal et al. [12] directly pre-training the ELECTRA model utilized biomedical corpora, and proposed the model. The performance of this model in tasks such as information extraction, sentence similarity calculation, and medical Q&A was significantly better than the BioBERT and PubMedBERT models.

As for the Chinese biomedical field, Zhang et al. [13] proposed the first Chinese biomedical language understanding evaluation benchmark (ChineseBLUE) and fine-tuned the BERT to obtain the MC-BERT model. In order to adapt to the complex and diverse structure of Chinese characters, they introduced whole entity masking and whole span masking strategies. The masking strategy adjustment significantly im-proved the model's performance in Chinese medical intent classification tasks. Cui et al. [14] proposed the MacBERT model, which modifies the masked language model (MLM) task in a language correction manner and masks words with similar meanings to reduce differences between pre-training and fine-tuning stages. To further improve the semantic understanding ability of the model, Wang et al. [15] proposed a new pre-training framework termed eHealth, which does not rely on external resources and is more suitable for fine-tuning model in different downstream tasks. Lan et al. [16] proposed a Chinese medical text classification method, ConKGNN, based on contrastive knowledge and graph neural networks (GNN), which constructed a medical knowledge graph to enable the model to learn text features by interacting with text through knowledge graphs and improve its ability to classify medical texts.

2.2 Joint Intent Classification and Slot Filling

Considering the associativity between intent classification and slot filling, Chen et al. [17] applied pre-training models in SLU tasks to propose the JointBERT model, where BERT is used to extract shared contextual embedding for intent classification and slot filling. Lu et al. [18] proposed a method to integrate the semantic information of intention and slot labels into the joint model. Experimental results on ATIS and SNIPS datasets show that this model could achieve better results in joint learning of two tasks. Ma et al. [19] pointed out the diversity of spoken language in joint modeling of intent classification and slot filling tasks, which leads to significant variations in entity positions for the same intent between different samples. They decompose the slot filling task into two stages: slot proposal and slot classification. The slot proposal network composed of BERT, Bi-LSTM, and CRF structures to label entity positions and further improved the accuracy of slot labeling by fusing slot and intent features in candidate slots. The two-stage fusion framework has provided new ideas and methods for the development of intent classification and slot filling tasks.

In the field of Chinese medical SLU, Yu et al. [20] used "Treatise on Febrile Diseases" as the medical textual corpus for analysis and proposed a knowledge distillation-based bidirectional Transformer encoder. This model utilized TinyBERT as the embedding and encoding layer, feeding the encoded feature information into a CNN to accomplish medical intent classification. Lee et al. [21] fine-tuned a BERT-based model using medical datasets. They added a softmax classifier on top of BERT to predict the intent labels. Additionally, they employed the final hidden state of the BERT model for sequence labeling tasks, combined the weights of both, and achieved user intent classification.

The modeling method based on pre-trained language models has extensively promoted the development of SLU. However, the current pre-training-based methods cannot fundamentally solve problems such as weak model interpretability, poor generalization ability, and insufficient reasoning ability. In terms of deep semantic acquisition and understanding, they still need to be closer to the level of human cognition.

2.3 Contrastive Learning

Contrastive learning is a self-supervised learning method. Its core theory is to pull samples with similar semantics closer together in the semantic space while pushing the semantics of unrelated samples farther away. The problem that contrastive learning is how to construct positive and negative sample pairs.

For data augmentation, Gao et al. [22] proposed SimCSE, a simple contrastive sentence embedding framework, which enhanced samples by introducing the dropout method. The model repeated the same sample twice as input to the encoder and used the dropout strategy to obtain two different embedding representations as positive samples. Other samples in the same batch were used as negative samples. Wu et al. [23] proposed ESimCSE based on SimCSE, which introduced momentum contrast to enlarge the number of negative pairs without additional calculations. Through contrastive learning, the quality of sentence embedding in sentence similarity tasks was dramatically improved. In addition, Wu et al. [24] believed that the randomness introduced by dropout caused inconsistency between model training and inference. They introduced a consistency training strategy to regularize dropout (R-Drop). Experiments on semantic understanding tasks proved that the R-Drop strategy significantly reduced inconsistency, especially when applied to fine-tuning pre-training models, and significant performance improvement was achieved.

To further enhance the effectiveness of contrastive learning, Xu et al. [25] proposed a new sentence vector representation method (ImSimCSE), which researched the impact of random noise generated by dropout strategy on generating positive and negative samples for the first time. Wang et al. [26] proposed a contrastive learning framework aimed at enhancing the semantic understanding capability of dialogue systems. By paraphrasing the context of key entities, the generated positive samples are semantically similar to the original samples but exhibit different lexical and syntactic expressions. Negative samples are generated by strategies such as randomly deletion and relevant replacement. Utilizing this contrastive learning framework, the model is able to effectively enhance the accuracy of the content generated by the dialogue system.

Contrastive learning methods reduced the performance gap with supervised methods in a self-supervised manner, where the supervisory signals are derived from augmented data. Therefore, the quality of the augmented data is crucial, and future research needs to find appropriate data augmentation methods to improve the quality of model semantic representation.

3 Method

3.1 Task Definition

Intent classification is a form of text classification task that classifies text into one or more specified categories. Slot filling is framed as a sequence labelling problem that outputs the corresponding label sequence based on the input samples. From a mathematical definition, we define a triple (x, s, y), where $x = (x_1, x_2, \ldots, x_m)$ is an utterance with m words, $s = (s_1, s_2, \ldots, s_m)$ is composed of slot labels of each word in x, and y represents the intent label of x. In few-shot scenarios, the training set $\mathcal{D} = \{(x_1, s_1, y_1), \ldots, (x_n, s_n, y_k)\}$, where $y_i \in \{1, \ldots, k\}$ is usually divided into a support set $\mathcal{D}_s$ and a query set $\mathcal{D}_q$. The model is trained in the support set and the loss is calculated using the query set. The support set $\mathcal{D}_s$ usually includes K samples (K-shot) for each N intent labels (N-way). The N-way K-shot task is then defined as follows:

Given a query set $x_q = (x_1, x_2, \ldots, x_m)$ and a support set $\mathcal{D}_s$ containing K samples, the final intent classification probability $\boldsymbol{y}^*$ of x_q: $\boldsymbol{y}^* = \mathrm{argmax}_y\, p(y|x_q, \mathcal{D}_s)$.

3.2 Model Overview

The PMNCL model architecture designed for few-shot Chinese medical SLU tasks consists of four parts: (1) Input module. (2) Encoder module. (3) Prototype generation and modification module. (4) Contrastive learning module. For a given support set and query set consisting of N intent categories, each word in the samples can obtain its word embedding by the encoder module. The prototype generation and modification module constructs prototypes for all medical intent and medical slots in the support set, with each prototype representing the common features of that class. The distance function is used to calculate the distance between the query set and all prototypes to represent the similarity between the sample and each category, and the cross-entropy loss function is used to calculate the classification loss. The contrastive learning module achieves data augmentation by constructing positive and negative samples and finally designs a contrastive learning loss function to separate different intent samples. The overview of the model is shown in Fig. 1.

3.3 Encoder

To capture the semantic and syntactic information, we used Roberta-wwm-ext as the encoder for both the support and query set samples. Compared with the BERT, Roberta-wwm-ext has improved parameters, computing power, and data scale. Its Chinese training method based on whole-word masking is more suitable for Chinese tasks. To capture the temporal dependencies between intent samples, we introduced a recurrent neural network (Bi-LSTM) after the output word embedding of the Roberta-wwm-ext model. Specifically, when sample x is input to the encoder module, x_i represents the i-th token in sample x, and $\boldsymbol{h}_i$ represents the representation vector obtained by x_i after Bi-LSTM, as shown in Eq. 1.

$$\begin{aligned} \overrightarrow{\boldsymbol{h}_i} &= LSTM_f\left(w_i, \overrightarrow{\boldsymbol{h}_{i-1}}; \theta_f\right) \\ \overleftarrow{\boldsymbol{h}_i} &= LSTM_b\left(w_i, \overleftarrow{\boldsymbol{h}_{i+1}}; \theta_b\right) \end{aligned} \qquad (1)$$

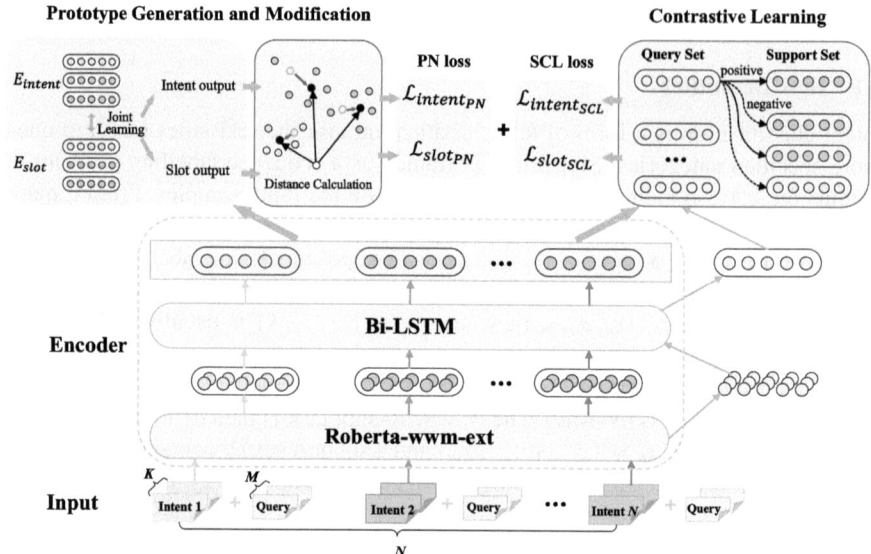

Fig. 1. PMNCL model architecture.

where $h_i = \overrightarrow{h_i} \oplus \overleftarrow{h_i}$, $\oplus$ means concatenating two vectors, θ_f and θ_b denote the parameters of forward and backward LSTM, respectively. $\overrightarrow{h_i}$ and $\overleftarrow{h_i}$ are the hidden states of the i-th word learned from forward and backward LSTM, respectively.

3.4 Prototypical Modification Network

Prototypical Networks (PN) is based on the idea that each category of samples has a prototype, and all samples of that category are distributed around the class prototype in the semantic space. To do this, PN learns a non-linear mapping of the input into an embedding space, calculating the mean c_i of each class sample and using c_i as the prototype in the embedding space, as shown in Eq. 2.

$$c_i = \frac{1}{n_i} \sum_{j=1}^{n_i} x_i^j \qquad (2)$$

Here, x_i^j represents the embedding of sample j corresponding to intent class i in the semantic space, and n_i represents the total number of samples in intent class i.

For query set sample x_q, by using a distance metric function to obtain the prototype closest to x_q, calculating the conditional probability $p_\theta(y = c_i | x_q)$ to classify query set samples, as shown in Eq. 3.

$$p_\theta(y = c_i | x_q) = \frac{exp(-d(f_\theta(x_q), c_i))}{\sum_{j=1}^{N} exp(-d(f_\theta(x_q), c_j))} \qquad (3)$$

where N represents the number of intent categories in the samples, $f(\cdot)$ represents the embedding function, and θ is the model parameter obtained through training. $d(\cdot)$

represents the distance metric function between the query set sample embedding and prototype. In PN, Euclidean Distance is usually used as a metric function.

In traditional prototypical networks, all features of intent and slot are given equal weight in the distance calculation. Research shows that not all features are adequate for tasks such as intent classification and slot filling. This problem leads to incomplete inclusion of information and association with a large number of irrelevant features in the sample embedding representation. As a result, obtaining informative sample embedding and measuring distances effectively becomes challenging. To enhance the representation ability of prototypical networks, we proposed a prototypical modification network based on distance weighting.

By calculating the distance between each intent class sample in the support set, different weights are assigned to each support set sample based on the distance, and the weights are used to modify the support set class prototype, as shown in Fig. 2.

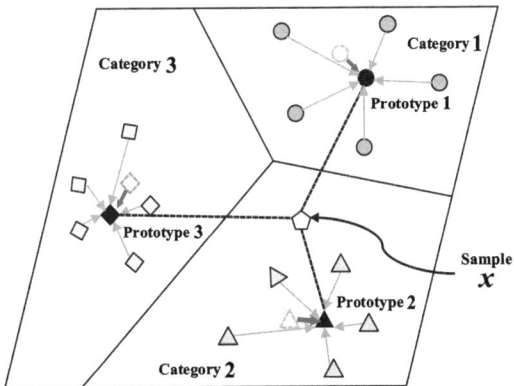

Fig. 2. Prototypical modification network architecture.

We used the Radial Basis Function (RBF) to calculate weighted prototypes. The RBF is a scalar function that is radially symmetric and can extend the input feature vector to an infinite-dimensional space. Commonly used radial basis kernel functions include Gaussian Kernel Function, Inverse Multivariate Quadratic Kernel Function (IMQ), etc. Because the IMQ has a robust anti-interference ability for noise contained in data, thus, we chose the IMQ function to calculate weighted prototypes based on the distance between samples of the same class, as shown in Eq. 4.

$$\varphi(x) = \frac{1}{\sqrt{d^2 + c^2}} \quad (4)$$

where d represents the distance between samples, and c represents the extended constant of the IMQ function. The more minor c is, the stronger the function's ability to separate noise and the more selective it is. When the degree of deviation of sample points from the sample center is more visible, $\varphi(x)$ takes a smaller value. Thus, it can be a filter for abnormal points.

For prototypical modification network, the encoder takes support set $\mathcal{D}_s$ and query set $\mathcal{D}_q$ as inputs and converts them into vector matrices S and Q, respectively. In the intent class i, calculate the sum of the distances D_i between the sample $x_i \in \mathcal{D}_s$ and the other sample x_j. The calculation equation is shown in 5.

$$D_i = \sum_{x_j \in \mathcal{D}_s} d(x_i, x_j) \tag{5}$$

where $d(x, y)$ is Euclidean Distance, the distance weight ω_i of each sample point is calculated using the IMQ function, as shown in Eq. 6.

$$\omega_i = \frac{\left(D_i^2 + c^2\right)^{-\frac{1}{2}}}{\sum_{x_j \in \mathcal{D}_s} \left(D_j^2 + c^2\right)^{-\frac{1}{2}}} \tag{6}$$

Finally, the sample prototype of each intent class is represented as:

$$p_k = \omega_i x_i \tag{7}$$

Using the IMQ to calculate weighted class prototypes reduces the influence of abnormal points and enhances algorithm robustness. Assuming that in the N-way K-shot task, Algorithm 1 shows the detailed process.

Algorithm 1 : Prototypical Modification Network

Input: Training set $\mathcal{D} = \{(x_1, s_1, y_1), \ldots, (x_n, s_n, y_k)\}, y_i \in \{1, \ldots, k\}$;
Output: Training loss $\mathcal{L}$;
1: Divide the training set $\mathcal{D}$ into support set $\mathcal{D}_s$ and query set $\mathcal{D}_q$;
2: **for** each *episode iteration* **do:**
3:    Calculate the sum of the distances D_i;
4:    Calculate the weight ω_i of each sample;
5:    Modify the prototype p_k by weight ω_i;
6:    Distance between query set and prototype $d(p_k, x_i)$;
7:    Calculate the classification probability $p(y = k|x_q)$;
8: **end for**
9: **return** loss $\mathcal{L} \leftarrow \mathcal{L} + \frac{1}{N} \log p(-d(p_k, x_q), y)$.

3.5 Intent and Slot Representation Based on Contrastive Learning

To separate text features of different intent categories, we use supervised contrastive learning to train the intent feature extractor. The crucial problem that contrastive learning needs to solve is constructing positive and negative samples. In this paper, a batch of support set samples from the same intent category are used as positive samples, with the query set sample as the anchor point. Support sets from different intent categories are used as negative samples. Contrastive learning is used to pull similar features closer together and make different intent category features move away from each other, thereby separating different intent information, as shown in Fig. 3.

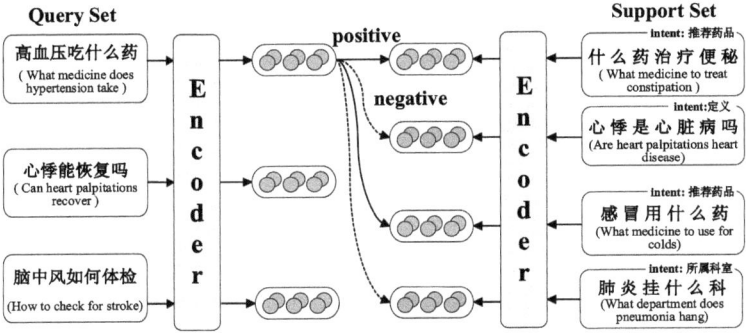

Fig. 3. The schematic diagram of the contrastive learning method.

For query set instances x, support set instances with the same label as x are used as positive samples, and support set instances with different labels are used as negative samples. Therefore, the contrastive loss function for intent classification is shown in Eq. 8.

$$\begin{aligned}\mathcal{L}_{intent_{SCL}} &= \frac{1}{|Q|}\sum_{x^i \in Q}\left[-\frac{1}{n_i}\sum_{x^j \in S} log \frac{exp(x^i \cdot x^j/\tau)}{\sum_{x^k \in S} exp(x^i \cdot x^k/\tau)}\right] \\ &= \frac{1}{|Q|}\sum_{x^i \in Q}\left[-\frac{1}{n_i}\sum_{x^j \in S} log \frac{exp(x^i \cdot x^j/\tau)}{\sum_{x^k \in S, k \neq i} exp(x^i \cdot x^k/\tau) + exp(x^i \cdot x^i/\tau)}\right]\end{aligned} \quad (8)$$

The slot contrastive loss function is constructed similarly, as shown in Eq. 9.

$$\mathcal{L}_{slot_{SCL}} = \frac{1}{|Q|}\sum_{x^i \in Q}\left[-\frac{1}{n_i}\sum_{x^j \in S} log \frac{exp(x^i \cdot x^j/\tau)}{\sum_{x^k \in S} exp(x^i \cdot x^k/\tau)}\right] \quad (9)$$

The final model loss function is represented as: $\mathcal{L} = \mathcal{L}_{intent_{PN}} + \mathcal{L}_{slot_{PN}} + \theta * (\mathcal{L}_{intent_{SCL}} + \mathcal{L}_{slot_{SCL}})$, where θ is a hyperparameter with a value range of (0, 1).

4 Experiments

This section describes the experiments designed to evaluate the PMNCL model, as well as the datasets, baseline methods, and experimental settings used for evaluation in detail.

4.1 Datasets and Data Pre-processing

Three Chinese medical SLU datasets were used in this experiment, namely IMCS-V2[1], KUAKE-QIC[2], and CMID[3]. Table 2 provides the detailed dataset statistics.

---
[1] https://github.com/lemuria-wchen/imcs21-cblue
[2] https://tianchi.aliyun.com/dataset/95414
[3] https://www.biendata.com/competition/ccks_2019_1/Evaluation/

Table 2. Detailed division of IMCS-V2, KUAKE-QIC, and CMID datasets.

Datasets	Train/Dev/Test	Intent classes	Slot classes
IMCS-V2	2472/833/811	16	5
KUAKE-QIC	6931/1955/994	11	–
CMID	8430/2459/1273	33	–

- **IMCS-V2**: An intelligent dialogue diagnosis and treatment dataset constructed by Fudan University, and the samples is derived from real online doctor-patient dialogue. After pre-processing, the sample size is 4116, including 16 types of medical conversation intentions, such as '诊断 (Diagnose)', '用药建议 (Medicine suggested)', '病因 (Etiology)', as well as '症状 (Symptom)', '操作 (Operation)', '药品 (Drug)' and other 5 types of medical entities.
- **KUAKE-QIC**: The intent classification dataset for medical retrieval questions, which samples are from the Alibaba Quark website, with a total of 9,880 samples containing 11 common intent categories, such as '病情诊断 (Diagnose)', '治疗方案 (Therapeutic schedule)', and '就医建议 (Medical advice)'.
- **CMID**: The Chinese medical intent classification dataset from CCKS-2019. After pre-processing, it contains 12,162 utterances, including 33 medical intents, such as '病症病因 (Disease etiology)', '药物作用 (Drug effect)', and '体检方案 (Physical examination protocol)'.

4.2 Episode Construction

In this paper, an episode strategy [27] was used to train the samples. First, N intent categories were selected from the training set $\mathcal{D}$, and K samples were sampled for each category to construct the support set $\mathcal{D}_s$ and query set $\mathcal{D}_q$ ($\mathcal{D}_s \cap \mathcal{D}_q = \varnothing$). One support set $\mathcal{D}_s$ and one query set $\mathcal{D}_q$ constitute an episode. In the design of comparative experiments in this paper, $N = 3$, K is set to 3 and 5 to form 3-way 3-shot and 5-shot few-shot classification tasks. Moreover, to simulate the uneven distribution of medical intents and slot categories in real scene, we designed a comparison experiment by randomly selecting N ($N \in [1, 5]$) intent categories of samples to construct episodes. We performed three repeated experiments to reduce randomness and reported the average performance as the final experimental result.

4.3 Baselines

We selected multiple few-shot classification methods as baselines:

- **Matching networks** [27] map sample representations into an embedding space by calculating the query and support set similarity. Combining attention mechanisms to obtain the predicted probability of each category.
- **Relation networks** [28] use neural network training to obtain a learnable nonlinear similarity metric function. It cascades feature information corresponding to support set and query set samples for similarity calculation.

- **Induction networks** [5] use capsule networks and dynamic routing methods to condense sample representations in each category into generalized class-level representations so that the model has better generalization ability in few-shot text classification tasks.
- **PROTAUGMENT** [8] is a meta-learning algorithm for short text classification applied to the intent classification task.
- **FSIC** [29] demonstrated that the cross-encoder architecture, trained with episodic training and featuring a parameterized similarity scoring function, performed well in few-shot intent classification tasks.
- **ERNIE3.0** [30], proposed by the Baidu team, it was trained on a 4 TB corpus composed of large-scale knowledge graphs with 10 billion parameters.
- **eHealth** [15] is a medical pre-training language model developed based on Baidu's knowledge-enhanced semantic understanding framework, ERNIE.
- **BERT-wwm** was released by the Harbin Institute of Technology iFLYTEK Joint Laboratory (HFL). This method increases the difficulty of MLM tasks and prompts models to learn more long-term dependencies to predict mask content.
- **MC-BERT** [13] is a Chinese medical pre-training model developed by the Alibaba team based on BERT. It was trained on biomedical language corpus.
- **Roberta-wwm-ext** is a Chinese pre-training model based on Roberta designed by HFL. The number of training samples, batch size, and model parameter quantity are larger than the BERT model.

4.4 Implementation Details

The experiment system used was Ubuntu 18.04.3 LTS, with Python3.6 as the experimental environment, CUDA version 10.1, Tesla V100 32G as the GPU, Pytorch version 1.7.1, and transformers version 4.18.0.

4.4.1 Parameter Settings

In this paper, the dimension of the hidden state is set to 1536. The number of iterations for model training and validation were 100 and 60, respectively, and a validation was performed every ten iterations to save the best model parameters for subsequent testing. The AdamW optimizer was used to optimize the model with a learning rate of 1e−4. To prevent overfitting during training, a dropout layer was added to the model to enhance its generalization ability, with a dropout ratio 0.1. For the IMQ extension constant $c = 0.01$, and hyperparameter τ, we set $\tau = 0.01$ consistently.

To determine the hyperparameter values in the weighted loss function and allocate better mixing weights, we simulated 9 experiments with θ as an increment of 0.1 from 0.1 to 0.9, and the results are shown in Fig. 4.

The experimental results showed that when $\theta = 0.3$, the intent classification accuracy and slot filling F1 value were highest, so the experimental hyperparameter θ was uniformly set to 0.3 in subsequent experiments.

4.4.2 Evaluation Metrics

Accuracy, Precision, and F1-score are universal evaluation metrics that can comprehensively reflect the overall performance of the model. Therefore, we mainly evaluated the

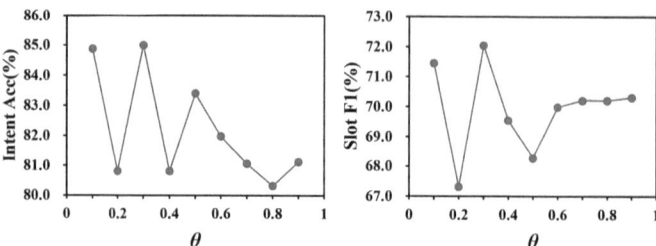

Fig. 4. Determination of mixing specific gravity θ.

performance of few-shot intent classification with accuracy and precision as references. We also evaluated the performance of few-shot slot filling, mainly with the F1 value as a reference.

4.5 Main Results and Analysis

4.5.1 Intent Classification

In IMCS-V2, KUAKE-QIC, and CMID Chinese medical SLU datasets, through comparative experiments with baseline methods for few-shot learning, it is proved that PMNCL has better performance than baseline methods. The experimental results are shown in Table 3.

The PMNCL model outperforms other baselines in IMCS-V2, KUAKE-QIC, and CMID datasets under 3-way 3-shot, and 5-shot sample settings. The PMNCL model is an improvement over the PNCL model (which integrates supervised contrastive learning methods based on the prototypical networks), and its performance is significantly better than the PNCL model. Especially in the IMCS-V2 dataset, under the 3-shot sample setting, the intent classification accuracy of the PMNCL model is improved by 3.88%, the precision is improved by 5.88%, and the F1 value is improved by 5.11%. This proves that using distance weight-corrected class prototypes is more representative than mean prototypes, improving the distance measurement effect of the prototypical networks.

Under the 3-shot and 5-shot sample settings, Relation Networks and Induction Networks have achieved more significant performance improvements than Matching Networks. This is because Matching Networks have always used a fixed distance measurement method and cannot effectively classify samples under limited data. Unlike fixed measurement methods, Relation Networks use neural networks to train nonlinear measurement functions, and Induction Networks match samples of the same class through capsule and dynamic routing algorithms. Both have strong recognition ability for unknown classes, and the model has better generalization ability.

In the IMCS-V2 dataset, under the 3-shot and 5-shot sample settings, compared to the PROTAUGMENT model, the PMNCL model improved the intent classification accuracy by 3.59% and 0.28%, respectively, and the F1 value by 3.82% and 5.68%, respectively; Compared to the FSIC model, the PMNCL model improved the intent classification accuracy by 4.48% and 3.62%, respectively, and the F1 value by 4.85% and 2.77%, respectively. This indicates that after integrating supervised contrastive learning

Table 3. Comparison of intent classification accuracy(%), precision(%), and F1(%) on datasets.

Dataset	Model		3-way 3-shot			3-way 5-shot		
			Acc	Pre	F1	Acc	Pre	F1
IMCS-V2	Matching Net	cosine	75.04	74.69	71.93	81.44	84.78	80.12
		euclidean	74.73	75.51	71.74	81.66	85.33	80.98
	Relation Networks		75.53	76.90	72.89	83.17	85.35	82.63
	Induction Networks		72.84	76.99	70.62	80.59	84.84	79.89
	PROTAUGMENT		80.48	80.83	79.60	86.83	84.54	81.26
	FSIC		79.59	81.55	78.57	83.49	86.94	84.17
	PNCL		80.19	81.02	78.31	84.56	86.64	84.05
	PMNCL		**84.07**	**86.90**	**83.42**	**87.11**	**89.52**	**86.94**
KUAKE-QIC	Matching Net	cosine	56.34	55.68	52.86	56.50	62.49	53.00
		euclidean	58.13	58.24	54.21	60.36	62.83	58.28
	Relation Networks		70.88	70.80	67.59	74.33	78.76	72.43
	Induction Networks		72.98	75.50	70.59	76.32	80.80	75.34
	PROTAUGMENT		78.33	81.46	76.99	83.78	87.02	83.38
	PNCL		81.67	84.31	80.42	86.56	88.98	86.32
	FSIC		83.17	85.35	82.63	84.19	89.85	85.04
	PMNCL		**84.15**	**89.85**	**85.04**	**89.18**	**91.35**	**89.41**
CMID	Matching Net	cosine	64.99	64.28	60.83	72.56	74.34	70.05
		euclidean	68.81	67.68	64.38	73.50	75.59	72.30
	Relation Networks		71.00	72.61	68.87	75.01	77.31	73.78
	Induction Networks		75.83	72.83	71.10	81.00	80.83	79.31
	PROTAUGMENT		79.59	81.55	78.57	83.08	84.97	82.74
	PNCL		78.47	80.76	76.83	80.60	80.63	78.03
	FSIC		79.66	**82.36**	78.50	80.83	84.54	81.26
	PMNCL		**80.33**	81.68	**78.87**	**83.49**	**86.94**	**84.17**

methods, better class discrimination representations can be obtained, and the model's ability to recognize same-class and different-class samples is further enhanced.

The experimental results of KUAKE-QIC and CMID datasets are similar to those of IMCS-V2, while different sample settings are also crucial factor affecting model performance. In the KUAKE-QIC dataset, compared with the 3-shot task, the PMNCL model improved intent classification accuracy by 5.03% and F1 value by 4.37% in the 5-shot task. The CMID dataset improved them by 3.16% and 5.3%, respectively. This indicates that as the number of training samples increases, models can learn more prior knowledge from samples. At the same time, larger data volumes can reduce the risk of overfitting, making their performance more reliable.

4.5.2 Intent Classification and Slot Filling

To further improve the performance of the PMNCL, this section jointly models intent information with slot information to obtain shared knowledge of both tasks. On the IMCS-V2 dataset, we compared the PMNCL with the PNCL method on different pre-training models to prove that slot information can assist models in improving intent classification accuracy. Meanwhile, it also proved that samples encoded through the Roberta-wwm-ext model have better effect. The results are shown in Table 4.

Table 4. Comparison of intent classification accuracy (%) and slot filling F1(%) on IMCS-V2.

Method	Model	3-way 3-shot		3-way 5-shot		Random	
		Acc	F1	Acc	F1	Acc	F1
PNCL	Ernie-3.0	79.07	58.56	85.56	63.75	86.72	66.16
	eHealth	83.52	65.26	86.44	70.91	88.11	71.26
	BERT-wwm	81.30	68.53	85.34	70.42	87.52	72.08
	MC-BERT	83.89	**70.31**	86.78	72.51	87.91	72.14
	Roberta-wwm-ext	**84.44**	70.08	**88.33**	**74.73**	**89.70**	**73.01**
PMNCL	Ernie 3.0	84.44	63.09	86.11	74.06	87.13	74.27
	eHealth	84.81	66.20	86.56	74.95	88.89	76.23
	BERT-wwm	85.55	70.93	87.78	75.00	89.59	72.97
	MC-BERT	85.74	72.78	89.89	77.05	90.07	75.07
	Roberta-wwm-ext	**86.48**	**73.62**	**90.33**	**77.29**	**90.96**	**77.53**

After adding slot information, using Roberta-wwm-ext as encoder, the PMNCL model achieved intent classification accuracy of 86.48% and 90.33% under 3-shot and 5-shot sample settings, respectively, which increased intent classification accuracy by 2.41% and 3.22% respectively compared to Table 3. Similarly, the PNCL model's intent classification accuracy increased by 4.25% and 3.77%. This indicates that slot information can improve intent classification performance to a certain extent.

Compared with the eHealth model, Ernie3.0 was not trained on the medical corpus, and its performance was not excellent in most cases. However, the eHealth model used the medical entity masking strategy to learn professional medical terms with more medical prior knowledge. Therefore, the eHealth model's performance was better than Ernie3.0 in most cases. Similarly, the MC-BERT model is a pre-training language model for Chinese medical language understanding with better performance than BERT-wwm.

Using Roberta-wwm-ext as an encoder, the PMNCL model achieved more remarkable performance improvement than baseline methods under three sample settings: 3-shot, 5-shot, and Random. This proves that Roberta-wwm-ext's whole word masking strategy can obtain richer semantic information, which helps improve the effect of models in Chinese medical SLU tasks.

4.6 Ablation Study

The PMNCL model has two essential components: prototypical modification network and supervised contrastive learning module. To verify the effectiveness of these two components, we make the ablation study by removing or replacing one of the components, respectively, on the IMCS-V2 dataset and comparing it with the original model. The experimental results are shown in Fig. 5.

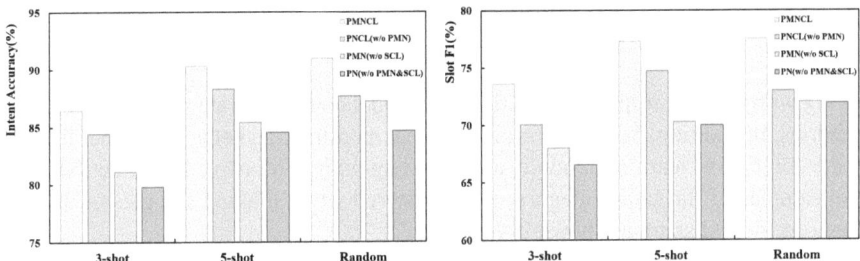

Fig. 5. Ablation study on IMCS-V2 dataset.

PN (w/o PMN&SCL) refers to using only the prototypical networks as a classifier. PNCL (w/o PMN) stands for adding the supervised contrastive learning method based on the prototypical networks. PMN (w/o SCL) represents using the prototypical modification network as a classifier. On the IMCS-V2 dataset, the PMNCL model achieved the best intent classification accuracy and slot filling F1 value under 3-shot, 5-shot, and Random sample settings. When the prototypical modification network was replaced with the traditional prototypical networks, the intent classification accuracy and slot filling F1 value decreased significantly in all experimental settings. This indicates that the prototypical modification network module is the core component of PMNCL, and the calculated class prototype is more representative. After removing the contrastive learning module, the performance of the model further declined. This is because using only the prototypical modification network as a classifier cannot effectively separate samples, and the model's ability to recognize same-class and different-class samples is weak. When both the prototypical modification network and the contrastive learning module are removed, the intent classification accuracy and slot filling F1 value both drops to the lowest point, indicating that the prototypical modification network module and the supervised contrastive learning module complement each other and are more effective than the baseline method in constructing class prototypes and improving classification performance.

To further demonstrate the effect of the prototypical modification network and supervised contrastive learning module on sentence embedding representation, we used the t-SNE algorithm to reduce high-dimensional sentence vectors on the IMCS-V2 dataset. The results are shown in Fig. 6.

In Fig. 6(a), when the model was not trained, directly inputting samples into the pre-trained model shows randomness and confusion in sentence embedding representation. However, in Fig. 6(b), after introducing the prototypical modification network and

(a) Roberta-wwm-ext　　　(b) Roberta-wwm-ext-PMN　　　(c) Roberta-wwm-ext-PMNCL

Fig. 6. Visualization analysis results of IMCS-V2 dataset.

training with cross-entropy loss function, the model could separate samples of different categories. In addition, based on the prototypical modification network, further integrating the contrastive learning module, after training with contrastive loss function, could make samples of the same category more clustered while making samples of different categories more distant, as shown in Fig. 6(c).

Through analysis of ablation experiments, it can be concluded that both the prototypical modification network and supervised contrastive learning module can improve the performance of the PMNCL model in Chinese medical SLU tasks.

5 Conclusion

To address the problem of distance measurement in traditional prototypical networks and reduce the impact of potential noise in each intent category, this paper explored prototype calculation and embedding space selection. It proposed a prototypical modification method based on IMQ function weighting. This method corrects class prototypes by calculating distance weights between support set samples, thereby improving the distance measurement efficiency of prototypical networks. To obtain deeper semantic representations, this paper introduced contrastive learning methods and designed a contrastive loss function to better separate samples of the same class from those of different classes. To verify the effectiveness of the method, we conducted experiments on three Chinese medical SLU datasets. The results show that the proposed prototypical modification network and supervised contrastive learning method can effectively improve the performance of models in few-shot Chinese medical SLU tasks.

Identifying medical entities is the core challenge in joint intent classification and slot filling tasks. Medical entity annotation relies more on professional doctors' knowledge and experience than entities in other fields. Different doctors may have different annotations for the same entity. It also requires more annotated resources for all entity categories to be extracted. Moreover, the varying lengths of medical entities make it difficult to determine entity boundaries, which poses significant challenges to entity recognition. In the future, more fine-grained research on medical entities is needed to improve the performance of models in medical SLU tasks further.

Acknowledgements. We are very grateful to the anonymous reviewers. Their insightful comments are very helpful to improve the paper. The work is supported by National Natural Science Foundation of China (62162001), Ningxia Provincial Natural Science Foundation (2021AAC03224), and 2024 Graduate Innovation Project of North Minzu University (YCX24122).

References

1. Son, G.Y., Kim, M.: A simple and efficient dialogue generation model incorporating commonsense knowledge. Expert Syst. Appl. **249**, 1–15 (2024). https://doi.org/10.1016/j.eswa.2024.123584
2. Hou, Y., Wang, X., Che, C., Li, B., Che, W., Chen, Z.: FewJoint: few-shot learning for joint dialogue understanding. Int. J. Mach. Learn. Cybern. **13**(11), 3409–3423 (2022). https://doi.org/10.1007/s13042-022-01604-9
3. Godslove, J.F., Nayak, A.K.: Trilingual conversational intent decoding for response retrieval. Knowl. Inf. Syst. 1–22 (2023). https://doi.org/10.1007/s10115-023-01972-w
4. Li, F., Fergus, R., Perona, P.: One-shot learning of object categories. IEEE Trans. Pattern Anal. Mach. Intell. **28**(4), 594–611 (2006). https://doi.org/10.1109/TPAMI.2006.79
5. Geng, R., Li, B., Li, Y., Zhu, X., Jian, P., Sun, J.: Induction networks for few-shot text classification. In: Proceedings of the 2019 Conference on Empirical Methods in Natural Language Processing, pp. 3895–3904 (2019). https://doi.org/10.18653/v1/D19-1403
6. Geng, R., Li, B., Li, Y., Sun, J., Zhu, X.: Dynamic memory induction networks for few-shot text classification. In: Proceedings of the 58th Annual Meeting of the Association for Computational Linguistics, pp. 1087–1094 (2020). https://doi.org/10.18653/v1/2020.acl-main.102
7. Snell, J., Swersky, K., Zemel, R.: Prototypical networks for few-shot learning. In: Advances in Neural Information Processing Systems, pp. 4077–4087 (2017)
8. Dopierre, T., Gravier, C., Logerais, W.: ProtAugment: unsupervised diverse short-texts paraphrasing for intent detection meta-learning. In: Proceedings of the 59th Annual Meeting of the Association for Computational Linguistics, pp. 2454–2466 (2021). https://doi.org/10.18653/v1/2021.acl-long.191
9. Wen, M., Xia, T., Liao, B., Tian, Y.: Few-shot relation classification using clustering-based prototype modification. Knowl.-Based Syst. **268**, 1–8 (2023). https://doi.org/10.1016/j.knosys.2023.110477
10. Lee, J., Yoon, W., Kim, S., Kim, D.: BioBERT: a pre-trained biomedical language representation model for biomedical text mining. Bioinformatics **36**(4), 1234–1240 (2020). https://doi.org/10.1093/bioinformatics/btz682
11. Gu, Y., Tinn, R., Cheng, H., Lucas, M.: Domain-specific language model pretraining for biomedical natural language processing. ACM Trans. Comput. Healthc. (HEALTH) **3**(1), 1–23 (2021). https://doi.org/10.1145/3458754
12. Kanakarajan, K., Kundumani, B., Sankarasubbu, M.: BioELECTRA: pretrained biomedical text encoder using discriminators. In: Proceedings of the 20th Workshop on Biomedical Language Processing, pp. 143–154 (2021). https://doi.org/10.18653/v1/2021.bionlp-1.16
13. Zhang, N., Jia, Q., Yin, K., Dong, L., Gao, F., Hua, N.: Conceptualized representation learning for Chinese biomedical text mining. In: International Conference on Web Search and Data Mining (WSDM), pp. 1–14 (2020). https://doi.org/10.48550/arXiv.2008.10813
14. Cui, Y., Che, W., Liu, T., Qin, B., Wang, S., Hu, G.: Revisiting pre-trained models for Chinese natural language processing. In: Proceedings of the 2020 Conference on Empirical Methods in Natural Language Processing, pp. 657–668 (2020). https://doi.org/10.18653/v1/2020.findings-emnlp.58

15. Wang, Q., Dai, S., Xu, B., Lyu, Y., Zhu, Y., Wu, H.: Building Chinese biomedical language models via multi-level text discrimination. arXiv preprint arXiv:2110.07244, pp. 1–14 (2022). https://doi.org/10.48550/arXiv.2110.07244
16. Lan, G., Hu, M., Li, Y., Zhang, Y.: Contrastive knowledge integrated graph neural networks for Chinese medical text classification. Eng. Appl. Artif. Intell. **122**, 1–14 (2023). https://doi.org/10.1016/j.engappai.2023.106057
17. Chen, Q., Zhuo, Z., Wang, W.: BERT for joint intent classification and slot filling, pp. 1–6 (2019). arXiv preprint arXiv:1902.10909. https://doi.org/10.48550/arXiv.1902.10909
18. Lu, Y., Zhao, Y., Cui, R., Jin, G.: Research on the joint learning method of intent detection and slot filling by fusing tag semantic information. In: IEEE International Conference on Control, Electronics and Computer Technology (ICCECT), pp. 838–842 (2023). https://doi.org/10.1109/ICCECT57938.2023.10141179
19. Ma, Z.Y., Sun, B., Li, S.T.: A two-stage selective fusion framework for joint intent detection and slot filling. IEEE Trans. Neural Netw. Learn. Syst. 3874–3885 (2024). https://doi.org/10.1109/TNNLS.2022.3202562
20. Yu, H.L., Liu, C.L., Zhang, L.: An intent classification method for questions in "Treatise on Febrile diseases" based on TinyBERT-CNN fusion model. Comput. Biol. Med. 1–11 (2023). https://doi.org/10.1016/j.compbiomed.2023.107075
21. Lee, J.H., Wu, E., Ou, Y.Y.: Anti-drugs chatbot: Chinese BERT-based cognitive intent analysis. IEEE Trans. Comput. Soc. Syst. 514–521 (2024). https://doi.org/10.1109/TCSS.2023.3238477
22. Gao, T., Yao, X., Chen, D.: SimCSE: simple contrastive learning of sentence embeddings. In: Proceedings of the 2021 Conference on Empirical Methods in Natural Language Processing, EMNLP 2021, pp. 6894–6910. Association for Computational Linguistics (ACL) (2021). https://doi.org/10.18653/v1/2021.emnlp-main.552
23. Wu, X., Gao, C., Zang, L., Han, J., Wang, Z., Hu, S.: ESimCSE: enhanced sample building method for contrastive learning of unsupervised sentence embedding. In: Proceedings of the 29th International Conference on Computational Linguistics, pp. 3898–3907 (2022). https://doi.org/10.48550/arXiv.2109.04380
24. Liang, X., Wu, L., Li, J., Wang, Y., Meng, Q., Qin, T.: R-drop: regularized dropout for neural networks. In: Neural Information Processing Systems 34, pp. 10890–10905 (2021). https://doi.org/10.48550/arXiv.2106.14448
25. Xu, J., Shao, W., Chen, L., Liu, L.: ImSimCSE: improving contrastive learning for sentence embeddings from two perspectives, pp. 1–12 (2023). arXiv preprint arXiv:2305.13192. https://doi.org/10.48550/arXiv.2305.13192
26. Wang, J., Qu, J., Wang, K., et al.: Improving the robustness of knowledge-grounded dialogue via contrastive learning. In: Proceedings of the AAAI Conference on Artificial Intelligence, pp. 19135–19143 (2024). https://doi.org/10.1609/aaai.v38i17.29881
27. Vinyals, O., Blundell, C., Lillicrap, T., Kavukcuoglu, K., Wierstra, D.: Matching networks for one shot learning. In: Advances in Neural Information Processing Systems 29, pp. 1–12 (2016)
28. Sung, F., Yang, Y., Zang, L., Xiang, T., Torr, P., Hospedales, T.: Learning to compare: relation network for few-shot learning. In: Proceedings of the IEEE Conference on Computer Vision and Pattern Recognition, pp. 1199–1208 (2018). https://doi.org/10.1109/CVPR.2018.00131
29. Mesgar, M., Tran, T., Glavas, G., et al.: The devil is in the details: on models and training regimes for few-shot intent classification. In: Proceedings of the 17th Conference of the European Chapter of the Association for Computational Linguistics, pp. 1846–1857 (2023). https://doi.org/10.18653/v1/2023.eacl-main.135
30. Sun, Y., Wang, S., Feng, S., Ding, S., Pang, C., Shang, J.: ERNIE 3.0 titan: exploring larger-scale knowledge enhanced pre-training for language understanding and generation, pp. 1–22 (2021). arXiv preprint arXiv:2112.12731. https://doi.org/10.48550/arXiv.2112.12731

Algorithm Application

Hierarchical Feature Selection Method Based on Sequential Backward Selection Algorithm for Fasting Blood Glucose Prediction

Wencheng Sun$^{(\boxtimes)}$ and Xiaoyong Chen

National University of Defense Technology, Nanjing 210039, China
sunwencheng@nudt.edu.cn

Abstract. It is important to identify people at high risk of diabetes, such as correlating them from physical examination data, and to intervene in advance in health management and medical treatment. In this paper, we employ both bagging and boosting methods to predict the patient's fasting blood glucose (FBG) based on physical examination data. A hierarchical feature selection method based on sequential backward selection (SBS) algorithm is presented to select an optimal feature subset. The results of extensive experiments on account of physical examination database suggest that the presented feature selection method has better performance.

Keywords: FBG · physical examination data · SBS · feature selection

1 Introduction

Diabetes mellitus is a typical chronic disease, often accompanied by hyperglycemia, which is also one of the criteria for clinical judgment. When the blood glucose level is high, it means that the patient is in a high-risk area for diabetes and needs to be treated as soon as possible, including lifestyle changes and appropriate medications. In the pre-onset of diabetes, patients do not feel much pain, which also makes patients less alert. However, a prolonged hyperglycemic state will bring about other malignant chain changes, such as the appearance of cardiovascular and cerebrovascular diseases.

At present, there are two main methods to predict FBG [1]. The first method, which is an expensive method of building a mathematical model by monitoring the key processes of glucose metabolism and insulin control, is mainly aimed at patients with more severe disease who need to monitor blood glucose changes at a very high frequency to prevent irreversible effects. However, the natural uncontrollable nature of physiological factors, such as mood swings, bacterial infections, fatigue and insomnia, makes this method encounter many limitations in the promotion of diabetes prevention and control. The second method uses other physiological data to construct a prediction model, which is based on the

Table 1. An overview of feature selection techniques.

Techniques	Methods	Advantages	Disadvantages	Examples
Filter	Univariate Methods	Simple	Overlook correlation between predictors	Information gain
		Independent of the prediction model	Overlook the prediction mode	Chi-square test
		Easy to understand output	Not a fully automatic procedure	Distance correlation
	Multivariate Methods	Considers predictor's correlations	Slow	Relief
		Independent of the prediction model	Overlooks the prediction model	CFS
		Fully automatic procedure		MBF
Wrapper	Deterministic Methods	Simple	Risk of over-fitting	SFS, SBS, BDS, LRS
		Interacts with the classifier	Classifier dependent selection	SBE
		Less computationally intensive		
	Randomized Methods	Less prone to local optima	Computationally intensive	Simulated annealing
		Interacts with the classifier	Classifier dependent selection	Randomized hill climbing
		Models feature dependencies	Higher risk of over-fitting	Genetic algorithms
Embedded	Embedded Methods	Interacts with the classifier	Classifier dependent selection	ID3, C4.5
		Lower computational complexity		SVM
		Models feature dependencies		CART

logical assumption that blood glucose metabolism is a complex process under the combined action of multiple physiological factors. Many current studies are based on the modeling of historical blood glucose data collected by medical professionals in diabetic patients to regress and predict blood glucose changes over the next period of time. The data-driven prediction method does not require the researcher to have sufficient medical knowledge and is more operational than the first method.

Insulin, blood pressure, lipids and other indicators are strongly correlated FBG, and if these data can be extracted, it is very helpful to predict FBG. However, this method is too costly and unpractical, and it will not be of much help to diabetes early warning in real life. When people go for a physical examination because of a cold and fever, or participate in an annual regular physical examination, they generally have blood routine, blood lipids, kidney function and other tests. The physiological cycle of the human body is a process of mutual influence and feedback, so it is reasonable to predict FBG based on physical examination data, and it is less expensive and easy to generalize.

2 Related Works

Due to the availability of data with the increasing dimension, feature selection methods are particularly important [2–4]. Effective feature selection methods can greatly reduce the computational cost by reducing the feature dimensions of the dataset, without degrading the prediction performance. The principle of the feature selection method is to select a feature subset from the input data, which can reduce the interference of noisy data and comprehensively describe the input data. In the current study, there are three feature selection methods that are widely used, including Filter, Wrapper and Embedded methods [5], as shown in Table 1.

- The filter method is a kind of heuristic method, and its main idea is to assign a weight value to each feature through statistical methods, which represents the

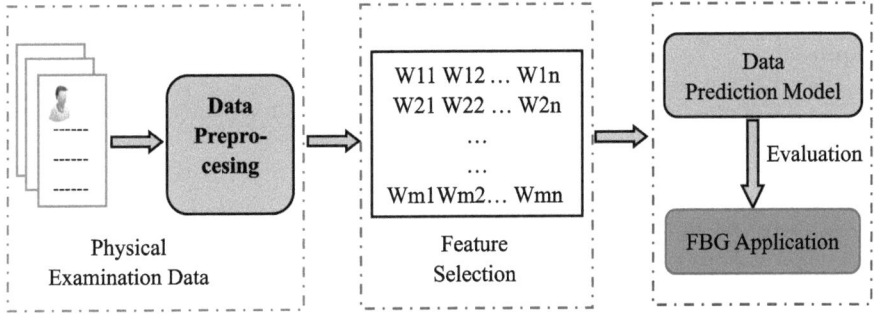

Fig. 1. Workflow demonstration of the proposed framework.

degree of influence of the feature on the target label and is the embodiment of the importance of the feature [6,7]. Features are sorted according to the weight values to form the optimal subset in the current state. The filter method only considers the relationship between the feature attributes and the target, which has the advantage of small computational cost, but the method does not consider the correlation between the feature attributes, which also leads to the neglect of some useful information.

- The wrapper method is characterized by the fact that the performance of the later model is used as an evaluation index for feature selection, and the front and back stages echo [8,9]. By comparing the differences in the combinations of various feature subsets, the best performing subset for the predictive model is the optimal subset.
- The embedded method is different from the first two methods, and the difference is reflected in the fact that the first two methods separate the feature selection process from the final learning model, and although there is mutual feedback, it is still carried out as two independent stages. The embedded method integrates the feature selection process and the tuning process of the learning model [10].

3 Methodology

The experimental framework in this paper is shown in Fig. 1, which is a process for predicting FBG based on physical examination data. In this framework, the data preprocessing process is carried out first, followed by a hierarchical feature selection method based on SBS algorithm. An improved prediction model based on the model fusion method are subsequently built.

3.1 Data Pre-processing

Data preprocessing steps include defaults filling and noise processing. When there is a missing value in a sample attribute, you can consider either deleting

Algorithm 1. Hierarchical Feature Selection Method based on SBS
Require:
　　The set of medical examination subjects, S_m;
　　The set of physical examination item in each subject, I_n;
　　The set of physical examination item in all subjects, IA;
Ensure:
　　The optimal subset of physical examination data, O;
1: Fit CatBoost to S_m, and calculate the importance score of each subject, W_1;
2: Fit XGBoot to I_n, and calculate the importance score of each item, W_2;
3: Calculate the global weight of each item in IA, $W_g = W_1 * W_2$;
4: Sort the items by W_g, the most important is at the top;
5: Based on SBS algorithm, delete the least weighted item each iteration and calculate the mean square error (MSE) value of the test set;
6: When the MSE value is the smallest, the optimal subset O can be obtained;
7: **return** O.

the sample or filling in the missing value, such as using the attribute mean or median to fill in the default value, or using machine learning model regression to fill in the missing value. Outlier analysis is a more efficient and more effective method of noise data processing.

3.2 Feature Selection

The Sequential Backward Selection (SBS) algorithm starts the loop from the full set of features. If the individual feature has the minimum classification accuracy, the feature will be excluded from the optimal subset. The remaining feature subset can obtain the best objective function value, and the subset can be considered as the optimal subset The naive SBS algorithm does not take into account the dependencies between features. In addition, the valuable relationship between features is easily ignored, resulting in over-fitting and poor performance. The current approach is to rank the importance of features first and then use the SBS algorithm to select features. W. Xao et al. [11] propose a feature selection algorithm, the Score-SBS method.

Physical examination data consists of the patient's basic information, such as age, sex, and physical examination date, and a variable number of physical examination items in different medical examination subjects. For example, renal function three includes UREA, uric acid(UA) and creatinine (CREA).

In the feature selection process, W. Xao et al. [11] only consider the relationship between physical examination items and blood glucose, and ignore the relationship between physical examination items and subjects, and the relationship between medical examination subjects and blood glucose. In view of this, we propose a hierarchical feature selection method based on SBS, as shown in Algorithm. 1.

3.3 Prediction Model Construction

After completing data processing and feature selection, we need to construct the regression models. For model selection, we plan to use XGBoost, LightGBM, CatBoost and the classical random forest model. The four models of XGBoost, LightGBM, CatBoost and Random Forest are tree based models. XGBoost, LightGBM and CatBoost belong to the boosting algorithm, which focus on reducing model deviations. The random forest belongs to the bagging

Table 2. Demographics of physical examination data

Subjects	Numbers of Items	Missing proportion	Scores
Liver function	8	21.6%	1
Renal function	3	24.4%	7/9
Blood routine	17	0.28%	2/3
Blood lipids	4	0.41%	7/9
Hepatitis B (HBV)	5	75.9%	7/9

Table 3. Importance scores of physical examination items.

Items	Our Method		Score-SBS method		Items	Our Method		Score-SBS method	
	Rank	Score	Rank	Score		Rank	Score	Rank	Score
AST	1	327	1	327	LDL	20	68	24	87
ALP	2	230	2	230	MCHC	21	67	19	101
ALT	3	177	5	177	PCV	22	63	20	94
r-GT	4	161	9	161	NEUT%	23	62	21	93
TG	5	156	3	200	MCH	24	61	22	92
Alb	6	155	10	155	PLT	25	60	23	90
UA	7	152	4	195	PDW	26	59	24	89
CR	8	137	6	176	MONO%	27	55	25	82
TP	9	131	12	131	MPV	28	53	26	79
WBC	10	116	7	174	LY%	29	52	27	78
UR	11	110	11	142	HbcAb	30	45	30	58
MCV	12	108	8	162	HBeAb	31	36	34	46
RBC	13	85	13	128	EO%	32	35	31	52
HDL	14	82	16	105	HBsAb	33	34	35	44
TC	15	82	17	105	PCT	34	34	32	51
GLB	16	77	28	77	BA%	35	33	33	50
RDW	17	74	15	111	HBsAg	36	26	36	33
HGB	18	74	14	111	HBeAg	37	21	37	27
A/G	19	72	29	72					

algorithm, which is biased to reduce the model variance. Comparison experiments on these models can better reflect the characteristics of these models. The common and effective fusion method is stacking or blending. However, due to the relatively small amount of data, multi-layer stacking/blending learning is prone to over-fitting.

4 Experiments

There are already many physical examination items, but only those items which have medical relationships with FBG are considered in this paper. The dataset extracted from real-world physical examination database [12], includes 229,240 individual values for 5,731 patients.

Table 4. Performance comparison between our method and the Score-SBS method using RF, XGBoost, LightGBM and CatBoost. MAE and RMSE are used as metric.

Criterias	FS Methods	Random Forest		XGBoost		LightGBM		CatBoost	
		Median fill	Mixed fill	Median fill	Mixed fill	Median fill	Mixed fill	Median fill	Mixed fill
MAE	Our method	0.7854	0.7881	0.7620	0.7681	0.7590	0.7590	0.7570	0.7603
	Score-SBS method	0.7844	0.7880	0.7640	0.7705	0.7594	0.7594	0.7571	0.7619
	All items	0.7866	0.7900	0.7638	0.7701	0.7596	0.7596	0.7596	0.7625
RMSE	Our method	1.0229	1.0254	1.0021	1.0080	1.0377	1.0393	0.9943	0.9985
	Score-SBS method	1.0234	1.0258	1.0066	1.0145	1.0379	1.0398	0.9955	0.9990
	All items	1.0260	1.0300	1.0034	1.0144	1.0377	1.0396	1.0007	0.9990

The importance scores of medical examination subjects are calculated with CatBoost algorithm and then standardized, as shown in Table 2. According to the above algorithm, the global weight of for all items can be calculated as shown in Table 3. We find that the model performs best when selecting the top 28 physical examination items. At the same time, we also calculate the importance score of all items according to the method of the Score-SBS method [11], as shown in Table 4. We find that the model performs best when selecting the top 31 physical examination items.

4.1 Evaluation Criteria

To evaluate the performance, we adopt two criteria that are widely used: mean absolute error (MAE) and root mean square error (RMSE). As shown in the following formulas, n is the total number, X_i' is the predicted FBG value of the i-th patient, and X_i is the actual FBG value of the i-th patient.

$$MAE = \frac{1}{n}\sum_{i=1}^{n}(|X_i' - X_i|) \tag{1}$$

$$MSE = \frac{1}{n}\sum_{i=1}^{n}(X_i' - X_i)^2 \tag{2}$$

$$RMSE = \sqrt{\frac{1}{n}\sum_{i=1}^{n}(X'_i - X_i)^2} = \sqrt{MSE} \qquad (3)$$

RMSE can evaluate the degree of change of data, the smaller the value of RMSE, indicating that the prediction model describes experimental data with better accuracy. MAE can better reflect the actual situation of prediction error.

In addition, we apply 5-fold cross validation method to evaluate our results, to ensure the reliability of the results. The smaller the result, the better the effect achieved.

4.2 Results and Evaluation

For the missing data which is inherent in the data set, we apply two methods for filling. The first one is relatively simple, using the median of attributes directly to fill. The second method belongs to the mixed filling. For the missing rate below 1%, we use the attribute's median to fill. For the missing rate over 70%, we choose to delete these items. For the remaining items, we fill the predicted value generated by random forest model. However, from the Table 4, we can see that the second mixed filling is generally not as effective as the first simple median filling. After analysis, we believe that the error between the predicted values generated by random forest and the true values is larger than the error between the attribute medians and the real values, thus affecting the final prediction results. In addition, the MAE and RMSE of the random forest model also generally surpass the other three models, which indicates that based on the physical examination data of FBG prediction, random forest model is not very good.

We use all items as the baseline for feature selection. Moreover, we use the Score-SBS method as a comparison, to evaluate the feature selection method we propose in this paper. We verify our FS method on four models, which are random forest (RF), XGBoost, LightGBM, and CatBoost, respectively. Besides, the MAE and RMSE of these models almost maintain the same trend.

As shown in Table 4, compared with the baseline method, the Score-SBS feature selection method has better effect on most of models, but it doesn't work well on all models and it is even worse on some models. For example, the Score-SBS method achieved the worst results on the XGBoost model. It indicates that the Score-SBS method is dependent on models, which doesn't have good scalability and stability.

Compared with the baseline method and the Score-SBS method, the proposed method has achieved better results on all models. Although the mixed filling method is not as effective as simple methods, the proposed method can still help the two filling methods improve results. It can also be seen that all the three Feature Selection methods achieve better results on the CatBoost model, which shows that the CatBoost model fits the data set most.

5 Conclusions

The aim of this paper is to select the most valuable features of physical examination data, and then use these features to predict the FBG value of patients. We extracted physical examination data from the cooperative hospitals. We adopt two methods to fill in the missing data. The first one is a simple attribute median filling and the other is a mixed filling method. The experimental results show that the former method has achieved better results. Further more, we use two evaluation criterions, MAE and RMSE, to evaluate and analyze the effect of feature selection methods. We use all items as the baseline for feature selection, and set up comparative tests for our method and Score-SBS method. Comparative experiments are carried out on four predictive models, which are random forest (RF), XGBoost, LightGBM, and CatBoost, respectively. Extensive experiments demonstrate that the optimal subset selected by the proposed method in this paper is more effective.

References

1. Wang, Y., Wu, X., Mo, X.: A novel adaptive-weighted-average framework for blood glucose prediction. Diabetes Technol. Ther. **15**(10), 792–801 (2013)
2. Li, J., et al.: Feature selection: a data perspective. ACM Comput. Surv. **50**(6), 1–45 (2017)
3. Xie, J., Wang, M., Grant, P.W., Pedrycz, W.: Feature selection with discernibility and independence criteria. IEEE Trans. Knowl. Data Eng. **1**, 1–15 (2024)
4. Xinwang, L., Lei, W., Jian, Z., Jianping, Y., Huan, L.: Global and local structure preservation for feature selection. IEEE Trans. Neural Netw. Learn. Syst. **25**(6), 1083–1095 (2014)
5. Girish, C., Ferat, S.: A survey on feature selection methods. Comput. Electr. Eng. **40**(1), 16–28 (2014)
6. Parlak, B., Uysal, A.K.: A novel filter feature selection method for text classification: extensive feature selector. J. Inf. Sci. **1**, 59–78 (2023)
7. Zheng, D., Tang, P., Danping, L., Han, L., Saberi, S.: A structured combination of ensemble classifier and filter-based feature selection to improve breast cancer diagnosis. J. Cancer Res. Clin. Oncol. **16**, 14519–14534 (2023)
8. Lee, S.J., Xu, Z., Li, T., Yang, Y.: A novel bagging C4.5 algorithm based on wrapper feature selection for supporting wise clinical decision making. J. Biomed. Inform. **78**, 144–155 (2017)
9. Jain, R., Wei, X.: Artificial intelligence based wrapper for high dimensional feature selection. BMC Bioinform. **24**(1), 392 (2023)
10. Shi, X., et al.: An ensemble-based feature selection framework to select risk factors of childhood obesity for policy decision making. BMC Med. Inform. Decis. Mak. **1**, 1–13 (2021)
11. Xiao, W., Ji, J., Shao, F., Sun, R., Xing, C.: Fasting blood glucose change prediction model based on medical examination data and data mining techniques. In: IEEE International Conference on Smart City/SocialCom/SustainCom 2016, pp. 742–747 (2016)
12. Aliyun: TIANCHI. https://tianchi.aliyun.com/dataset/3964?t=1689217278709

Personalized Recommendation Algorithm Based on Knowledge Graphs with High-Order Information

Siyao Zhang, Zhihui Wang, Jinru Hu, and Jianrui Chen(✉)

School of Computer Science, Shaanxi Normal University, Xi'an 710199, China
jianrui_chen@snnu.edu.cn

Abstract. With the rapid development of network technology, recommendation systems attract increasing research because of its wide applications in e-commerce. Nevertheless, most existing recommendation models based on graph neural networks do not consider the transitivity of subgraph structures in interactive data. This makes the models unable to capture the complex dependencies and mutual influences between users and items, resulting in the inability to achieve high-quality personalized recommendations. To address the above challenge, we propose a novel recommendation algorithm based on knowledge graph with high-order graph convolutional network, named KG^2CN. Firstly, we introduce the subgraph structure on the knowledge graph to capture high-order contextual information between users and items. Secondly, the mined subgraph information and graph convolutional network are combined to learn high-order features of users and items. Finally, the decoder is applied to predict the ratings of target users on the uninteracted items, thereby recommending the Top-K items. Experimental results on the Book-Crossing and Last.FM datasets show that the proposed KG^2CN obtains better performance in F1 score and AUC metrics.

Keywords: Recommendation Algorithm · Knowledge Graph · Graph Convolutional Network · High-order Pattern

1 Introduction

With the rapid development of information technology, information overload has become a critical issue that can not be ignored at present [1]. To alleviate this issue, recommendation system is receiving amount of attention because of its higher efficiency and accuracy [2]. For most target users, recommendation system not only recommend the items they have browsed according to their historical behavior records [3], but also recommend new items for them, which is called item cold start recommendation [4]. Recommendation system greatly reduces the behavior cost of users and improves the efficiency of searching [5]. Traditional recommendation algorithms are divided into content-based recommendation [6], collaborative filtering (CF) [7], and hybrid recommendation [8]. CF is widely used in recommendation systems, which aims to recommend items that users may be interested in by exploiting their historical behavioral data and behavioral similarities between users. To some extent, CF-based methods have alleviated the issues of the data sparsity [9], cold start [10] and other issues [11]. Recently, researchers try to combine CF and deep learning to further explore the intrinsic relations between users and items. Graph Convolution Networks (GCNs) have become the hot topic of recommendation systems. Based on a deeper understanding of GCN, researchers attempt to make GCN-based recommendation system more complete and satisfactory. Unlike the traditional network models, Long Short Term Memory [12] and Convolutional Neural Network [13] are only used for grid-based data, GCN processes data with generalized topological graph structure and deeply explores its attributes. For most GCN-based recommendation models, they are centered on the target node aggregating sufficiently reliable neighbor information and embedding these in the network [14] for convolution.

Faced with the surge in network data, most existing recommendation algorithms face some challenges, such as uneven distribution of interaction data between users and items and inability to effectively recommend for new users without interaction records [15]. These issues lead to poor recommendation performance. To address these issues, knowledge graph technology is introduced for recommendation systems. Knowledge graph is a directed heterogeneous graph, where nodes represent entities and edges correspond to relations between entities. Knowledge graph aims to enhance the relevance of its search engine results, thereby optimizing the search experience of users [8]. Normally, a knowledge graph is a semantic network that formalizes the description of entities and their relations in the real world. Knowledge graph contains rich semantic information and the associated data between entities, so they can effectively enhance the representation capability of items and compensate for the sparsity of interaction data between users and items [16]. By combining users personal characteristics and contextual information, knowledge graph also helps alleviate the cold start problem in user recommendation. Furthermore, Knowledge graph improves the accuracy of recommendation algorithms and provides interpretability [17].

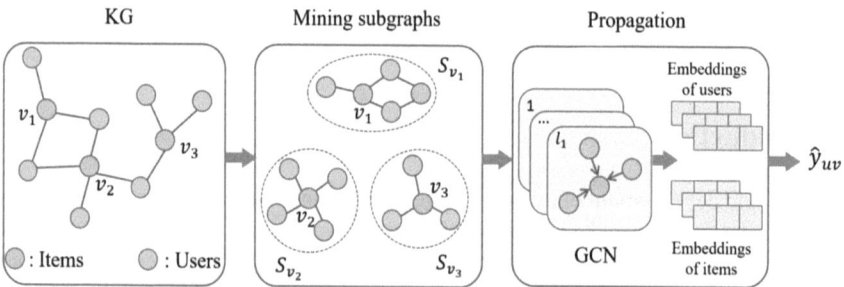

Fig. 1. Overall framework of the proposed KG^{2}CN.

However, most previous efforts have been limited to propagating neighborhood information in pairwise interactions, and have not considered the powerful role of subgraph structures in recommendation systems. As a result, GCNs can only capture the propagation of information between local nodes, and are unable to utilize global information to aid node representation learning. This limitation makes the recommendation model insufficiently understand the structure and context of the entire graph, leading to poor recommendation performance.

To address the above issue, this paper proposes a novel recommendation algorithm, and the main contributions are summarized as follows:

- We introduce subgraph structures in the knowledge graph and model high-order patterns by the number of subgraphs on different nodes.
- We design a novel recommendation algorithm based on high-order GCN to obtain more comprehensive and enriched high-order features by aggregating subgraph structural information.
- Diverse experiments and analyses demonstrate that KG^{2}CN outperforms existing better recommendation algorithms on two datasets.

The remainder of this article is organized as follows. Section 2 provides a detailed introduction to our proposed recommendation algorithm. Subsequently, the experimental results are presented in Sect. 3. Finally, Sect. 4 provides the conclusions and sketches future work.

2 Our Proposed Algorithm

In this section, we comprehensively elaborate on the proposed KG^{2}CN based on knowledge graph with high-order graph convolutional network. This model deeply explores the high-order patterns in the knowledge graph. Uppercase bold (e.g., $\mathbf{X}$), lowercase bold (e.g., $\mathbf{x}$), lowercase italics (e.g., x), and uppercase italics (e.g., X) represent matrices, vectors, constants, and sets, respectively.

2.1 Problem Formalization

In a recommendation system, there are m users, denoted as $U = \{u_1, u_2, \ldots, u_m\}$, and n items, denoted as $V = \{v_1, v_2, \ldots, v_n\}$. The interaction matrix between users and items is defined as $\mathbf{Y} \in \mathbb{R}^{m \times n}$, where $\mathbf{Y}_{uv} = 1$ if there is an interaction behavior between user u and item v (e.g., click, purchase, selection), otherwise $\mathbf{Y}_{uv} = 0$.

Generally, the knowledge graph $G = (E_1, E_2, R)$ is composed of several triplets in the form of entity-relation-entity (h, r, t), where $h \in E_1, r \in R, t \in E_2$ represent the head entity, relation, and tail entity of the triplet, respectively. Moreover, E_1, E_2, and R represent the sets of head entities, tail entities, and relations in the knowledge graph. In this paper, the head entity of the knowledge graph triplet is the item, the tail entity is the attribute of the item, and the relation is the attribute relation of the item. For example, in Book-Crossing dataset, h, r, t is respectively book, author, author name. In other words, $E_1 = V$ in this case. Once the user-item interaction matrix $\mathbf{Y}$ and the related knowledge graph G are determined, the task of recommendation algorithm is to recommend items that the target user may be interested in, which exist in a set of items they have not interacted with before. Importantly, without special designation, the following entities are head entities.

Hence, we design a prediction function

$$\hat{y}_{uv} = \mathcal{F}(u, v | \theta, \mathbf{Y}, G) \tag{1}$$

where $\hat{y}_{uv}$ is the probability of user u likes item v, and θ represents the model parameters of the function $\mathcal{F}$.

Figure 1 presents the overall framework of the model. The inputs of KG^{2}CN include the user-item interaction matrix $\mathbf{Y}$, the knowledge graph G, and the node neighborhood sampling set $S(v)$ of item v. The output is a prediction function $\mathcal{F}$. The purpose of KG^{2}CN is to capture the high-order patterns between entities in the knowledge graph. In the candidate pair set of user u and item v, we use $N_{(v)}$ to represent the set of items directly connected to item v. Besides, r_{v_i,e_j} represents the relation between item v_i and attribute e_j, using a vector inner product $g : \mathbb{R}^d \times \mathbb{R}^d \rightarrow \mathbb{R}$ to evaluate the score between the user u and the relation r.

$$\pi_r^u = g(\mathbf{u}, \mathbf{r}) \qquad (2)$$

where $\mathbf{u} \in \mathbb{R}^d, \mathbf{r} \in \mathbb{R}^d$ represent the embedding of the user u and the relation r, respectively. d denotes the dimension of the embedding vector. Thus, π_r^u is the evaluation metric for the importance of the relation r to user u.

Further, KG^{2}CN explores the high-order patterns of items (i.e., $\mathbf{v}_{N_{(v)}}^u$) by computing the linear combination of neighbors:

$$\mathbf{v}_{N_{(v)}}^u = \sum_{e \in N_{(v)}} \tilde{\pi}_{r_{v,e}}^u \mathbf{e} \qquad (3)$$

Here, $\tilde{\pi}_{r_{v,e}}^u$ represents the normalized importance of the score $\pi_{r_{v,e}}^u$ for the user u to relation $r_{v,e}$, $\mathbf{e}$ is the embedding of entity e (i.e., item).

$$\tilde{\pi}_{r_{v,e}}^u = \frac{exp(\pi_{r_{v,e}}^u)}{\sum_{e \in N(v)} exp(\pi_{r_{v,e}}^u)} \qquad (4)$$

As the neighborhood embedding of entities is constructed, the user-relation score π_r^u is utilized as a personalized filter to aggregate neighbors that have biases towards specific ratings from users.

2.2 Constructing High-Order Neighborhood of Subgraphs

In the knowledge graph, the size of neighborhood $N(v)$ varies according to the item v. In the specific process, each entity uniformly samples a fixed-size set of neighbors. For example, the neighborhood embedding of an item v is $\mathbf{v}_{S(v)}^u$, where $S(v) \triangleq \{e|e \sim N(v)\}$ represents the set of entities in the neighborhood of item v. The selection of neighbors for each entity is achieved by traversing the subgraph of nodes and selecting a fixed number of subgraph nodes as the neighborhood of the source node.

High-order patterns in the knowledge graph enrich the semantic information contained in the graph and convey more collaborative relations. Figure 2 illustrates an example of the high-order patterns expanded from user u_1. If the high-order pattern $u_2 \rightarrow v_1 \rightarrow u_1$ represent users u_1 and u_2 that have interacted with item v_1 in the past, then the high-order pattern $v_3 \rightarrow u_2 \rightarrow v_1 \rightarrow u_1$ representations of item v_3 will be preferred by user u_1. Similarly, if the high-order pattern $v_4 \rightarrow v_3 \rightarrow u_2 \rightarrow v_1 \rightarrow u_1$

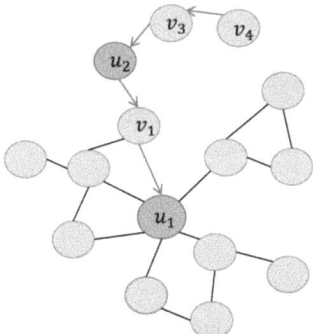

Fig. 2. Simple example of subgraph structure.

represents a set of entities where item v_3 is related to item v_4 via relation (e.g., they have similar themes or share the same authors and singers.), then item v_4 will also be preferred by user u_1.

The original model fixed the selection of neighboring nodes in the node neighborhood at a fixed order, without considering the influence of non-adjacent nodes in a subgraph on the completeness of source node attributes, as well as the influence of different subgraph selections on nodes.

2.3 Aggregation Methods

The model eventually aggregates the representation of item v and its neighborhood representation $\mathbf{v}_{S(v)}^u$ into a single vector. The sum aggregator sums the two representation vectors and then undergoes a non-linear transformation, as shown in Eq. (5).

$$\mathbf{v}^u = \sigma(\mathbf{W} \cdot (\mathbf{v} + \mathbf{v}_{S(v)}^u) + \mathbf{b}) \tag{5}$$

where $\mathbf{W}$ and $\mathbf{b}$ are the learnable network weights and σ denotes the ReLU activation function. $\mathbf{v}^u$ is the final embedding of item v of user u. Then, we gain ratings of user u for item v:

$$\hat{y}_{uv} = \mathbf{u} \cdot \mathbf{v}^u \tag{6}$$

where $\hat{y}_{uv}$ represents the score of user u for item v. The user's embedding $\mathbf{u}$ is used as a parameter for training, so the model learns the features of the item.

2.4 Loss Function

The complete loss function defined by the model is:

$$loss = \sum_{u \in U} \left(\sum_{v:y_{uv}=1} \tau(y_{uv}, \hat{y}_{uv}) - \sum_{i=1}^{T^u} E_{v_i \sim p(v_i)} \tau(y_{uv_i}, \hat{y}_{uv_i}) \right) + \lambda ||\mathcal{F}||_2^2 \tag{7}$$

where $\tau(\cdot)$ represents the cross-entropy loss function, $p(\cdot)$ is the distribution of negative samples, and T^u represents the number of negative samples for user u. Besides, y_{uv} is the true label, $y_{uv} = 1$ if user u and item v interacted in the test set, otherwise $y_{uv} = 0$.

In this section, we mainly introduces the overall framework of KG²CN and the improvements made to the original model, which involve selecting nodes from subgraphs as neighborhoods of original nodes. Leveraging the rich semantic relations between subgraph nodes in the knowledge graph, we further enhance the completeness of attributes for each original entity, thus providing personalized feedback and recommendations for users.

3 Experiments

In this paper, we validate the recommendation performance of KG²CN through extensive experiments. Specifically, we use two different datasets and four recommendation algorithms as baselines for comparison, aiming to comprehensively evaluate the recommendation performance of KG²CN.

3.1 Datasets

In this article, we apply the **Book-Crossing** and **Last.FM** datasets for experiments. The Book-Crossing dataset consists of book rating data, including user information, book attributes, and ratings from 3,709 users. The ratings range from 1 to 10, and there are 77,903 books with 25 types of book relations. The Last.FM dataset contains music-related data from the Last.FM online music website, including user information, music attributes, and user listening records. It includes listening data from 1,872 users, 9,366 songs, and 60 types of song relations. The properties of the datasets are shown in Table 1.

To improve the accuracy of the recommendation model, we convert the explicit feedback in both datasets into implicit feedback, using binary numbers 0 and 1 to represent the interaction evaluations between users and items. '1' indicates a positive evaluation from the user for the item, while '0' indicates a negative evaluation or no interaction record between the user and the item.

Table 1. Properties of different datasets.

Datasets	Book-Crossing	Last.FM
Number of users	17,860	1,872
Number of items	77,903	9,366
Number of relations	25	60
Number of triples	151,500	15,518

3.2 Experimental Settings

During the experimental process, the datasets are divided into training (60%), validation (20%), and testing (20%) sets for both datasets. The code implementation of KG²CN is

Table 2. Hyperparameter settings for different datasets.

Datasets	Book-Crossing	Last.FM
k	8	50
d	64	16
λ	2×10^{-5}	10^{-4}
η	2×10^{-4}	5×10^{-4}

k: Sample size of neighbor, d: Embedding dimension,
λ: L2 regularization weight, η: Learning rate.

done in Python 3.6, TensorFlow 1.12.0, and NumPy 1.14.3. The specific hyperparameter settings for the experiments are shown in Table 2.

Combining the model content of this experiment with common model evaluation metrics, F1 score, and Area Under the Curve (AUC) are selected as evaluation metrics for assessing the recommendation model.

The higher the AUC and F1 metrics, the better the recommendation performance of the model.

3.3 Experimental Baselines

To validate the effectiveness of KG²CN, the experimental results of KG²CN are compared with those of common recommendation algorithm models. The parameters of baselines for comparison are set the same as those in the original paper. The baselines for comparison include NCF [7], PER [8], SVD [11], CKE [16], and KGCN 2. The detailed descriptions of the baselines are as follows:

- CKE [16] adopts a collaborative filtering module that utilizes heterogeneous information to extract semantic representations of items with structural, textual, and visual information.
- SVD [11] is a traditional collaborative filtering recommendation model through singular value decomposition. It uses inner products to construct interaction models between users and items.
- PER [8] treats the knowledge graph as a heterogeneous information network and describes the connectivity between users and items by extracting features based on meta-paths.
- NCF [7] learns embedding parameters by treating users and items as embedding parameters and reconstructing historical interaction information between users and items.
- KGCN 2 uses graph convolutional networks to aggregate information from the knowledge graph, creating rich, informed representations of users and items.

3.4 Overall Performance

According to the experiment settings, we conduct performance comparison, and the experimental results are shown in Table 3.

As shown in Table 3, KG²CN shown a certain degree of improvement in both AUC and F1 scores compared to other baselines. Compared to traditional recommendation algorithm models, the AUC values have respectively increased by 1%–8% and 3%–9% on the Book-Crossing and Last.FM datasets. Similarly, compared to traditional recommendation models, the F1 scores have shown improvements of 1%–8% and 2%–12%, respectively. This indicates that KG²CN can effectively predict users preferences for items in different domains and styles.

Horizontal comparison of experimental results shows a greater improvement in recommendation performance on the Last.FM dataset. This dataset is sparser compared to the Book-Crossing dataset, suggesting that KG²CN alleviates the data sparsity issue to some extent by introducing semantic information from knowledge graphs and high-order subgraph structures.

Table 3. Prediction performance of different models.

Models	Book-Crossing		Last.FM	
	AUC	F1	AUC	F1
NCF 2	0.663	0.608	0.758	0.632
SVD [11]	0.672	0.635	0.766	0.696
PER [8]	0.617	0.562	0.632	0.596
CKE [16]	0.676	0.611	0.744	0.674
KGCN 2	0.721	0.680	0.794	0.719
KG²CN	**0.682**	**0.641**	**0.796**	**0.722**

Traditional collaborative filtering-based recommendation algorithms such as NCF, SVD, and PER mainly rely on user-item interaction data. They use deep learning networks or singular value decomposition techniques to capture the nonlinear features of interaction data. However, these models do not utilize additional information inherent in the relations between items themselves, limiting their recommendation performance. KG²CN leverages knowledge graph technology, which provides rich semantic information to better understand the complex relations between items and user preferences, thereby enhancing the recommendation effectiveness.

Compared to the CKE and KGCN recommendation algorithms, which also use knowledge graph technology, KG²CN processes the high-order patterns of knowledge graphs. By selecting nodes from the node neighborhood in the construction of neighborhoods, KG²CN enhances node similarity and effectively improves feature extraction in nodes. Additionally, by combining convolutional networks to simulate the interaction between users and items, the model enhances the accuracy of recommendation. KG²CN is slightly inferior to KGCN in Book-Crossing. This is due to KGCN mines better semantic information based on Knowledge graph while KG²CN only learns the topological information.

To explore the impact of different numbers of neighbor nodes on the recommendation results, comparative experiments are conducted separately for the Book-Crossing and Last.FM datasets. The experimental results are presented in Fig. 3.

As shown in Fig. 3, on the Book-Crossing dataset, the AUC value exhibits the greatest change when the number of neighbor nodes increases from 4 to 8, with further increases having a smaller impact on the experimental results. Similarly, on the Last.FM dataset, the AUC value shows the most significant change when the number of neighbor nodes increases from 4 to 50. However, when the value of k becomes too large, having too many neighbor nodes can introduce noise interference to the model. Therefore, it can be concluded that appropriately increasing the number of neighbor nodes can enhance the recommendation performance of the model.

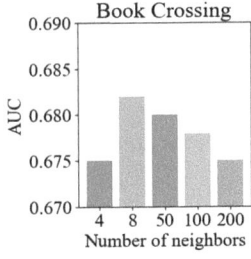 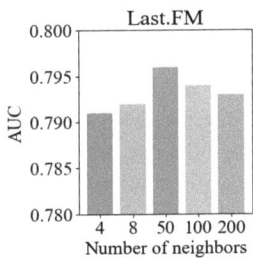

Fig. 3. Different numbers of neighbor nodes of KG^2CN.

As shown in Table 3, KG^2CN performs less effectively on the Book-Crossing dataset compared to KGCN. Due to the higher sparsity relative to Last.FM, interactions between users and books are fewer and more singular. This results in greater influence of individuals when constructing node subgraphs, which makes the model more susceptible to noise and thus yields suboptimal outcomes.

3.5 Ablation Study

To demonstrate the effectiveness of KG^2CN in capturing high-order neighborhood subgraphs, we conducte ablation experiments on the Last.fm dataset against KGCN models of varying orders, as shown in Table 4. KGCN-$i(i = 1, 2, 3)$ means KGCN with i-order patterns.

Table 4. Model comparisons of different orders

	KG^2CN	KGCN-1	KGCN-2	KGCN-3
AUC	0.796	0.794	0.725	0.563

From the experimental results, it is observed that as the fixed order of neighborhood construction increases, the AUC value actually decreases, attributed to the noise introduced with higher orders. The KG^2CN model, by not fixing the order of neighborhood selection and instead choosing nodes from node subgraphs, effectively reduces the impact of noise.

4 Conclusions

To break the problem that most existing graph convolutional networks are limited to pairwise interactions, we propose a novel KG^2CN for recommendation systems. KG^2CN integrates knowledge graphs and graph convolutional networks to learn high-quality embeddings of users and items. By exploring high-order neighbors in the knowledge graph and applying graph convolutional networks, KG^2CN simulates interactions between users and items, thereby promoting the accuracy of recommendation and effectively alleviating data sparsity issues to some extent. In the experimental process, we compare KG^2CN with four recommendation algorithms on the Book-Crossing and Last.FM datasets. The experimental results demonstrate that KG^2CN exhibits improvements in multiple metrics compared to other models. In the future, we further explore the high-order patterns influence both in topological information and semantic information to enhance the recommendation performance.

Acknowledgements. This research was supported through National Natural Science Foundation of China (No. 62273219); Program for Innovative Research Team in Universities of Inner Mongolia Autonomous Region (NMGIRT2317); Key Laboratory of Infinite dimensional Hamiltonian System and Its Algorithm Application (Inner Mongolia Normal University), Ministry of Education (No. 2023KFJD02).

References

1. Jannach, D., Manzoor, A., Cai, W., Chen, L.: A survey on conversational recommender systems. ACM Comput. Surv. **54**(5), 1–36 (2022)
2. Wang, S., Cao, L., Wang, Y., Sheng, Q.Z., Orgun, M.A., Lian, D.: A survey on session-based recommender systems. ACM Comput. Surv. **54**(7), 1–38 (2022)
3. Sun, F., et al.: BERT4Rec: sequential recommendation with bidirectional encoder representations from transformer. In: Proceedings of the 28th ACM International Conference on Information and Knowledge Management, pp. 1441–1450 (2019)
4. Lu, Y., Fang, Y., Shi, C.: Meta-learning on heterogeneous information networks for cold-start recommendation. In: Proceedings of the 26th ACM SIGKDD International Conference on Knowledge Discovery and Data Mining, pp. 1563–1573 (2020)
5. Ying, R., He, R., Chen, K., Eksombatchai, P., Hamilton, W.L., Leskovec, J.: Graph convolutional neural networks for web-scale recommender systems. In: Proceedings of the 24th ACM SIGKDD International Conference on Knowledge Discovery and Data Mining, pp. 974–983 (2018)
6. Wang, D., Liang, Y., Xu, D., Feng, X., Guan, R.: A content-based recommender system for computer science publications. Knowl.-Based Syst. **157**(1), 1–9 (2018)
7. He, X., Liao, L., Zhang, H., et al.: Neural collaborative filtering. In: Proceedings of the 26th International Conference on World Wide Web, pp. 173–182 (2017)

8. Yu, X., Ren, X., Sun, Y., et al.: Personalized entity recommendation: a heterogeneous information network approach. In: Proceedings of the 7th ACM International Conference on Web Search and Data Mining, pp. 283–292 (2014)
9. Pan, Y., He, F., Yu, H.: Learning social representations with deep autoencoder for recommender system. World Wide Web **23**, 2259–2279 (2020)
10. Lee, H., Im, J., Jang, S., Cho, H., Chung, S.: MeLU: meta-learned user preference estimator for cold-start recommendation. In: Proceedings of the 25th ACM SIGKDD International Conference on Knowledge Discovery and Data Mining, pp. 1073–1082 (2019)
11. Badrul, S., George, K., Joseph, K., et al.: Incremental singular value decomposition algorithms for highly scalable recommender systems. In: Fifth International Conference on Computer and Information Science, vol. 1, no. 012002, p. 27-8 (2002)
12. Shi, X., Chen, Z., Wang, H., Yeung, D.-Y., Wong, W., Woo, W.: Convolutional LSTM network: a machine learning approach for precipitation nowcasting. In: Proceedings of the 28th International Conference on Neural Information Processing Systems, vol. 1, pp. 802–810 (2015)
13. Bhuvanya, R., Kavitha, M.: Integrated image recommendation based on category and color utilizing CNN and VGG-16. In: Proceedings of the International Conference on Cognitive and Intelligent Computing, pp. 785–799 (2022)
14. Wang, X., He, X., Wang, M., Feng, F., Chua, T.-S.: Neural graph collaborative filtering. In: Proceedings of the 42nd International ACM SIGIR Conference on Research and Development in Information Retrieval, pp. 165–174 (2019)
15. Li, Z., Liu, F., Yang, W., et al.: A survey of convolutional neural networks: analysis, applications, and prospects. IEEE Trans. Neural Netw. Learn. Syst. **33**(12), 6999–7019 (2021)
16. Zhang, F., Yuan, N., Lian, D., et al.: Collaborative knowledge base embedding for recommender systems. In: Proceedings of the 22nd ACM SIGKDD International Conference on Knowledge Discovery and Data Mining, pp. 353–362 (2016)
17. Wang, H., Zhao, M., Xie, X., et al.: Knowledge graph convolutional networks for recommender systems. In: The World Wide Web Conference, pp. 3307–3313 (2019)

Author Index

B
Bu, Dongbo 30

C
Chen, Jianrui 169
Chen, Xiaoyong 161
Chen, Yinhua 68

D
Dao, Lu 140
Diao, Zhuo 47
Ding, Shizhe 30
Ding, Zhenxin 30
Du, Yu 123

G
Guo, Hao 3

H
He, Qing 95
Hu, Jinru 169
Huang, Zihao 30

L
Li, Chen 140
Li, Jianglin 68
Li, Weidong 14
Li, Yongming 81, 95
Liu, Na 140
Liu, Ruizhi 30
Liu, Wuniu 81
Luo, Rongchuan 58
Lv, Xiao 123

M
Mu, Chuanjiang 81

P
Pan, Wenyan 111

Q
Qin, Jiaohua 111

S
Shao, Kuncheng 3
Sui, Jingyan 30
Sun, Fuchun 123
Sun, Wencheng 161

T
Tang, Zhongzheng 47

W
Wang, Chao 30
Wang, Wencheng 68
Wang, Zhihui 169
Wen, Ying 95

X
Xia, Zhihua 111
Xiao, Man 14
Xu, Liming 30

Y
Yang, Jie 140
Yu, Chungong 30

Z
Zhang, Haicang 30
Zhang, Siyao 169
Zhang, Tongquan 68
Zhang, Xian 123
Zheng, Guofeng 140
Zou, Haoyang 47

If you have any concerns about our products,
you can contact us on
ProductSafety@springernature.com

In case Publisher is established outside the EU,
the EU authorized representative is:
Springer Nature Customer Service Center GmbH
Europaplatz 3, 69115 Heidelberg, Germany

Printed by Libri Plureos GmbH
in Hamburg, Germany